JESUS
UNLEASHED

JESUS UNLEASHED

Luke's Gospel for Emerging Christians

RON CLARK

CASCADE Books • Eugene, Oregon

JESUS UNLEASHED
Luke's Gospel for Emerging Christians

Copyright © 2013 Ron Clark. All rights reserved. Except for brief quotations in critical publications or reviews, no part of this book may be reproduced in any manner without prior written permission from the publisher. Write: Permissions. Wipf and Stock Publishers, 199 W. 8th Ave., Suite 3, Eugene, OR 97401.

Cascade Books
An Imprint of Wipf and Stock Publishers
199 W. 8th Ave., Suite 3
Eugene, OR 97401

www.wipfandstock.com

ISBN 13: 978-1-61097-989-4

Cataloguing-in-Publication Data

Clark, Ron.

    Jesus unleashed : Luke's Gospel for emerging Christians / Ron Clark.

    viii + 222 p. ; 23 cm. Includes bibliographical references.

    ISBN 13: 978-1-61097-989-4

    1. Bible. N. T. Luke and Acts—Criticism, interpretation, etc. 2. Emerging church movement. I. Title.

BS2589 .C50 2013

Manufactured in the U.S.A.

Contents

Acknowledgments | vii

SECTION 1: **INTRODUCING JESUS**
1 How Did We Get Here? | 3
2 Jesus Unleashed | 21
3 Introducing the Cast | 43
4 Introducing Jesus | 54

SECTION 2: **INTRODUCING THE JOURNEY**
5 Reaching Those on the Margins | 69
6 Mentoring on the Margins | 95

SECTION 3: **JOINING JESUS ON THE JOURNEY TO JERUSALEM**
7 Joining Jesus on the Margins | 109
8 Repentance and Healing in the Margins | 128
9 Undesirables on the Margins of the Empire | 143
10 Taking Risks on the Margins | 160

SECTION 4: **THE LONG JOURNEY HOME**
11 Jesus Comes Home | 175
12 Jesus Is Evicted | 188
13 Jesus Returns | 201
14 The Church Continues Onward | 210

Bibliography | 215

Acknowledgments

This is the second in a series of three books for emerging Christians. With the release of *The God of Second Chances: Finding Hope in the Prophets of Exile*, I realized that the backdrop of exile was present in Luke's Gospel as well as Acts. *Jesus Unleashed: Luke's Gospel for Emerging Christians* carries forward that theme of the marginalized experiencing salvation. Many of the stories from Agape and our years of ministry fit well into this Gospel and are added to help read the text in a different light.

Thanks go to my best friend, partner in ministry, and wife, Lori. God has blessed me with a wonderful minister to work beside and you are deeply embedded in many of these stories as well as my views of the Bible. Thank you for challenging me to think differently and more clearly. To my oldest son Nathan and his new wife Nyla: I look forward to watching you both continue to grow as a family and as adults. You are both wonderful and you have been with us in this journey as well. To Hunter and Caleb, I hope that you will continue to see Jesus as a hero and continue to show courage in your faith, love, and friendships. All of our boys have been a joy to raise.

Agape Church of Christ, AS IS Church, and Agape Rockwood have been great places to share these stories and biblical texts. Preaching and working with you all has been a great blessing. You have not only embraced Luke but you live it as well. I would also like to thank Dr. Mark Hamilton, Dr. Walter Brueggemann, Dr. Michael Frost, Shane Claiborne, and Kevin Palau for their help and support in this work. To K. C. Hanson, James Stock, Christian Amondson, Rodney Clapp, Ian Creeger and Laura Poncy: thanks for all your help and work publishing my books and supporting our ministry.

SECTION 1
Introducing Jesus

1

How Did We Get Here?

It was a sunny Saturday morning in Portland. We had taken a team from our supporting church in Tulsa, Oklahoma, downtown to Pioneer Courthouse Square to see the city and make one last connection with people before we launched our new church, Agape Church of Christ. This year Easter was in early April and we were lucky to have a sunny day that early in the year. Even more, those helping us were very excited to see us launch this new work. My wife Lori and I had been meeting in our home for nine months with four families, preparing to launch a church that would reach people on the margins. I had made many trips downtown to connect with others and listen to what they needed from a church.

We had split up into small groups to hand out invitations throughout the heart of Portland and I had my two year old son, Caleb, with me along with two Tulsa women. Caleb was riding on my shoulders and I was quickly walking along the light rail (MAX) tracks to the center of the square. As with any sunny Portland day, people and their children, homeless youth, and others were gathered throughout the square visiting, eating, or soaking up the sunshine.

"Spare some change?" a quiet female voice asked as I passed. I stopped, turned around, and saw a young woman, dressed in black with black fingernails and thick black eyeliner. She was in her early twenties and took the spot where many young people sit while spanging (begging for spare change). I had been downtown many times but had never noticed her before. I was walking so fast and preoccupied with the church launch that I almost missed her.

"Sorry, I don't have any money to give you. Would you like something to eat?" I asked. She responded, "No, I'm not hungry, but would like some change for something to drink." I said, "I can go to the Starbucks over there and get you some coffee or juice. Would that be okay?" She said, "No, that would be too expensive." I replied, "No problem, I don't mind." "Okay," she smiled. "I would like some juice."

I walked the fifty yards to Starbucks with Caleb on my shoulders and brought back apple juice. She drank it, thanked me, and then we talked. She told me she had lived in the Midwest and had come to Portland for work and adventure. Unfortunately life was hard for her and her boyfriend and they were sleeping in his car under one of the bridges. She talked to Caleb, said he was cute, and asked what I was doing. I told her about Agape as a new church and invited her. "Nah," she said, "my boyfriend and I don't do church—that's cool for everyone else but not us."

"No problem," I said. "I will probably see you around. My name's Ron."

"Cassy," she said. "Thank you for stopping and listening. A lot of people don't do that, you know." I smiled, waved to her, and walked away. I had to smile because I was almost one of those who didn't stop, listen, and offer help. It was convicting. I almost told myself she was just another street punk and walked by, because I was too busy getting ready to fulfill a calling from the Spirit to start a new church. I was so focused on doing something for Jesus that I almost ignored someone on the margins of my life.

HISTORY LESSON NUMBER ONE

In my previous book, *The God of Second Chances*, I discussed the history of the Jewish nation as it returned from Babylonian exile. The nation of Judah had violated their covenant/relationship with Yahweh (the name of the Jewish God) by becoming unfaithful, practicing injustice among their people, and abusing/neglecting their relationship with their God (Jer 3:8). Therefore God divorced them and allowed the Babylonian army to enter Jerusalem to destroy the city, temple, and a large portion of the population. In addition to this, the majority of the remaining Jews (those who were socially and intellectually elite) were taken captive in 590–587 BCE, transported to Babylon, and expected to live in that country as servants of the king. Some stayed in Jerusalem and scratched out a minimal existence. Others fled to Egypt or other countries and began new communities practicing a form of their Jewish faith. There was no temple for Yahweh and the land was given rest for seventy years. Yahweh, however, continued to live among the people of faith in these areas and rescued them from persecution, death, and suffering. Some became valuable leaders for their governments. Many compromised their faith. Others kept their faith in their God and dreamed for a day when they would return to their homeland.

At the end of the sixth century BCE, after the Persians defeated the Babylonians and became the world rulers, the Jewish refugees were allowed to return home and rebuild their temple. Nehemiah, Ezra, Haggai, and Zechariah were prophets and leaders who encouraged their people to rebuild their city, lives, and Yahweh's temple. During this time the nation struggled for its survival due to the threats of its enemies, legal disputes with the Persian government, its own fatigue and exhaustion, as well as fear of the large task ahead. However, with the support of their leaders the nation finished its work and returned to becoming a people serving Yahweh. As time unfolded the prophet Malachi indicated that the nation was once again returning to worship other Gods, possibly *Asherah*, the "wife of El" (which means God). The people also continued to neglect Yahweh in their sacrifices, practice of justice in the land, and follow the renewed covenant enacted by their earlier leaders. Judah was once again headed for destruction (Mal 2:17; 3:5, 15).

However, Yahweh warned the nation that they would again have a visit from its Lord.

> Hey, the day is coming, burning like a firepot, when all the arrogant ones and evildoers will be kindling. The day that is coming shall set them on fire, says Yahweh of hosts, so that there will be no roots or branches left behind. For you who fear my name, the righteous sun will rise with healing wings. You shall go out leaping like calves from the pen. You will crush the wicked ones like ashes under your feet, on the day when I act, says Yahweh of hosts. Remember the law/Torah of my servant Moses which I commanded to him and all Israel at Mount Horeb. Hey, I will send Elijah the prophet to you before the great and awesome day of Yahweh comes. He will turn the hearts of fathers to their children and the hearts of children to their fathers so that I won't come and completely destroy the land. (Mal 4:1–6)[1]

Since the nation had again turned from Yahweh, the Lord promised to send a prophet to prepare the people for a divine visit. Some would listen and repent while others would not. This same text was uttered decades later by God's angel (*malachi* in Hebrew) to Zechariah the priest concerning his son John (known as John the Baptist). "He will go before him [the Lord], in the spirit and power of Elijah. He will turn the hearts of the fathers/parents

---

1. All scripture quotations are my translation of *Biblia Hebraica* and *Novum Testamentum Graece*.

to their children and the disobedient to the wisdom of the righteous—to prepare the people to be ready for the Lord" (Luke 1:17). Preparing people for the coming of Jesus involved the remnant of those who were faithful/righteous, teaching and turning others to God's wisdom. As John's father Zechariah said, John was going to teach salvation through forgiveness of sins. This would be due to God's mercy: "You, child, will be called a prophet of the Most High; because you will go in front of the Lord to prepare his way and give his people the knowledge of salvation by the forgiveness of their sins, because of the compassionate mercy of our God" (Luke 1:76–78).

John came at a time when the Judeans needed a visit from their God. Between the book of Malachi and the birth of Jesus the Jewish nation had been through years of turmoil. Jerusalem was located between Egypt and Persia. It was once again caught in the middle of the wars involving Persia, Greece, Egypt, and other Syrian nations. After Alexander the Great died and had lost control of his empire, the Romans conquered the land which surrounded and included Jerusalem. The Jewish nation had fought small battles by their terrorist cell groups and driven the Greeks out of Palestine. However, the Romans were too strong and eventually took charge of the region. After many civil wars in Jerusalem Herod Antipas, a non-Jewish Edomite, was given the rule of Jerusalem by mixing politics with Rome and power over his own people. He became the "king of the Jews" and appointed high priests (rather than one high priest) to care for the temple. Herod refurbished the Jewish temple, rebuilt some of the Jewish cities in the Roman style, and built many Roman palaces, summer homes, and sports and theater structures in Jerusalem as well as the surrounding areas of Judea.[2] His massive building projects created a heavy tax burden on the people. However, Rome did allow Jerusalem and Joppa to be exempt from taxes when they rebuilt these structures and during their sabbatical years.[3]

Politically the Jewish nation was under the rule of Rome. The land was no longer theirs and their temple system was corrupted. By the time Jesus became an adult Herod had died but his son Herod Antipater had become a tetrarch (one of four rulers) of the Northern region of Judea named Galilee. Pilate, a Roman, was in charge of southern Judea and Jerusalem, Philip (also Herod the Great's son) was tetrarch of Iturea and Trachonitus (north of Galilee), and Lysanius was tetrarch of Abilene (west of Galilee). Pilate's headquarters was next to the Jewish temple serving as a reminder to everyone worshiping that Caesar was in charge, rather than Yahweh.

---

2. Netzer, *The Architecture of Herod*, 302–4.

3. Udoh, *To Caesar What is Caesar's*, 43–46, 50.

Roman Power and Colonies

Rome wanted to control Palestine. This area of the world was a strategic location to keep Egypt in check and confiscate metals and other materials that would benefit the Roman Empire. Rome occupied many countries and offered a patron/client type of relationship. Patron/client relationships were common in ancient cultures and involved a wealthy benefactor or supporter (patron) entering into a legal covenant with someone who was in need (client). Typically the patron provided support, finances, and troops for those who were in need. In return the clients offered loyalty, paid taxes, and agreed to allow occupation of their cities. This operated on both a larger community level as well as an individual one. While this arrangement had advantages, the problem was that the clients became colonized by their supportive powers. As Jae Won Lee writes, "What is more, the Empire advertised itself as divinely destined not merely to rule the world but to bring to the people it conquered the blessings of its supposedly superior culture. The conquerors blessed the conquered with peace, justice, and well-being, and saved them where they could not save themselves."[4] While Rome claimed to offer peace (*Pax Romana* in Latin) this peace came with a price. Most cities paid enormously high taxes and found that they could be treated unjustly by Romans or the government. The colonizers established a relationship where the colonized were vulnerable and dependent upon their patrons. Typically the colonized felt oppressed, mistreated, and humiliated.

While they may have been told that they would be cared for and that they would experience peace, a system of oppression, privilege, and power still existed in the Judean country. To be colonized was a price some might pay if they were faced with fighting the war machine that the Roman military had so effectively established. It would also be a price people might pay if their country was economically struggling to exist. While the peace of Rome was not a decision made by the people, it was one made by their leaders.[5]

The Holy Land

Palestine lay along the Mediterranean coast. The Judean region included Jerusalem (the capitol city which lay sixty kilometers east of the coast), Samaria (north of Jerusalem) and the Decapolis (known as the ten cities surrounding Galilee), Galilee (one hundred kilometers north of Jerusalem and

---

4. Lee, "Pilate and the Crucifixion of Jesus," 97–98.
5. Ibid., 95.

including the Lake of Galilee), the Jordan River plains, Perea (mountainous region east of the Jordan River) bordering the river and Arabia, Abilene and Batanea (bordering Northern Arabia), and Iturea (bordering the Syro Phoenecian coast along the Mediterranean). This region was extremely diverse, consisting of the fertile valley of the Jordan River, the dry arid regions near Arabia, and the coastal cities along the Mediterranean. In the days of Jesus, king Herod Antipas (known as Herod the great) built large shipping harbors at Caesarea so that Roman and Egyptian grain ships could dock and provide Judea with food. This area was both rugged, and fertile. Walking long distances involved hilly regions, however with Roman occupation the direct route from Galilee to Jerusalem would have been paved, dotted with Roman mile markers, and cluttered with inns for weary travelers. Jesus mentioned that the disciples should not just carry someone's pack (more than likely a Roman soldier) one mile (marker) but go two (Matt 5:41). Jesus also mentioned inns, the construction of buildings, and paths, indicating that the region of Judea was experiencing growth and reconstruction as a colonized nation (Matt 5:15, 7:24–27; Luke 10:35). However, this came with a price. Taxes would have increased, causing the tax collectors to be hated even more than they had been. In addition to this Roman soldiers would have also been in positions to take advantage of those who were colonized and vulnerable. Judea was like a powder keg waiting to explode.

Religious Groups Living Under *Pax Romana*

Religious/Political Groups

In response to this colonization and political turmoil that the Judeans faced, various groups formed as an attempt to maintain faith and promote salvation toward God. First, there were religious groups that emerged as an attempt to preserve the Jewish nation and the practice of the *Torah*. Essenes have been thought to practice strict principles of self denial, sacrifice, and conservative interpretations of the law. Some have suggested that these groups/sects were part of a community called Qumran (the city where the Dead Sea Scrolls were found).[6] These monks lived in community in the desert and practiced writing, translating the scriptures, and maintaining ritual purity. A second group may have been the Sadducees.[7] These leaders were among the elite of

---

6. Roetzel, *The World that Shaped the New Testament*, 49–51; Witherington, *New Testament History*, 93–95.

7. Roetzel, *The World that Shaped the New Testament*, 43–44; Saldarini, *Pharisees, Scribes, and Sadducees*, 116–18.

the community, were conservative interpreters of the Torah, and accepted only the first five books of Moses as authoritative. Some served as scribes, others on the council, and others held positions of power in the community. The Pharisees were another group similar to the Sadducees who also served as scribes, leaders in the community, and rabbis. They were more progressive than the Sadducees in that they allowed Greek culture to influence their teaching. They were scholars who served as retainers, leaders who served he governing class but "wrestled power from the authorities and tried to keep the traditions active among the people."[8] In addition to this they believed that the Prophetic books of the Bible were authoritative and believed in angels. Other smaller groups existed in Palestine but all served a similar purpose. These sects were making an attempt to keep the Jewish nation devoted to their God and loyal to the community. They also tried to bridge the gap between leaders and people in the community. While it is tempting to see these leaders as trouble makers or spiritually blind, it is important to realize that they had good intentions for their community.

During the years of turmoil between Jerusalem and the rest of the world Jews were tortured and killed for their faith. Their desire to worship exclusively one God, and their refusal to eat or sacrifice pork, worship any idol or image, work on the Sabbath (Saturday—the day of rest), or not circumcise their baby boys was considered by some nations an act of rebellion. These individuals died for their faith, their practices, and their devotion to their God, Yahweh. They had compromised their faith concerning these issues in the past and were punished in Babylonian captivity. This time, they would not give in. Because of Palestine's location with respect to the rest of the world, the Judeans had become targets for bullies and oppressive rulers and suffered for it. The Jewish religious sects were in place to prepare the people to be strong and confront evil.

Militaristic Groups

Other militaristic groups formed during this time. One notable group was the *Zealots* or *Sicarii*.[9] This group was comprised of assassins who attempted to overthrow the Romans, as well as the corrupt Jewish governments, by violence. One of Jesus's disciples, Simon (known as Zealot), and possibly Judas Iscariot (similar to Sicarii), may have been members of assassin groups at one time. The Apostle Matthew, a former tax collector, would have been a target of these men since he was a servant of the Roman government.

---

8. Saldarini, *Pharisees, Scribes, and Sadducees*, xiii, 9.
9. Roetzel, *The World that Shaped the New Testament*, 31–32.

Soldiers and temple guards were important as a police force in the city. While Rome controlled Jerusalem, it was up to the local governments, especially in Galilee and the surrounding territories, to use their armies and police forces to keep peace.[10] If they could not, a Roman detachment would be sent to investigate. Local authorities did not want any Roman interference and many times tended to be over zealous in their practice of justice rather than have to answer to Rome.

It is important to realize that these groups existed to preserve their faith and prevent another destruction, as with Babylon in 587 BCE. Unfortunately this happened again in 70 CE as the Roman General Titus led an army to destroy the temple. The actions of the terrorists drew the attention of Rome and the might of their army. While many of us who read the Gospels may draw negative conclusions concerning rabbis, Pharisees, Sadduccess, and others, they had a responsibility to maintain peace and squelch any political uprisings.

Issues that Brought Stress to Authorities

Since the authorities had to maintain peace, prevent Roman intervention, and protect the people, a high level of anxiety existed in ruling portions of Palestine. There were many issues that would bring intervention by authorities and heighten anxiety among the leaders.

Opposing Caesar or claiming to be a king. When Jesus spoke about the kingdom/empire of God, claimed to be Savior, mentioned "his kingdom/empire," spoke of true peace, called himself Lord or Son of God, and performed miracles he would have been viewed by those maintaining order as threatening Caesar. While most Judeans would not have felt he was betraying their loyalty, accusing Jesus of treason would have become a convenient tool for threatened leaders to use with the Roman authorities.

Causing an uprising and/or threatening the safety of a community. This would involve gathering large crowds together, causing a disturbance, and behaving in ways not accepted by the community.[11] In addition to this, *opposing accepted traditions or religious practices/teachings of a community* also created anxiety in area leaders. The first Christian martyr, Stephen, was falsely accused of trying to turn the Jewish people from following their traditions. "We have heard him say that this Jesus of Nazareth will destroy this place and change the customs Moses handed down to us" (Acts 6:14).

---

10. Lee, "Pilate and the Crucifixion of Jesus," 94.

11. De Vos, *Church and Community Conflicts*, 87–116; Saldarini, *Pharisees, Scribes, and Sadducees*, 51–57.

The community was expected to uphold any rules/laws from the authorities. Many of the traditions practiced by a community were designed to keep a sense of order and stability among the people.

Another situation creating anxiety involved a high status male *associating with women, children, slaves, and lower class people.* These individuals were assigned a position in society that involved strict boundaries between the honorable and the humble or those considered shameful. The word for humility/humble/humiliated does not suggest a psychological state of remorse for an individual but a position of status. To be humble meant that one associated with the humiliated or shamed of society. The word for *humble* in the Greek version of the Hebrew Bible also referred to someone who had been sexually assaulted.[12] To be in a position of status/honor and associate with the "dishonorable" of the community was not only a violation of personal boundaries, but it was a devaluation of ideological boundaries. In addition to this, for the superior to engage the lower class on their level mean that those in the lower class became vulnerable and open to further oppression and abuse.[13] People had their own social locations and needed to accept this state and respect the boundaries dividing the humble and those of high status.

Finally, *violating honor/shame codes within a community caused one to become a target in the city.* Honor was an important commodity in the ancient world. Honor was like the American value of "credit." If I have good "credit" or a high "credit score" I am able to have many blessings in my life. I can secure loans, credit cards, a house, vehicles, and many other items based on the fact that I have good credit. With good credit, I am seen as having a higher status in society and am able to access many things that make my life much more comfortable. However, if my credit is deemed "low" or I am labeled "a risk" then I am typically punished and expected to pay greater amounts with higher interest rates.

Honor and Shame

In the ancient world honor was their form of credit. A person with a high value of honor had access to many opportunities not available to those without honor, the shameful or the humiliated of society. Honor was obtained in one of two ways. Those born to noble families were born with a level of honor, called *ascribed honor*. Those who publicly challenged or shamed an honorable person received honor from others and *acquired honor* for

12. Reid, "Women Prophets of God's Alternative Reign," 55.
13. Saldarini, *Pharisees, Scribes, and Sadducees*, 37.

themselves. If a person with honor paid a debt for an individual, invited them to a dinner/banquet, gave them a position of authority, or entered into a relationship/friendship with them, they were blessing the other person by helping them "move up the honor scale" in the eyes of their community. If a person of low status challenged an honorable person publicly, took something valuable from them, threatened them, or broke a relationship with them, they would shame or dishonor that noble. When Jesus argued with the religious leaders publicly and "put them to shame" he was *acquiring honor* from them. The offended party, for the sake of honor, needed to punish, defend, or confront the other individual lest they become dishonored among their people.

In the ancient world honor was a valuable and limited commodity.[14] Those who had honor not only had to defend what they held, but many times sought to increase their status by taking honor from others.

> Since the honor system is a mode of social ranking, it produces competition for and defense of honor. Most people in a peasant society are of the same class and lack clear criteria for assigning prestige, so they engage in constant challenge and riposte in a quest for more honor among their fellow citizens.[15]

Bargaining, developing higher status relationships and contracts, and submitting to the wishes of nobles were all methods to gain honor and put oneself, as well as their children, at a higher status level in the eyes of others. Due to this the ancient world was known as an *agonistic* (competitive) society. In addition to this, maintaining and keeping one's status, as well as the status of one's family and friends, was of high importance. It is important to note that individuals were not viewed as individuals with personal choice (as are North Americans today), but as part of a group where status was defined by one's group/community. To act dishonorably or outside tradition brought anxiety on an individual's family, friends, and community.

Maintaining Honor and Faith

While we have traditionally been extremely negative toward the religious leaders in the Gospels and Acts, it is important to understand what lay behind their behavior. First, the Pharisees, Saducess, and other spiritual leaders arose out of a need to prevent the Jewish nation from returning to their

---

14. Malina, *The New Testament World*, 27–56; De Silva, *Honor, Patronage, Kinship and Purity*, 43–94; Malina and Neyrey, "Honor and Shame in Luke-Acts," 25–66.

15. Saldarini, *Pharisees, Scribes, and Sadducees*, 55.

old ways of worshiping idols, practicing injustice, working on the Sabbath, and turning from God and the Torah.[16] These men had the role of guiding the Judean people closer to God and to learn the Torah and its regulations. In addition to this, they had to work within the current Roman political system as those colonized by an oppressive force. These leaders tended to focus on three major issues with their people: *food, idolatry, and ritual/social impurity.*

First, *food was an issue that distinguished the Jewish people from other nations.* The Jewish nation was called to follow dietary laws that separated them from Gentiles and other non-practicing Jews (Lev 11). While Gentiles saw no problem in eating pork or other unclean animals, the Jews were forbidden by Torah and rabbinical teachings from ingesting these foods. Outside of Jerusalem where Jews were less populous this became a serious issue. It was safer for Jews to host dinners for Gentiles than it was to accept an invitation to their home, since they could not control what was being served. Food, eating, and dinner company became serious sources of anxiety for religious leaders/teachers and practicing Jews.

Second, *idols, images, statues, and pictures on coins were also important issues for the people of God.* Roman coins included images of Caesar, the goddess Roma, and other divinities. Many of the images of Caesar included inscriptions claiming that the emperors were divine or sons of Zeus, or representing Ceres, the goddess of grain.[17] While this was a common form of propaganda for the Roman Empire, it became a problem for the Jews who resisted any form of idolatry or claims that images were divine representations of human leaders. Pilate also tried to place Roman insignia, eagles, in the Jewish temple, causing a strong resistance from the leaders and their people. While the religious leaders may have had a difficult time monitoring statues and reverence toward them, in the Jewish cities occupied by the Romans, the presence of idolatry on currency continued to raise their levels of anxiety.

Finally, *associating with those who were ritually unclean* was another source of anxiety for Jewish leaders. Jews had to associate with Gentiles and while they may have developed strict laws protecting their holiness, being colonized by Gentiles meant that there were times when they had to navigate the boundaries of separateness required by the Torah. "[Peter] said to them, 'You understand how unlawful it is for a Jew to associate with or go visit anyone of another nation, however God has shown me to not call any person common or unclean'" (Acts 10:28). "When Peter went up to

---

16. Ibid., 6.
17. Lee, "Pilate and the Crucifixion of Jesus," 98.

Jerusalem, the circumcision party criticized/condemned him, saying, 'You went to uncircumcised men and ate with them'" (Acts 11:2–3). In Luke's Gospel, the Pharisees also introduce "sinner" as referring to a class of people and those marginalized by the religious group as a way of separating those practicing the holiness codes from those unable to do so.[18]

These issues among occupied Palestine heightened a level of fear of fear, anxiety, compulsion, and controlling behavior for those observing strict regulations of purity and separation from Gentiles. The religious leaders of the Jewish nation, especially in the areas outside Jerusalem which tended to be more relaxed in observing Torah, had a difficult job in keeping the people holy, undefiled, and devoted to Yahweh. It is easy for us, in the twenty-first century, to condemn their behavior, but it was an incredibly difficult task. They felt called by their God to lead, guide, and protect Yahweh's people in case God returned. The prophet Malachi had warned the nation from deviating from Torah and the religious leaders seemed focused on upholding God's commands (Mal 4:4–6).

Unfortunately, as with many in positions of power, some of the Jewish leaders had become corrupt. In the Hebrew scriptures one of the problems the prophets faced was the corruption of the people because of their religious and political leaders (Jer 36; Ezek 8). Yahweh sent the prophets to address the oppression of the vulnerable in their communities, hypocrisy in their faith, their hidden sin, and their greed and injustice (Amos 1–2). The problem was not any one leader, but those leaders who, contrary to the true Torah, had oppressed and exploited God's people. Corruption combined with fear, anxiety, and injustice created a class of leaders who used their position of power to care for themselves to the neglect of those who needed their guidance.

> Woe to you, scribes and Pharisees, hypocrites! You are like whitewashed tombs, which are beautiful on the outside, but within are full of dead people's bones and all uncleanness. You also appear righteous to others on the outside, but within you are full of hypocrisy and lawlessness. (Matt 23:27–28)

Not only had these leaders become corrupt, but they began to use their Sacred Texts (Torah, Prophets, Writings, and their Rabbinical Traditions) to justify their conduct and forms of injustice.[19]

---

18. Adams, *The Sinner in Luke*, xiv.

19. The typical division of the Hebrew/Jewish Bible was the Torah (Moses—Deuteronomy) which was considered the inspired scripture by all religious sects, followed by the Prophets and Writings (considered by some sects to be inspired), as well as the traditions of the rabbis (which were respected and honored among all the sects). Even

How Did We Get Here? 15

> He was teaching in one of the synagogues on the Sabbath, and there was a woman who had had a sickness for eighteen years. She was bent over and could not straighten herself. When Jesus saw her, he called her over and said to her, "Woman, you are freed from your sickness/disability." He laid his hands on her, and immediately she straightened up and glorified God. But the ruler of the synagogue was irritated because Jesus had healed on the Sabbath, and said to the people, "There are six days to work, come on those days and be healed, but not on the Sabbath." Then the Lord answered him, "You hypocrites! Each of you on the Sabbath unties his ox or his donkey from the food trough and leads it to water. Shouldn't this woman, a daughter of Abraham bound by Satan for eighteen years, be freed from this bond on the Sabbath day?" When he said these things, all his opponents were put to shame, but the people rejoiced at all the honorable things that were done by him. (Luke 13:10–17)

These leaders struggled to lead the nation of Judah forward, however when those in higher forms of leadership became corrupt they wielded power to oppress others both spiritually and doctrinally. As Jesus confronted the corrupt leadership system, some among the leaders who had open hearts and truly loved Yahweh and the people continued to seek the true path.

> There was a Pharisee named Nicodemus, a ruler of the Jews. He came to Jesus at night and said to him, "Rabbi, we know that you are a teacher who has come from God, because no one can do these signs that you do unless God is with him." Jesus answered, "I am telling you the truth, unless someone is born from above they cannot see the empire of God." (John 3:1–3)

> Nicodemus . . . said to them, "Does our law judge a man without first giving him a hearing and learning what he does?" They replied, "Are you from Galilee? Search and see that no prophet arises from Galilee." (John 7:50–52)

> The word of God continued to increase, and the number of the disciples multiplied greatly in Jerusalem, and a many priests became obedient to the faith. (Acts 6:7)

Other leaders, however, tried to destroy Jesus and those joining his cause. Jesus was hated by some of the leaders, not because he criticized the

---

thought the Torah was considered the sacred text, the other sections were held in respect as God's revelation to the Jewish nation.

scriptures, Jewish nation, or Yahweh. They hated him because he, like the prophets before, confronted corrupt leaders for their sins and oppression of others. This is why the Gospel writers portrayed him publicly arguing with leaders and condemning their behavior, rather than doing the same to the poor, oppressed, and those struggling to find peace in their daily lives. By confronting the religious leaders, Jesus obtained honor in the eyes of the crowds but also brought shame on the corrupt who were esteemed in their community.

LIVING IN A WORLD WITH ANXIETY

Today's world is similar to the world in Jesus's day. While we may be more technologically advanced than they were two thousand years ago our problems are basically the same. *First, we too are colonized and exploited in a world seeking peace, hope, love, and respect through possessions.* During the Christmas season, a time meant to celebrate the birth of Jesus, we are bombarded by images that ask us to buy material possessions that, we are told, will make us happy, give us worth, or suggest that we are valuable to those who are supposed to love us. Parents are persuaded that if we give expensive and multiple gifts, we will show our children that they are valuable to us. Couples are encouraged to believe that the expensive gifts show our worth and love toward each other. One reason that we are told this is because the Christmas season reaps the highest sales for businesses. The more we spend/give, the better they do. However, this pressure to spend only creates anxiety, tension, and fear—that continue after the holiday season. This was not the purpose behind the Incarnation.

At Agape we have joined the Advent Conspiracy as an attempt to help people focus on the true meaning of the Christmas season. Advent Conspiracy is a movement which encourages Christians, during the Christmas holiday season, to give one gift less, avoid the temptation of materialism, spend more time with family and people, and give the money saved to a charitable organization (Living Water International) that impacts a community or country where people in need live. This has been a great opportunity to help our people keep their focus on the giving life of Jesus rather than the marketing blitz during this holiday.

However, this exploitation continues throughout the year as people learn from media, culture, and merchants that our worth is based on looks, body size, image, youth, and what we possess. Unfortunately this system creates a longing for more items and a desire to "fit in" with like minded people. What we believe offers peace and contentment only offers loneliness, fear, and a high level of anxiety.

We are also colonized because there exists a perception of control in our communities. Diets, exercise, sports, weight loss programs, and foods have become a problem in our culture. While I support our United States President and his wife's efforts to address childhood obesity, I am amazed that the most practical method for activity (athletics, arts, and physical education in our public schools) has been removed due to budget cuts. Emphasis is now being placed upon controlling what we eat, where we eat, and who we eat with. When I was young eating was a social time. Now, it is a cautious time. While I admit that we as a nation have become lackadaisical in our eating habits, I also admit that we have created a sense of anxiety around food. There are many people who have dietary regulations for their health, but I notice that when some of them walk into a group of people and read what is on the label for their food, others become uncomfortable and tense. Some cannot simply eat with their friends but need to control what everyone else eats, in addition to what they eat. This high level of fear and anxiety over food creates control, fear, and oppression of others. I worked with a minister who was diabetic. He never made an issue of it and when we would have church potluck meals someone would make him a special pie. Sometimes people forgot, so he chose to eat what he could. He was much different than others I know who proclaim that they can't eat certain foods and create a panic in the room.

This control has been transferred to the scriptures and our faith communities. Visit a Christian bookstore and notice how many spiritual weight loss, exercise, or personal health books are displayed. Even more, many of these target females. Compare the number of these books to those encouraging us to reach out to the poor, the oppressed, or encouraging us to feed the thousands of people starving in our country. Mary Louise Bringle once wrote, "If religion has to do with the state of being 'ultimately concerned' . . . then the figures about our figure-consciousness shows us to be pouring our money, our energies, and ourselves into a 'religious' pursuit of the pseudo-ultimate concern for thinness."[20] We, as a faith community, have once again found a way to use food to control and shame others, especially females. We have also found a way to create a sense of guilt in those who do not dress, look, or act like we do.

Finally, we have found a way to avoid outsiders. I have enjoyed the many publications over the past few decades that have challenged Jesus's people to develop relationships with those who don't know Him. I am indebted to

---

20. Bringle, *The God of Thinness*, 27.

Dan Kimball, Shane Claiborne, Alan Hirsch, Michael Frost, John Burke, Rick Warren, and many others who have called Christians to become relational with those outside our doors.

> The difficulty for the church today is not in encouraging people to ask what Jesus would do but in getting them to break out of their domesticated and sanitized ideas about Jesus in order to answer that question.[21]

> The core theme of American evangelicalism is the change in the personal lives of people through the transforming power and presence of Jesus Christ, the living Lord. We rejoice in this gospel of transformation; and yet we regret that too often it can remain merely personal and does not also find expression in relationship, in community, and in the public practice of faith.[22]

> We in the past told new Christians to leave their friends. We need to encourage them to "live out their faith boldly without disconnecting from the old tribe," and we will see larger groups converted.[23]

> It seems incredibly ironic that as we mature and get to know Scripture better and get to know Jesus better and are transformed all the more by the Spirit, fewer non-Christians get to experience those things through relationships with us.[24]

However, a climate in the church still exists where Christians spend less time with those "not their own" than developing new relationships in their communities. While these authors have called us to rethink our spirituality, the church continues to focus inward. Is this partly because we want to control our relationships, keeping them "safe" and conformed?

Maintaining Order

Through all this control we have found a way to maintain order. The research on Christianity in North America suggests that not only are we declining as a movement, we are only ministering to ourselves. In addition to this people who express their faith as Christians are choosing not to identify

---

21. Frost and Hirsch, *ReJesus*, 19–20.
22. Robinson and Wall, *Called to Be Church*, 6.
23. Burke, *No Perfect People Allowed*, 191.
24. Kimball, *They Like Jesus But Not the Church*, 43.

with denominations, making "unaffiliated" the fastest growing segment of Christians.[25] While the number of megachurches in North America are growing, the number of smaller churches is dying. We, like the people of Genesis 11, have decided to *come together* and form our own place to hide. As God called the people of the earth to scatter and fill the land (Gen 1:28, 9:1, 7), so we have been sent out to fill the earth, as well as our cities and neighborhoods, with the message of Jesus. Unfortunately we have decided to maintain order rather than peace/*shalom*. In the name of "unity" we serve each other. We, like the early religious leaders of Jesus's day, enact sects to keep us faithful, holy, and separate from the "heathen."

We also maintain order by *exclusion*. We exclude those who do not speak our language (even though God is the author of languages), who do not hold our same beliefs, who do not look like us, and who do not carry the same sense of honor that we feel we ourselves own. Through exclusion we have created people who live on the margins of our communities. Aliens, immigrants, people who don't fit our body molds and seat cushions, those who don't uphold our traditions, those who don't have 2.3 children or aren't a couple feel the pressure. We have little place for them. I see it all around us:

- When we go to a restaurant a single person or one with more than two children seems out of place in our society.
- Smokers have to sit outside in the cold.
- Airline seats are too small . . . period.
- Women who don't look like Barbie are considered heavy, while men can be whatever size they want.
- People who don't speak English are an inconvenience.
- Years ago the "Blue Law" would not allow stores to sell non-food items on Sunday. Those who worship on Saturday or who don't attend church were neglected.

Those who don't fit are excluded. Those who are excluded are marginalized. Those who are marginalized are forgotten both by us and themselves. However, the gospel of Jesus came to those excluded, marginalized, and forgotten. God came to live among those on the margins of society. Born to a blue-collar construction worker family, he was raised among those on the margins. God came to live among the captives—not those in geographical captivity, but social captivity. Jesus came to bring order, honor, courage, *shalom*, and value to those society said were "shameful." Even more importantly, he stopped to offer people a sense of honor. He was not so focused on

---

25. Woodward, *Creating a Missional Culture*, 29.

this new movement that he ignored the small voices by the side of the road. He listened to them.

Cassy came to Agape one Sunday morning, about four months after I had met her. I had taken her and her boyfriend Mike to lunch a couple of times and visited with them on the street. She and my oldest son Nathan made a nice connection when we visited them downtown. One Sunday morning in August she came to worship wearing very tight shorts and a tank top, displaying her many tattoos. That weekend Mike had been arrested and sent back to the Midwest to be incarcerated. Cassy spent those days binging on alcohol and heroin because she was pregnant and didn't know what to do. When all else failed she came to church.

She kept coming back. Our younger and older women made her part of the family. My wife Lori spent a lot of time with her and she became a regular at Agape. She even sang one day on our praise team. Lori was in the hospital with Cassy for a week as the baby was born. I was invited to witness the birth. Cassy and Lori had a good friendship. She had a job, went through treatment, and through time and struggles has graduated from college and married Mike. They have two daughters now. They have moved back to the Midwest but we don't believe for one minute that our love and energy as a church was wasted. Agape people smile when they mention Cassy. She once told us that she felt accepted at Agape. When she was in the maternity ward she told the nurses, "I go to Agape. They are a church that loves pregnant girls and drug addicts."

What if I would have walked by Cassy and said, "I'm too busy to help?"

What if I would have loved starting the new church more than listening to the small voice on the road to Pioneer Courthouse Square?

I realized that we got here because we listened to someone on the margins.

2

Jesus Unleashed

The Gospel of Luke is a fascinating work. The more one studies it, the more one realizes its inexhaustible richness.[1]

THE GOSPEL OF LUKE is one of four Gospels accepted in many Christian circles. While the Gospel of Thomas and other smaller works have helped give a broader picture of the early Christian movement, Matthew, Mark, Luke, and John continue to be the standard works accepted by the early church and most Christian scholars. The Gospels provide an interesting balance to understanding not only the life of Jesus, but the authors' messages to the church.

Each Gospel writer not only suggested his intent but provided the reader with clues concerning issues that the church faced during their writing. Matthew has been attributed to the follower and apostle of Jesus, also known as Levi, who had been a tax collector. This Gospel provides us with clues concerning the early community that read his work. The author often used passages from the Hebrew Bible, commonly known as the Old Testament,[2] used Jewish phrases without interpretation, and emphasized

---

1. Croatta, "Jesus, Prophet Like Elijah," 451.

2. In this work I will avoid the commonly used terms Old Testament and New Testament. These phrases, while used for centuries by Christians, are couched in terms that present problems for students of the Bible. Testament is another term for covenant, used by the author of the Letter to the Hebrews to refer to the relationship/covenants with God and the nation's violation of them. Due to our misunderstanding some would suggest that the common Old Testament is fulfilled in the New Testament, which is not true. In my previous work, *The God of Second Chances*, I explain the difference between the covenants and the use of "renewed" instead of "new" to help us understand this

that Jesus had come for Jewish Christians, possibly those reading the document.

Mark is much shorter than Matthew and has been attributed to John-Mark, who followed the Apostle Paul on his first mission trip and later partnered with Barnabas and with the Apostle Peter in his ministry at Rome (Acts 15:37–38; 1 Pet 5:13; Col 4:10). Papias, an early follower of the Apostle John, suggested that Mark accompanied Peter to Rome and became his scribe as he delivered the story of Jesus to the Roman Christians.[3] This might suggest that the Gospel of Mark was actually the Gospel according to Peter. Mark left clues to the reader that his audience was Gentile as he translated Jewish terms, offered interpretations for Gentiles, and modeled the story of Jesus in light of literature praising the Roman emperors.[4]

John's Gospel is believed by some to be the latest written of the four and has been attributed to Jesus's apostle who was the brother of James the Apostle, and a fisherman in a co-op with Peter and his brother Andrew (Luke 5:9). John is thought to be later than the other three because it follows a theme that Jesus is God, divine, and of the Father. While many scholars suggest that John was written near the end of the first century, a growing consensus continues to place John earlier and suggests that this work may have been used by one or more of the other Gospel writers.[5]

THE GOSPELS AS LITERATURE

Since the eighteenth century the Gospels have been studied as literature and discussed as texts for the early church. *Synoptic Gospels* has been a term used to describe Matthew, Mark, and Luke. This word means "to see together" or "view with," suggesting that these three books not only have strong similarities, but that all three writers relied on a common written source, whether each other's writings and/or written traditions that predated their manuscript. Most scholars suggest that Mark was the first document written, since it is the shortest, and was later used and edited by Matthew and Luke.[6] These variations suggest that Matthew was written second, followed

---

better. I am choosing to use the terms Hebrew scriptures and Christian scriptures for the Bible as I believe they give us a broader and complete understanding of this sacred book. Clark, *The God of Second Chances*, 9–10.

3. Papias, "Fragments," 3:15.
4. Schmidt, *A Scandalous Beauty*, 31–37.
5. Anderson, *The Fourth Gospel and the Quest for Jesus*, 29.
6. Peabody, Cope, and McNicol, *One Gospel from Two*; Moo, "'Gospel Origins': A Reply to J. W. Wenham," 24–36.

by Luke, vice versa, or that Mark used Matthew and Luke.[7] Views also suggest that various prototypes of writings or sayings of Jesus existed that were used by the writers. While this involves literary examination, investigation of the texts, some guesswork, and academic debate, it is clear that these three Gospels have a high degree of similarity. A quick reading of these three books leaves the reader with parallels and a common timeline for the life of Jesus.

Paul Anderson is one of a growing number of scholars who suggests that John be placed in this group as well. Traditionally John has been excluded from the Synoptic Gospels and viewed as a unique and later creation, yet Anderson gives compelling evidence that John may have predated Luke and Matthew while carrying many similarities with the other three Gospels. If Anderson and others are correct, we can assume that all four writers share a common source or have produced common sources for the early Christian community.[8]

The Gospel of Luke has been attributed to Luke, the physician and companion of the Apostle Paul (Col 4:14; Acts 16:9). According to Luke's other volume (Acts) he joined Paul on his mission trip to Macedonia (Acts 16:11). Luke may have been included on the team after Paul passed through the Greek city Troas as the story switched from "Paul and his companions," to "we." If this is true, Paul was wise to add a physician to his team, especially since he had received many physical beatings while traveling. While Luke had no direct access to or knowledge of Jesus, he clearly wrote as someone who was influenced and taught the Way according to Paul, was familiar with the Greek version of the Hebrew Bible, and had researched his community well.[9]

Luke as Author

While much has been written concerning the identity of the author of Luke, either in original or edited form, I am choosing the perspective that Luke, the companion of Paul and the physician, was the author of these two works. First, there is controversy concerning the style of Luke/Acts. Some suggest it is historiography, others biography or novel, and some believe it is a romantic epic.[10] Suggestions as to the identity of Luke have been based

---

7. Carson, Moo, and Morris, *An Introduction to the New Testament*, 19–60.

8. Anderson, *The Fourth Gospel and the Quest for Jesus*, 134–35.

9. Marshall suggested that a historian did not always have direct contact with evidence, but chose what to record as a basis of his belief. I. Howard Marshall, *Luke*, 22.

10. Witherington, *The Acts of the Apostles*; Palmer, "Acts and the Ancient Historical

on this discussion as well. However, this work is not designed to explore this further. It is not illogical to accept that the early Christian testimony that Luke was a physician and evangelist is valid. It also can explain Luke/Acts both as historical document and/or literary narrative reflecting the work of someone trained in research.

Second, in the ancient world many doctors were Gentile slaves. Most slaves/servants were well treated in the Roman Empire and often earned enough money (*peculium*) to buy their freedom. Many had the opportunity to obtain leadership positions in their community and were well educated. Those educated were employed as teachers, scribes, financial managers, and business owners. These servants were trained in Greek literature and language, rhetoric, and other sciences. Since Asklepios was the god of healing most doctors worked in or through an Asklepion (the temple for this god). These Asklepions contained libraries suggesting that these physicians were skilled in research and highly educated. Philippi had a well-known medical school. Since Luke joined Paul's mission team at Troas, just outside of Philippi, and spoke more highly of the city than any other towns where they visited, it seems that Luke may have been from this area (Acts 16:12). In Luke 1:3, the author used a word for "investigate" indicating that he was able to do research. The writer of Luke displayed the skills of a highly trained author as well as one who was able to research and interview people.[11] Luke's texts prove to be the product of an educated individual who associated with elite individuals in society.[12] It is also interesting that Luke conveyed people's thoughts and opinions, suggesting that he also interviewed and spoke to people as sources in the Gospel (Luke 1; 2).

Luke demonstrated his skills as a writer by retelling the story of the female hemophiliac. Mark claimed that she "suffered much under the care of doctors and spent all of her money," but Luke protected the profession when he wrote that "she couldn't be healed" (Mark 5:36; Luke 8:43). Luke also used medical terms concerning tools, demoniacs, and sickness.[13]

As a Gentile, Luke also reminded the reader that Jesus came to free Jews and Gentiles.

> He [Simeon] took him in his arms and blessed God, saying:
> "Master, let your servant leave in peace according to your word.
> My eyes have seen your salvation, which you have prepared in

---

Monograph," 28–29; and Penner, *In Praise of Christian Origins*, 45.

11. Conway, *Behold the Man*, 137; Spencer, *Journeying through Acts*, 14.
12. Witherington, *Acts*, 55.
13. Ibid., 349.

the presence of all people: a light to be revealed to the Gentiles, and the glory of your people Israel." (Luke 2:28–32)

Throughout Luke's Gospel the author reflected his perspectives on life, the Messiah, and his experiences of the early Christian community. However, the main focus of both Luke and Acts was the beginning, development, and growth of the church as a new movement. As with many other ancient authors, history was written to describe the growth of new institutions and religions.[14]

Luke and His Gospel

There are many discussions concerning the type of genre of the Gospels. Some would suggest that the Gospels are a history of the life of Jesus, called *bios*.[15] While this has merits, difficulties arise when scientific tools are applied to the stories. Each writer had a theological bent to telling the story and this collides with historical writing as we in the twenty-first century understand it to be.

Other scholars indicate that the Gospels were Greco-Roman biographies (*encomiums*) of Jesus. This also finds merit in Gospel studies but fails to explain the heavy emphasis on other minor characters as well as the believing community. Another suggestion is that the Gospels were another type of Torah such as the first five books of Moses in the Hebrew Bible, which became the church's law and foundation. As with many conservative Jewish rabbis who saw only the Torah as inspired and authoritative for the community, many church leaders throughout the centuries viewed the four Gospels as the inspired rule for the church. I am currently working with over forty ancient Ethiopic scrolls (Ge'ez) of the four Gospels and learning how foundational and authoritative these books have been in their churches. However, Luke's second volume and his teacher, Paul, claim to also provide a strong source of authority and inspiration to the Christian community as well.

A fourth suggestion, and one which I will embrace, is that the Gospels were a combination of sermons, biography, and historiographic drama for the reading community. Luke, like many other ancient writers, provided an epic story of Jesus, Christianity, and God's interaction with a new people. Ancient students and writers were acquainted with classical writings such

---

14. Cancik, "The History of Culture, Religion, and Institutions," 673.

15. Burridge, *What Are the Gospels?* 12–15; Nolland, *Luke 1–9:20*, xxviii-xxxii; Bonz, *The Past as Legacy*, 1–25.

as the ancient Babylonian creation epic *Enuma Elish*, Homer's Greek classics *Iliad* and *Odyssey*, as well as Virgil's history of Rome also known as *The Aeneid*. Marianne Bonz indicates that Virgil's historical description of the emergence of Rome in the *Aeneid* was not only a commonly used literary classic, but Virgil himself actually wrote this narrative using common themes from Homer's and other author's works.

> In the case of the *Aeneid*, it must even be assumed that this work was read and admired by the empire's Greek subjects—at least by the time of the apostle Paul—for the Roman philosopher Lucius Annaeus Seneca wrote a letter to the imperial slave Polybius, in which he notes the important tasks that Polybius has undertaken in translating Virgil's poetry into Greek and Homer's works into Latin.[16]

For Bonz, Luke, like Virgil, was retelling a history, not just of Jesus, the hero, but the movement known as Christianity.

> It is my contention that the author known to us as "Luke" was one of those authors upon whom Virgil's epic of Roman origins and divinely guided destiny had a profound influence. Accordingly, the analysis of the *Aeneid* that follows serves not only to illustrate the major themes of Virgil's work but also to isolate a number of the dramatic devices that he employed so effectively and that can also be discerned in the later prose epic, Luke-Acts.[17]

This suggests that Luke's work be viewed not just as history, or a literary creation, but as both. Even more, Luke's emphasis is less on the personal qualities of Jesus as Savior than an overview of the growth of the kingdom of God, the church, and Christianity in general.[18]

While some may suspect that I am taking the emphasis off of Jesus in the Gospel of Luke, this is not my intention. My intention is to suggest that Luke's emphasis is on Jesus as leader and Savior of a movement, which grew and thrived in his earthly absence in the book of Acts.

First, Luke used Savior (*soter* in Greek) and Lord an overwhelming number of times compared to the other Gospel writers. While Gentiles would not have understood the Jewish concept of the Messiah, Savior and Lord were terms reserved for Caesar. A savior was one who set all things in order, was the visible representative of God/Zeus, a benefactor, and brought

---

16. Bonz, *The Past as Legacy*, 24.
17. Ibid., 39.
18. Cancik, "The History of Culture, Religion, and Institutions," 674.

good news (Gospel) to his people.[19] Luke used many Roman Empire terms of Jesus to suggest that he was the leader of a new empire/movement. Luke also suggested that Jesus brought peace (*shalom*), salvation, unity, and power, like accomplishments credited to Caesar as he sought to maintain peace in a world subservient to chaos.

Second, Luke introduced Jesus against the backdrop of a nation returning from captivity. As the Roman Caesars claimed to extend their borders geographically and establish peace (*Pax Romana*) and order through force and military power, Luke suggested that Jesus extended his borders socially to provide freedom and peace through forgiveness and sharing the Spirit. As Caesar expanded power through political proclamation, Jesus expanded power through prophetic preaching and the global influence of the Spirit. In addition he visited those on the margins of society. For Luke, Jesus was more prophet than Messiah.[20] Instead of the Jewish nation returning to worship in and rebuild the temple, Jesus became the Lord who led the captives into a relationship through repentance, forgiveness, and the pouring out of the Spirit. This movement grew to become a powerful institution.

Finally, Luke/Acts must be viewed as two works in one. Luke's Gospel introduced themes which were later fulfilled by the early Christian community after Jesus ascended to heaven. Luke focused on fulfillment not only in the Gospel but in Acts. The Book of Acts illustrated the movement's imitation of their Lord. In Luke's Gospel Jesus began to disseminate power, authority, and leadership while among the disciples. The story resumes in Acts as the apostles led and disseminated power, authority, and leadership while Jesus was "taken up to heaven."

Viewing Luke as this type of literature calls the reader to engage the movement rather than simply observe the life and times of Jesus and the church of old.

Luke's Epic Writing

> Many have set their hand to narrate an account of what has happened among us, just as they were passed down to us by those who were, in the beginning, eyewitnesses and servants of the word. It seemed good to me, since I myself have carefully investigated everything from the beginning, to write an orderly account for you, most excellent Theophilus, so that you may know that what you have been taught is safe/trustworthy. (Luke 1:1–4)

---

19. Cartlidge and Dungan, eds., *Documents for the Study of the Gospels*, 5–6.
20. Croatto, "Jesus, Prophet Like Elijah," 453.

Luke seemed to craft his history through both research and narrative. In Luke 1:1–4 he suggested that the following were true. *First, there were other versions of the Jesus story in circulation among the church.* Whether this was one or all three of the other Gospels, their original sources, and/or oral stories, Luke claimed to deliver another account in addition to existing stories. Concerning the introduction of Luke (Luke 1: 1–4) Donald Juel stated that, "The Greek is elegant and quite distinct from the prose that follows."[21] Whether Luke was referring to Mark, Matthew, and/or John is unclear. He did indicate that the tradition had been "handed down," suggesting that these stories/writings were viewed as authoritative teachings. However, he believed that the community needed another account of Jesus. Luke would have viewed his books as scripture as he did the others.[22] We can assume that the Jesus tradition was alive and well orally, but also in shorter segments collected and distributed in the early first century. The short collections of sayings of Jesus in the Gospel of Thomas, a writing found in the archives of ancient Syrian churches, indicated that shorter collections of Jesus's sayings and stories existed in the earliest stages of the church.

Second, Luke claimed to investigate or "follow again" the story.[23] While not present during Jesus's ministry, Luke indicated that he interviewed others and shared their personal stories in his writing. He shared Mary's thoughts and personal accounts of her encounters with an angel, Elizabeth, the shepherds, and Simeon (Luke 1–2). While Luke claimed not to be an eyewitness to the Jesus story, he did relate eyewitness accounts suggesting that his research involved personal testimonies, interviews, and reading other stories, and discussion with the community.[24]

Third, Luke claimed that these accounts discussed "what happened among us." This is usually translated "the affairs among us," and was a business phrase indicating that Luke counted himself among the believers and that this history was his/their history. He had somehow gained enough information to understand the faith and possibly was viewed as a person with credibility among the Christian community. The word for "affairs" also suggested that he saw the movement as a credible organization in an empire that held new religious groups with suspicion. Luke seemed less concerned with the "truth about Jesus" and more with the events of the church.

Fourth, Luke wrote an orderly narrative. Luke's writing style is sophisticated and reflects his training and education as a writer. He also wrote that

---

21. Juel, *Luke-Acts*, 13–14.
22. Smith, "When Did the Gospels Become Scripture?," 9.
23. Marshall, *Luke*, 39; Adams, *The Sinner in Luke*, xxiii.
24. Marshall, *Luke*, 41; Adams, *The Sinner in Luke*, xxxiii.

this Gospel was a "narrative."²⁵ Narrative suggests advanced training. When historians such as Homer and Virgil delivered epics of their culture, these epics became widely read and copied. These writers set out to prove to their world that their empires were divinely ordained and highly successful. They used persuasion to engage their audience/readers. Similarly, Luke used an orderly or step by step method to persuade his readers that Jesus was the founding emperor of a renewed empire.²⁶ Luke also in the style of these authors believed that the Jesus empire was an epic and divine event that changed the face of history. As narratives Luke and Acts were not meant to be scientific or simply historical documents, nor were they meant to be training manuals. Both works share a literary form understood as an epic adventure according to Luke's perspective of the Jesus story and the birth of the church—the new people of God.

Finally, Luke's account was written to Theophilus to assure him that what they knew about the faith was safe. He was possibly a high ranking Gentile official. His name means "lover of God" in Greek. The term could have been. The term could have been for a high ranking official, suggested by the preceding phrase "most excellent." The term Luke used for "most excellent," *kratiste*, was also a term for someone in the equestrian units in Rome.²⁷ It is likely that Theophilus was a Christian of noble status who was in charge of speaking to the Christian community with which he was affiliated. Theophilus may also have been a wealthy patron who funded Luke's writings.²⁸ The word for "safe" was a legal term that indicated one was financially in good standing. As a gentile Theophilus and his community would have been struggling to avoid the "riches and cares of their world" in order to further the kingdom of Jesus. Safe also indicated, to Theophilus and the community, that Christianity could be a legitimate movement/religion, sometimes labeled by the Romans as *religio licita* (legal religion).

It seems that Luke's Gospel was an epic story of the ministry of Jesus that changed the course of history. Like Homer and Virgil, Luke used common themes, symbols, and selected stories to indicate that Jesus, the divine emperor, inaugurated this new empire of compassion and mercy rather than violence and power. This empire spawned a religious faith that was safe, peaceful, and one that grew and promoted good in their world.

25. Marshall, *Luke*, 41; Adams, *The Sinner in Luke*, xxxiii; Shepherd, *The Narrative Function of the Holy Spirit*, 1.

26. Maxwell, "The Role of the Audience," 171–80; Shepherd, *The Narrative Function of the Holy Spirit*, 108.

27. Shepherd, *The Narrative Function of the Holy Spirit*, 103.

28. Robinson and Wall, *Called to Be Church*, 19: Moxnes, "Patron-Client Relations," 267.

> For Luke, writing more than twenty years after Mark and living in a predominantly gentile Christian community, now wholly separate from the synagogue, Jesus' death and resurrection were no longer seen as the immediate prelude to the cataclysmic end of history or the eschatological turning of the ages. Rather, Jesus' death had triggered God's final judgment against unbelieving Israel, and Jesus' resurrection and ascension had signaled the transformation of the old ethnic ideal of the people of God into a newly universalized concept of community.[29]

A Hybrid Gospel

As I studied through this work and while working on *The God of Second Chances*, it became clear to me that the Jewish exile, periods of reform, and templeless age had a profound effect on the Judeans' view of themselves and their faith.[30] As N.T. Wright suggests, the people of first-century Judaism saw themselves as being in exile. Wright also indicates that the people of Jesus saw themselves as this restored community and that true restoration did not happen in the Hebrew Scriptures but that the author of Luke and Acts saw this fulfilled in Jesus and the church.[31]

In 587 BCE the Babylonian army began to take the Jerusalem inhabitants captive and transported them to their capitol city.[32] A century and a half before this event, the Israelite Kingdom (also known as the Northern Kingdom or Samaria) was taken captive and exiled to the Assyrian capitol of Nineveh. Both nations saw this as a punishment for neglecting Yahweh by worshiping other gods and acting unjustly with those who were poor and oppressed. In both events some were taken captive by their victors, others fled to form new communities outside of their country, some remained in the capital as squatters, and many others were killed either during the destruction and army invasion, or during the four-month travel to their host country. During this time prophets offered hope and vision for restoration, laments and psalms were written to express the grief of a people over shame, sin, and suffering, and new leaders, such as Daniel, Ezra, Nehemiah, Esther,

---

29. Bonz, *The Past as Legacy*, 193.

30. Clark, *The God of Second Chances*, 25–33.

31. Wright, *Jesus and the Victory of God*, xvii-xviii; Evans, "Jesus and the Continuing Exile of Israel," 77–100.

32. I have chosen BCE (Before the Common Era) instead of BC (Before Christ) as this term is now the standard term used in dating the Bible and history. CE (Common Era) will replace AD (*Anno Domini*).

Mordecai, Hananiah, Azariah, and Mishael emerged in a new culture. This exile/templeless period provided a creative outlet for the Jewish people to reflect on their relationship with God as well as their sin, guilt, and shame. This period also refined the Jewish views of Yahweh, faithfulness, and a renewed relationship/covenant.

However, when Cyrus the Persian led the defeat at Babylon, the Jews returned to their homeland to rebuild their temple. During this period prophets such as Zechariah, Haggai, and Malachi called their people to turn back to Yahweh. The political leaders Nehemiah, Ezra, Zerubabel, and Joshua the high priest also led the nation to reestablish their covenant with God. The temple was rebuilt and Yahweh promised that the restored community was loved by their God and Savior.

> "The glory of this present house will be greater than the glory of the former house. In this place I will give peace," declares Yahweh Almighty (Hag 2:9).

Unfortunately the book of Malachi suggested that the nation quickly returned to their old ways. God reminded the nation that, as before, they would receive a divine visit to judge the good as well as the evil (Mal 4:5–6).

This left the door open for repeated cycles of exile and restoration. With the rise of the Greek and Roman Empires the nation of Judah continued to find themselves, once again, between warring cultures (Egypt versus the rest of the world). During the time of Jesus the nation was scattered, colonized, and longing for redemption. However, this was not only geographical exile, they were colonized and socially exiled from their own land.

> He raised up a horn of salvation for us in the house of his servant David. As in the old days he spoke through his holy prophets—salvation from our enemies and from the hand of all who hate us—to show mercy to our ancestors and to remember his holy covenant, the oath he swore to our father Abraham: to rescue us and help us not fear our enemies, to serve before him all our days in holiness and righteousness. (Luke 1:69–75)

> There was a man in Jerusalem named Simeon, who was righteous and devoted. He was waiting for the encouragement/comfort of Israel, and the Holy Spirit was on him. (Luke 2:25)

While Wright and others suggests that the Jewish nation never saw the restoration as complete and believed themselves to remain in exile, I would suggest that they saw themselves in "another exile." First, restoration in Haggai and Zechariah had less to do with the temple and its construction and more to do with the renewal of Yahweh's covenant with the people. The renewal of the Spirit, forgiveness, and having Yahweh as Lord were key components to the restoration of the Jewish nation as Yahweh's people.

> From this day on (the twenty-fourth day of the ninth month), put this in your heart . . . From this day on I will bless you (Hag 2:18–19).

> I will remove the sin of this land in a day (Zech 3:9).

Second, the Hebrew for "new" (*chadesh*) can also mean "renewed." The Jewish nation was not limited by one covenant, but was sanctified by renewed covenants. Finally, the promise of Haggai 2 and Zechariah 3 suggested that restoration happened during the prophets' day. Yahweh restored the nation to holiness not by the rebuilding of the temple but through the obedience and repentance of the people/nation and their leaders.

Luke heavily used exile and restoration language in both his Gospel and Acts. Terms such as repentance, empire, redemption, restoration, comfort, consolation, the prophetic nature of Jesus and the Holy Spirit, and the revival of the twelve Jewish tribes indicate that he viewed the coming of Jesus and the Spirit as another restoration of God's people. As the Jewish nation was gathered home during the templeless period, so the nation was united by the preaching of the Gospel, the Holy Spirit, and the church. This is evident by Luke's description of John and the baptism of Jesus.

> In the fifteenth year of the reign of Tiberius Caesar, Pontius Pilate was the governor of Judea, Herod was tetrarch of Galilee, his brother Philip was tetrarch of the region of Ituraea and Trachonitis, and Lysanias was the tetrarch of Abilene. During the high priesthood of Annas and Caiaphas, the word of God came to John, the son of Zechariah, in the wilderness. He went to all the region surrounding the Jordan, proclaiming a baptism of repentance for the forgiveness of sins. (Luke 3:1—3)

The setting of this narrative suggested that a movement began during the reign of a powerful emperor. First, John was preaching a baptism of repentance for the forgiveness of sins at the Jordan River, a river that the Jews crossed to pass into a new time of history for their nation (Josh 3). Second, the word of God came through John, who was the one to lead God's people back to their Lord (Luke 1:16–17). John, like the prophet Elijah, was to prepare people for the coming of God (Mal 4:3–4; Luke 1:17; 76–77).

> The sound of one crying in the wilderness: "Prepare the Lord's way, and straighten out the paths. Every valley shall be filled in,

> and every mountain and hill shall be made low, and the crooked shall be straightened, the rough places will become level roads, and all flesh/people will see the salvation of God." (Luke 3:4–6)

This passage, also found in Isaiah 40:3–5, was used to promise the return of the Jews from Babylonian captivity. In the Isaiah passage the return of the nation was also a sign that Yahweh was coming in glory to show forgiveness, mercy, and reconciliation, to a nation that had violated its covenant with its Lord. In the time of Jesus, Luke, and the other Gospel writers, presented John baptizing Jesus, along with the crowds who came to hear him, as a sign that the Son of God offered forgiveness, mercy, and righteousness.

Third, John also suggested that Jesus was Yahweh coming to judge and reconcile people to a relationship with their Lord.

> On the one hand, I baptize you with water. On the other hand the one who is mightier than I is coming, I am not worthy to untie the strap of his sandals. He will baptize you with the Holy Spirit and fire. His winnowing fork [rake] is in his hand, to clear [the chaff/husks from] his threshing floor and gather the wheat into his barn. The chaff/husks will be burned with an unquenchable fire. (3:16–17)

The baptism of the spirit and fire were metaphors found in the Hebrew prophets that suggested both judgment (pouring out fire, anger, wrath) or reconciliation (pouring out the Spirit, water, peace) at the hand of Yahweh (Isa 4:4–5; 42:1–3; Joel 2:28–32; Mic 3:8; Zech 12:10). John was suggesting that Jesus was Yahweh who judged the disobedient and offered a renewed relationship to those in captivity. "Luke-Acts often deals with the reintegration of marginalized people to the social order . . . which is a restoration of Israel's social order."[33]

Fourth, Jesus was baptized, suggesting that he not only offered judgment and forgiveness, but he led the captives/marginalized in glory by going before them and becoming their leader, Lord, and Savior. Finally, John's baptism and call to repentance echoed the prophet's call in the Hebrew Bible, to return to Yahweh and seek salvation (Ezek 18:32). While not everyone in ancient captivity was guilty of sin, the nation as a whole needed to turn back to God and seek relationship with its Lord (Dan 9).

I believe that Luke wrote his Gospel and Acts as an epic story of another redemption of spiritual Israel, which included both Jews and Gentiles. Jesus was Yahweh who came to a marginalized people longing for inclusion and acceptance. He came among them to empower them to once again

---

33. Lee, "Pilate and the Crucifixion of Jesus," 90.

become an empire of marginalized people who could "turn the world upside down" (Ezek 37:1–14; Acts 17:6) and show that it was more blessed to give than receive.

LUKE'S GOSPEL IN AN EMERGING CULTURE

This story of exile, redemption, and emergence was written for an existing Christian community. Little is known of this community but we can assume that important people were part of this audience as we read the introduction to Luke's Gospel. Theophilus and his church needed to know that their instruction was sound/safe/healthy. In addition to this Luke also seemed to suggest that they needed more than their existing beliefs. First, since "most excellent Theophilus" was an honorific title for a Gentile leader, I am assuming that he was also a leader for this church, and would have been a wealthy patron for the group.[34] This leader needed more of Jesus than what they already knew.

Second, Luke's emphasis on the poor, repentance, salvation, Gentiles, outcasts, and peace occur in greater number than the other Gospels and suggest that these may be issues that the Theophilus community either neglected to develop or had missed from other eyewitness accounts. Luke may have been challenging an emerging and possibly established church to be restored/renewed as a marginalized community by addressing the neglected teachings of Jesus, and his church. As ancient Judah was exiled for neglecting social justice and Yahweh, so this community may have been struggling with the same fate. They may also have been enmeshed in a culture that neglected those on the margins.

Finally, the retelling of the Jesus story through post-exilic and restoration themes suggests to the community that the church gathers those on the margins and presents them before Yahweh to be blessed in the pouring out of the Spirit, sanctification, repentance, forgiveness, and economic redistribution. The church was to become the "restored empire" that drew all nations to Jesus/Yahweh, rather than those who drove others into exile.

> Gathering together they asked him, "Lord, are you restoring the empire of Israel at this time?" He said to them: "It is not for you to know the times or dates set by the Father's own authority. You will receive power when the Holy Spirit comes on you; and you will be my witnesses in Jerusalem, Judea, Samaria, and to the ends of the earth." (Acts 1:6–8)

---

34. Shepherd, *The Narrative Function of the Holy Spirit*, 103; Moxnes, "Patron-Client Relations," 267.

Paul and Barnabas boldly said: "We had to speak the word of God to you first. Since you reject it and do not consider yourselves worth eternal life, we turn to the Gentiles. For this is what the Lord commanded us: "I have placed you as a light for the Gentiles, that you may bring salvation to the ends of the earth." When the Gentiles heard this, they were glad and honored the word of the Lord . . . (Acts 13:46–49)

Modern Exiles

Luke's Gospel has a powerful message to the modern reader. The church today sometimes reads Luke and Acts almost as a book for church doctrine or as a book to "get saved." Instead of finding texts and verses to use in worship on Sunday mornings the Gospel was meant to teach us about restoration, relationship, and freeing those in captivity. Few of us would believe that we were in exile. Yet with one trip to a shopping mall or health gym, or by watching advertising on television, we realize that we live in a world that presents a false sense of reality. Our world, our empire, our reality is power, tension, anxiety, fear, and oppression. It is a world that promises much and delivers little. It is a world where relationships are shallow and objects are priceless. It is a reality where those who have, keep and hoard, and those who have not, desire. It is a world that promises power over peace. People who do not fit into our reality's view of body size, looks, and financial stability are people without power. In this system peace is an illusion, temporary freedom from anxiety, and a mist.

In the world of exile God promised peace/*shalom* to the refugees. This *shalom* was a safe place where God's love empowered people to be accepted, loved, and secure. Ancient Rome promised peace (*Pax Romana*) at the expense of military power, the threat of violence, and submission to the Roman emperor. This peace caused the elite to become more powerful and the vulnerable to become marginalized. However, Jesus promised *shalom* (*Pax Christi*) to those who were on the margins of society, powerless, vulnerable, and without hope.

- Luke wrote this Gospel to people in this world.
- Luke wrote this Gospel to the church in this same world.
- Luke wrote this Gospel to people called to do ministry in this world.
- Luke wrote this Gospel to the church which had forgotten to reach people on the margins of this world.

Unfortunately the church of Luke's day was very similar to the modern church. We too have heard the Gospel of Jesus. We too have the traditions and doctrines passed down from generation to generation. We too have our accepted texts and scriptures concerning Jesus. As North Americans we have prided ourselves in the fact that we have been known as a Christian nation. Yet something has gone drastically wrong.

> Leighton Ford indicates that North America now holds the distinguished honor of being the third largest mission field in the English-speaking world. And the United States has more secular, unchurched people than most nations of the world, yet many churches don't seem to operate in light of this fact.[35]

In addition to this, we who have heard the message and chosen not to proclaim it have also forgotten the Jesus whom Luke wanted us to embrace. This Jesus can revive the church because he calls us to a radical love for God and our neighbors, especially those marginalized by society. For some this "social justice" or "social gospel" has become a dirty word, but for Luke, this was Jesus the friend of outcasts.

> Christians cannot turn away from any form of inhumanity without separating themselves from the humanity of God. Most Christians would be scandalized to be told that abandoning the homeless, overlooking the deep injustice of poverty and systematically excluding the socially unacceptable is the moral and spiritual equivalent of apartheid.[36]

> Social justice is not an abstract principle, nor is it an ideal to be pursued. Social justice is the core of human experience. It is the bread and water; it is blood and bones; it is brothers and sisters who unlearn the knowledge of how to hurt and how to kill and who learn to live in power, the freedom and the hope with which God intended that we should live. If there is any basis for social justice, it lies between us, within our humanity; it is anthropological. Social justice is a divinely ordained order of human existence. Humanity is essentially cohumanity.[37]

Or, as the nineteenth-century theologian Walter Rauschenbusch once stated concerning the social gospel, "The social gospel needs a theology to

---

35. Burke, *No Perfect People Allowed*, 20.
36. Anderson, *The Shape of Practical Theology*, 179.
37. Ibid., 312.

make it effective but theology needs the social gospel to vitalize it."[38] For Rauschenbusch the church during the American Industrial Revolution had lost its way and became focused on theological ideas that separated them from their neighbors.

> The dogmas and theological ideas of the early church were those ideas which at that time were needed to hold the church together, to rally its forces and to give it victorious energy against antagonistic powers. Today many of those ideas are without present significance. Our reverence for them is a kind of ancestor worship. The social gospel gets hold of our heart now—as the Nicene Creed did in the fourth century.[39]

The modern church needs to recapture the real Jesus and become friends of the outcasts, as their master continues to be a friend to these. In addition to this, the church must model this Jesus as we continue to see future generations leaving churches.

> A generation of young Christians believes that the churches in which they were raised are not safe and hospitable places to express doubts. Many feel that they have been offered slick or half-baked answers to their thorny, honest questions, and they are rejecting the "talking heads" and "talking points" they see among the older generation.[40]

This takes sacrifice and courage not just from young people, but older, mature Christians, especially those in leadership.

> The difficulty for the church today is not in encouraging people to ask what Jesus would do but in getting them to break out of their domesticated and sanitized ideas about Jesus in order to answer that question.[41]

The modern church, even after years of being challenged to reach out to a hurting world, still needs to reexamine the Lukan Jesus and the call to live on the margins with the outcasts. As Martin Luther King, Jr. once stated, our young people's future has, for decades, been affected by the present mission of the church.

> The judgment of God is upon the church as never before. If today's church does not recapture the sacrificial spirit of the early

---

38. Rauschenbusch, *A Theology for the Social Gospel*, 1.
39. Ibid., 13.
40. Kinnaman, *You Lost Me*, 11.
41. Frost and Hirsch, *ReJesus*, 19–20.

> church, it will lose its authenticity, forfeit the loyalty of millions, and be dismissed as an irrelevant social club with no meaning for the twentieth century. Every day I meet young people whose disappointment with the church has turned into outright disgust.[42]

King said it well: if we want our young people to embrace Christianity then it must be one that addresses social, theological, and justice issues as a core of its being. We must accept that social justice issues are the gospel and issues for Jesus's followers to embrace.

> In the midst of blatant injustices inflicted upon the Negro, I have watched white churchmen stand on the sideline and mouth pious irrelevancies and sanctimonious trivialities. In the midst of a mighty struggle to rid our nation of racial and economic injustice, I have heard many ministers say: "Those are social issues, with which the gospel has no real concern." And I have watched many churches commit themselves to a completely otherworldly religion which makes a strange, un-Biblical distinction between body and soul, between the sacred and the secular.[43]

This means that Christians, especially leaders and other mature Christians, must become a people who feel called to live on the margins of life so that they can practice the ministry of the Lord, who had the reputation of being a friend of sinners. It is a dark place, a dangerous place, and a risky place. Yet it is the place where Luke reminded the early reader that Jesus lived. It is also the place where we must live so that the empire of Jesus can create new life and new ministries to a world suffering in social captivity. "The church today must exist at the edge of chaos, between anarchy and rigidity."[44]

THEMES WE WILL SEE IN LUKE

I understand that Theophilus and his community were aware of the story of Jesus. I also understand that Luke added stories to his narrative that were unique to his Gospel as well as Acts. I also understand that this ancient church, not unlike many churches today, needed to be reminded that Jesus did ministry to a community marginalized by their environment and possibly the church.

---

42. King, Jr., *Why We Can't Wait*, 93.
43. Ibid., 92.
44. Woodward, *Creating a Missional Culture*, 72.

Is it possible that Luke included "neglected" stories from the Jesus narratives? I do not mean those stories "neglected" by eyewitnesses, but those "neglected" by the church. Is it possible that the church had forgotten to minister to the marginalized in their communities? History suggests that this is not unlikely.

Many years ago I sat on an airplane with a couple and their toddler from Portugal. They were a nice family and the woman was comfortable speaking English. They worked at a car dealership that his father owned and had lived in a large city in Portugal all of their life. They loved selling cars and they were good at it. I asked the woman a lot of questions about cars in Portugal and America and we had a nice visit until lunch was brought.

After a while she asked about my job and I told her I was a minister. I shared with them that I was going on a mission trip to Albania to do some work and teaching. We began to talk about church and they expressed that they were very active in the Catholic church at home. They, their parents, and their grandparents had attended all their life. They were committed to the teachings, but they didn't always understand them. However, one point she discussed with me for about an hour concerned the church buildings and the homeless and impoverished neighborhoods surrounding these churches. She mentioned often that the church buildings were beautiful, covered in precious metals and stones, and had fences to keep out the neighborhood. Her main concern was that Christianity was not changing with their neighborhoods and not reaching those in need. I had to agree and felt that their world was not much different than mine. Churches have been viewed by communities, as well as those who are members, as avoiding those on the margins of society. We began as a movement that met in caves and then became an institution that resides in castles.

Are we accomplishing anything in our churches when we have big, elaborate beautiful buildings in the slums? Are we accomplishing anything when we sink so much money into our buildings rather than our neighborhoods? Oh, but we do it for God, we say. I understand. We do it because we want God to have the best. But somehow when I read my Bible I find that God lived in a tent, in a building, and in a human body raised in a common home.

After the book of Haggai and Zechariah God lived in a shabby building that king Herod had to rebuild. The Gospel of John states that God lived in a human body (John 1:14). Humble dwellings of God in a humble world, maybe in some way communicating to God's people, "I'm willing to live as you live and I'm willing to understand what you understand."

Christian history is filled with stories that describe abuses of power, neglect, and oppression. However, when God's people return to the Gospels and the life of Jesus, the church seems to revive its concern for the poor, oppressed, and marginalized. Our history is also filled with liberation, social justice, and acts of compassion by God's people. Luke seems to be one of the early evangelists calling the church to return to Jesus through a story emphasizing important themes.

First, repentance is a major theme in Luke and Acts. The word for repent (*metanoeo*) appears fourteen times in Luke and eleven times in Acts, which is more often than the other Gospels combined.[45] At times Luke even adds repentance to stories concerning forgiveness. For Luke, Jesus and the church, like the prophets of old, called people to change their behavior in order to embrace the Gospel. This repentance involved connecting with God and humans and developing relationships. Repentance is similar to making amends and strengthens relationships so that others can forgive. *Shalom* occurred fourteen times, heart forty-five times, and compassion or mercy occur more than the other Gospels combined.[46] It is clear that Luke believed that the people of God were being called back into relationship with their creator. It is also clear that Luke wanted the reader to understand that forgiveness was not possible without repentance. A key component of discipleship was repentance. True justice and *shalom* can only exist when individuals and communities repent, make amends, and offer justice to those they have wronged.

Second, Luke emphasized the work of the Holy Spirit. The Spirit worked with prayer and offered power to preach and proclaim the message of Jesus. The Holy Spirit was a common theme in the exilic and post-exilic prophets and was the vehicle of restoration. The Holy Spirit also accompanied Jesus and the church through preaching and healing, also terms occurring together and more frequently than any of the other Gospels.[47]

Another theme in Luke was Jesus as Savior. While Gentiles may not have been aware that the Jewish Messiah was to come and set things in order, they did know that Caesar (as emperor and Savior) would be the powerful Father of the state who would establish order, peace, and justice in the land. Luke used "today" more often than any other Gospel writer, suggesting that the Savior's call to follow him was an immediate offer extended for peace. He also used "glorified/amazed" as a response to this Savior from the crowds more often than the other writers. These crowds responded to his and the Holy Spirit's work with praise and amazement. Luke used "call"

---

45. Grassi, *Peace on Earth*, 28.
46. Ibid., 27, 58, 68.
47. Bailey, "Looking for Luke's Fingerprints," 148; Marshall, *Luke*, 12.

or "name" over forty-two times, suggesting that Jesus offered not just salvation but relationship and healing. He was truly missional.

Luke emphasized the poor, oppressed, outsiders, Gentiles, and Samaritans more than any other writer. He had the Pharisees assign the label of sinner and identify Jesus in sinners' company more than the other Gospels combined. For Luke, Jesus's main ministry was to include those who were socially marginalized by their communities.

Meal scenes were more common in Luke and Acts than the other Gospels (Luke 4:38; 5:27–39; 7:36–48; 9:10–17; 11:37–54; 14:1–24; 19:1–10; 22:7–38; 24:28–32). In Luke's writings Jesus violated the traditional boundaries of separation by eating with both the righteous and unrighteous. He called his hosts to repent of their neglect, criticisms, and resistance to showing mercy. He accepted people to the table who were shunned by the religious leaders of his day. He taught his disciples that in the meal the key tenets of discipleship are unleashed to a world desiring relationship.

Luke's Gospel began and ended at the temple while Acts began and ended in a home or apartment. In Jesus's day the temple was the public location for prayer, worship, and obedience to Yahweh. The home was the private sphere where hidden sins existed. It was also the place for those steeped in sin, shame, and guilt to hide from God, their leaders, and relationship. *However, Luke indicated that the home became the vehicle of the church, salvation, the good news of God, and family spirituality.* The temple had become corrupt but would soon be destroyed. The home/family would become the new location for prayer, worship, and obedience to Yahweh. As John the Baptist would call the fathers to return to their children/families, so Jesus called the family/house/home the place for spirituality and healing. The temple had lost its power but the family would become an engine which opened the door for the growth of this new empire.

Finally, Luke used the "journey" theme, prophecy, and divine mission to suggest the motion of the hero (Jesus, then in Acts Peter, Paul, and the church) and the emphasis of his ministry. In the ancient Greek and Roman stories, during the journey the heroes confronted those on the margins of society: monsters and beasts. In the end they defeated these marginalized entities. In Luke Jesus met those on margins of society—the poor, the lame, the outcasts, women, and others who were oppressed. In the end he called them. He healed them. He loved them and showed mercy to them. He offered them relationship. He saved them.

Luke's themes suggest to us that he had an agenda in writing his Gospel. This agenda not only sought to teach the reader about Jesus, but also sought to prove that Jesus began a great movement that continues today as long as the disciples follow in the footsteps of their Lord and imitates his actions. For Luke the ancient church must have been neglecting the important things of God—repentance, *shalom*, conversion of the heart, salvation, discipleship, and those on the margins. This involved reaching all people, especially those shunned by the dominant entity in society. They were themes neglected then as well as our day today.

What will it take to unleash Jesus today? What would it mean for Jesus to be unleashed today? What can we do when Jesus is once again calling us to be unleashed in our lives, hearts, churches, and communities?

3

Introducing the Cast
Luke 1–2

THE STARTING LINEUP

ONE YEAR ALL THREE of our sons performed in a high school play. The choice that year was *The Pajama Game* and our oldest son and his girlfriend (who is now his wife), both juniors in high school, played the played significant roles in the production. Our oldest son encouraged his brothers, kindergarten and second grade, to play the children in the performance, and helped the boys with their lines. The boys bought a compact disc of the music and would listen to the songs every night while in bed. The first song was always an introduction that played highlights from all songs in the play. While the characters were introduced at the end of the performance, the songs are typically introduced in the beginning. Before they would go to sleep at night they would ask me to play their CD and the first song, since it "tells us what songs will be coming . . ."

Luke tells the reader what themes will come in his narrative. The first two chapters of his Gospel do not introduce the characters, but the major themes of his work. In fact only John and Jesus play a major role in the Gospel after the introduction; the others fade into the background.[1] Here Luke exposes the reader to the themes that will be discussed throughout his work. In addition to this, two threads weave the story of Jesus and the church together.

---

1. Juel, *Luke-Acts*, 9–10.

The Righteous Remnant

The story began at the Jerusalem temple during the reign of a horribly corrupt king named Herod Antipater. Luke reminded his reader that Herod was the king of the Jewish nation. The name Herod would remind those familiar with Jewish history of the events of the times.

As mentioned earlier, Herod had appointed his own priests in the Jewish temple.[2] He became friends with Marc Antony who overthrew Julius Caesar, the emperor of Rome. Antony was so impressed with his building projects that he sent engineers, artisans, and soldiers to help with the construction.[3] After Antony was defeated in Egypt by the Roman general Octavian, who became Caesar Augustus, Herod was concerned about the future of his political career. In Judea he was rejected by the community and was in fear of losing his throne, which was given to him by Julius, and supported by Marc Antony. Herod made the long trip to Rome and convinced Augustus to allow him to rule Judea by asking, "Please don't judge what friend I was loyal to [Antony] but please judge me by what kind of loyalty I will show my friends." He impressed Caesar enough to return to rule Jerusalem.[4] Herod constructed many great buildings in honor of Caesar in many towns including the port city Caesarea Maritima. However, this construction was costly and resulted in heavy taxes for Herod's people.[5]

Through time Herod became paranoid and hypersensitive to perceived plots which he interpreted as being against his authority. He ordered action throughout the city seeking to torture and kill any would-be assassins.[6] At one point he had his wife Miriam murdered, for fear she wanted his throne, and then later murdered Aristobulus and Alexander, his sons, because he was afraid they would take revenge for their mother. The slaughter of the infant boys, in Matthew 2:14–18, was an event that was reflective of Herod's character. Herod died a bitter and paranoid man.

During this time God, once again, began to act. Luke's story began at the temple, the center of the Jewish universe and home of Yahweh, during a priestly sacrifice. Each day the priests, those in the Levite family, took turns serving at the Jerusalem temple. There were twenty-six divisions of priests during this time and each week one of the divisions served in the temple by cleaning, offering sacrifices, helping people find their way, and making

---

2. Skarsaune, *In the Shadow of the Temple*, 99.
3. Netzer, *Herod the Great*, 15.
4. Roetzel, *The World that Shaped the New Testament*, 25.
5. Ibid., 28.
6. Ibid., 26.

preparations for the Sabbath or holy days. Usually fifty-six priests worked in the temple each day while on the Sabbath an additional twenty-eight priests helped fulfill this holy day ministry.[7] All of them were chosen randomly to do their weekly service. Only one was allowed to enter the Holy Place, where Yahweh was believed to live.

This day Zechariah was given a once in a lifetime opportunity to serve in this Holy Place. Luke wrote that Zechariah and his wife, Elizabeth, were both righteous, followed Yahweh's teachings, and were blameless before their God. Luke also tells us that they were older and had no children because Elizabeth was sterile. In this world, even though they were good people, they would still have felt a sense of shame and dishonor. To be barren in a world where survival depended on raising children was considered by some a sign of sin, shame, or evil.[8] They also were not able to secure their family presence in the priestly tribe by producing an heir. While they may have been accepted by friends, family, and close colleagues the reality in an honor/shame culture suggests that they would have carried a great sense of social shame and sadness over their inability to have children.

In Luke's Gospel God acted in the Holy Place by sending an angel to tell Zechariah that his prayers had been answered. Even though he and Elizabeth did not have children, they continued to pray for a child. Imagine their prayers, their tears, and their hopes. These would have been prayers that reflected the anguish and pain of those who felt marginalized by their society. While they would have had comfort from friends and family, their cultural views kept them on the edges of normal life. God's angel, however, appeared on the side of the altar, which would startle anyone. Because security was so tight with the priests in the temple Zechariah would understand that this had to be divine activity. Zechariah, in the middle of his once in a lifetime opportunity, was told:

> Do not be afraid, Zechariah, because your prayers have been heard, and your wife Elizabeth will give birth to a son, and you will call him John. There will be a lot of joy and celebration and many in your family will be happy. He will be great before the Lord, will not drink wine or strong drink, will be full of the Holy Spirit in his mother's womb, and will turn the children of Israel to the Lord their God. He will go ahead of them in the spirit and power of Elijah and will turn the hearts of the fathers to their children and the disobedient to righteous minds, to prepare people to worship their Lord. (Luke 1:13–17)

---

7. Skarsaune, *In the Shadow of the Temple*, 99.
8. Nolland, *Luke 1:1–9*, 27.

The experience must have caught this older priest off guard because his response was one of faithlessness. The man who had been praying for a child regularly responded with, "No way can this happen—I am too old." He responded with doubt rather than faith. It is easy on the one hand to understand Zechariah's question, but hard to understand how someone who has been praying for God to act for so long could not believe that prayers could be answered. Gabriel's response was, "I am Gabriel, the one who stands in front of God and has been sent to share this good news with you. But you will be silent and not able to speak until the time this happens since you did not believe me." It seems like such a hard rebuke for a man who was told incredible news. However, Gabriel challenged Zechariah concerning his faith.

Crowds, including the other priests, were waiting outside the Holy Place, for Zechariah to finish his job. The task was simple: get in, change the incense, and get out. There was no need to dawdle in the place where Yahweh lived. This was a "place of fear." However, Gabriel began his speech to Zechariah with "don't be afraid." Zechariah's short conversation with the angel was long enough to cause people concern. The text claimed twice that a group was waiting and praying outside (1:10, 21). God's people were not just attending worship, they were worshiping and expecting something to happen. As Zechariah emerged, unable to speak, they assumed he had seen or experienced something from God. However, Zechariah went home, slept with Elizabeth (as he had done so many times before), and saw that God was true. She became pregnant and hid from people, as her husband also must have had to do since he couldn't speak. If their shame before was great, it must have been even greater now. No one wants a priest who can't give a blessing, nor do they want to be around a wife who is hiding during her pregnancy. In some way they both stood in opposition to God—Zechariah by his failure to believe and Elizabeth by her desire to "get even with God" (1:24).

Luke introduced us to those I would call the *righteous remnant*. There were people in these dark Herodian times who still believed. Some prayed for children, others prayed outside the temple and waited for God to act. Some went into hiding when God blessed, others questioned when God offered hope. Zechariah, Elizabeth, and the faithful crowd were the people who stayed with God, even in dark days. Whether it was a family living in cultural shame, people wondering if this would be the time God would act, or others wanting to rejoice at the birth of a baby—God moved and spoke to those who looked for hope. These were the righteous people of God who, unlike many of their community, chose to believe even in times of doubt. While Zechariah was speechless and Elizabeth was in hiding, they at least had the opportunity to reflect, listen, and find the power of God in silence.

The righteous remnant will be one major thread in Luke's writings. These men and women were raised in a faithful environment who lived with the belief and hope that God blessed the faithful. They experienced God's power and knew that God would act and come to save the people. They, like many others today, were those who "grew up" in a home where faithfulness, loyalty, and spirituality were nurtured and practiced. When they saw Jesus, they were expecting and hoping for him to show.

The Marginalized

The same angel came six months later to a different region of Judea and a different person named Mary. We don't know Mary's age. Some traditions suggest that she was an early teenager while Joseph, her fiancé, was a widowed older man (this may have been an attempt to explain why he was not present in the ministry of Jesus since he would have been thought to die).[9] However, this does not have to be true. Ancient historians claim that men and women in their late teens were engaged to be married during this time in history.[10]

The encounter also did not happen in the temple but in the small town of Nazareth. Nazareth was located south of Sepphoris, a town destroyed by the Roman Governor Varus and rebuilt by Herod Antipas (the son of Herod Antipater). Due to the city's resistance to Roman leadership at the death of his father Rome taught the city a lesson by destroying the people and buildings. Herod also, as was his practice, rebuilt the city as a Roman town, and renamed it Autocratis. During the days of Joseph and Mary this city experienced massive construction. As a carpenter (the Greek word also means builder), Joseph, and of course his son Jesus, would have made the three-mile commute from Nazareth to work each day. Thus the angel Gabriel appeared to this young girl, in a common blue collar neighborhood, who was engaged to a construction worker. She, unlike Zechariah, was the least likely person to expect a visit from an angel.

The angel seemed to make Mary somewhat uncomfortable. In apocalyptic or prophetic literature, those who experienced an encounter with angels found them to be mighty beings. However, when angels met people on the ground they were indistinguishable from normal people. Zechariah would have been startled seeing an angel because it would take a divine

---

9. *The Proto-Gospel of James*, 9.

10. *Mishnah, 'Abot* 5:21, 32; *Babylonian Talmud, Qiddishin* 29b-30a; Keener, *A Commentary on the Gospel of Matthew*, 88.

miracle for anyone to enter God's Holy Place. At Nazareth, the angelic encounter seemed to be one that disturbed Mary.

First, the angel greeted her with "Be happy, favored one, the Lord is with you . . ." Any women who were engaged would have been cautious as they were vulnerable to rape, attack, or seduction. The Torah expressed that there were incidents when engaged women were raped by other males (Deut 22:23–29) and women in Nazareth, as today, were taught to protect themselves. Roman soldiers were also present in this area. Being greeted by a strange male was a boundary issue for women in the ancient world. The angel also mentioned that Mary was special to God. Luke tells us that Mary wondered "what sort of greeting" this was, suggesting that he had interviewed her and that she may have been confused by what seemed like a proposition. Finally the angel said she would conceive and give birth to a child, which must have raised her anxiety level even higher. In the end the angel shared that this would be a divine promise and her son would be a great leader.

Mary's response was not unusual. In light of the fact that she was not married pregnancy would have been an impossible occurrence. She made it clear that she was a virgin, setting boundaries as she would have been expected. When the news was given to Zechariah, he had no excuse to question, but Mary did. Zechariah had also asked for an encounter with God, while Mary had not. However, she believed the promise of the angel. Mary confessed she would believe and submit to what was said. Was she in a vulnerable position and stating she would not resist or was she truly believing this was from God? The text only tells us that Mary, as a vulnerable female, made the decision to believe and submit to the promise of God, even though it presented a great risk.

After the angel left Mary, she erupted with a song that expressed her faith as well as her vulnerability. The song was similar to the one uttered by the prophet Samuel's mother Hannah, when she was given a child and believed it was a sign that God defended the oppressed (1 Sam 2:1–10). Mary's song displayed elements of praise from those on the margins. First, she described God as one who protected the marginalized, the humiliated, those who fear God, and those without food (Luke 1:48, 50, 52–53). As mentioned earlier, the word Luke used for "the humiliated state of God's servant" was a term for a sexual abuse victim. Mary stated that God opposed the powerful, rich, and proud, and offered mercy (1:50, 52, 54). Finally, she called God her savior (1:48). Warren Carter claims that people who are colonized or oppressed find ways to resist their powerful overlords through song, poetry, and writing.[11] Mary's subversive language suggested that even though Rome offered the Jews peace/shalom, they were still suffering under their reign.[12] As slaves on the American frontier used songs mixed with biblical imagery to express hope of the day of freedom and justice, so those in oppression sing of the day when they will be free and their oppressor fallen. Mary's song was a form of resistance to oppression and suffering from those on the margins of society. For Mary, God as Savior would enact a form of justice that would involve the redistribution of resources and universal salvation for all people.[13]

The marginalized community is also a major thread in Luke's writings. These individuals may have been raised in a spiritual environment, but the spiritual community had socially labeled them as "unrighteous" and placed them in the "shame" class of society. They typically would not expect to experience God nor would they expect a divine encounter. When they saw Jesus, they rejoiced because they had lived life on the outer boundaries of their world. "When Mary sings of God sending the rich away empty she introduced a theme that runs strongly throughout the Gospel. In an empire where two or three percent of the population possessed most of the wealth and where the majority constantly struggled to sustain a subsistence-level existence, Mary articulates an end to economic structures that are exploitive and unjust."[14]

The Threads Cross

These two lines/threads, marginalized and righteous remnant, intersect when Mary visits her cousin Elizabeth. One can almost hear their joy as Mary saw that Elizabeth had finally become pregnant and as Elizabeth realized that Mary was carrying the Messiah in her womb. The unborn baby John jumped for joy in the presence of the in-wombed Jesus and Elizabeth erupted with praise. Luke predicted that John would be a servant of Jesus and that he would again testify to the divinity and authority of his cousin. Mary stayed with Elizabeth and, after the birth of John, returned to her home—six months pregnant.

---

11. Carter, "Singing in the Reign," 28–29.
12. Ibid., 31.
13. Pickett, "Luke and Empire," 9.
14. Reid, "Women Prophets of God," 57.

The Marginalized

Luke 2 began with an introduction to the setting and history of Luke's world. While Luke discussed the Roman Empire's attempt to enact control and enlist all people on their role, God continued to be active in the life of Mary and Joseph, Zechariah and Elizabeth. Luke suggested that Rome was expanding its control by enrolling people for a census. While evidence from scholars suggests that there was not Empire-wide enrollment policy or that Luke's description my have been found in Roman records, local authorities did enroll people for tax purposes and military service. Caesar used the census to ensure peace, control, and submission.[15] Luke indicated that Judea was under the rule of Rome both politically and economically. Luke also suggested that Joseph, the guardian for Jesus, was a man who followed the laws of the land. While Joseph may have been a very common construction worker he faithfully practiced his religious and legal customs. Joseph followed Roman law (2:1–4); went to Jerusalem each Passover (2:41); offered the prescribed tithes and ritual sacrifices (2:21–25); and attended synagogue (4:16). Jesus was raised by a man and woman who practiced their faith and modeled courage and loyalty to both Yahweh and the Jewish religion.

The story in Luke 2 is quite different from the typical birth narratives told during the Christmas season. First, Joseph and Mary went to Bethlehem to enroll in the census. Second, they stayed in a home (not an inn) which had a small section for animals.[16] Third, because the house was crowded they laid their new baby in a feed trough. Fourth, Mary wrapped Jesus in rags. The birth was not a miraculous event. It was a very normal, quiet, birth in a common crowded home.

In addition to this an army of angels appeared to shepherds. Shepherds were common, unclean, and seen as dishonest workers. The Jewish traditions taught that shepherds were not viewed as trustworthy people.[17] As they were taking different watches over the sheep (this is why it is assumed that Jesus was born in the summer, since it would be too cold to do this in winter), the angel appeared to them and told them that they would find the baby in a feed trough wrapped in rags—nothing spectacular, just a common baby in a common house. The sign for the shepherds was that their Savior would be like them, a common person living in a common family. The angels also shared with them a promise from God: "Glory to the highest God

---

15. Grassi, *Peace on Earth*, 1.
16. Bailey, *Jesus Through Mediterranean Eyes*, 28–29.
17. *Mishnah, Kiddushin* 4:14, "A man should not teach his son to be a donkey or camel driver, a barber, a sailor, or a herdsman, or shopkeeper. Their craft is the craft of robbers."

and *shalom* on earth to those whom God favors" (2:14). The announcement promised peace to those whom God loves. This was a powerful message to the shepherds. Not only did they have the chance to see the Messiah, who was like them, but they were favored by God.

Luke used these shepherds to again express the marginalized theme of the Gospel. Like Mary and Joseph, the shepherds were people on the margins of society. Like Mary, they exhibited faith as they followed the angel's command to see the baby and share the message of God with those in the house. Their amazement and excitement also erupted with praise to God.

Luke again indicated that the gospel came to the most unlikely people. Shepherds were unclean and viewed as dishonest, disgusting, and unspiritual. Yet they, rather than the rulers and religious leaders of the day, had the opportunity to see the baby Jesus. They had permission to view their Savior, God, in a most vulnerable state. In turn God gave them hope, faith, and mercy.

The Righteous Remnant

The righteous remnant theme continued as Mary and Joseph took Jesus to the temple when he was forty days old. While there a righteous man, named Simeon, encountered this family. The text doesn't tell us that Simeon was a priest but it indicates that he was righteous and "waiting for the comfort" of Israel. This language was used for the return of the Jewish nation from captivity: "Comfort, comfort my people Israel. Tell her that her captivity has ended and that she has received double for her sins . . ." (Isa 40:1–2). Israel was again believed to be in captivity, marginalized, colonized, and outcast. God's people hoped for a day when they would return as a nation. However, their captivity was not in a foreign land, it was among their own people. Simeon was simply a godly man who was led by the Spirit to take Jesus and bless him. Imagine Mary and Joseph's faces as this man asked to hold Jesus, then held him up and prayed,

> Lord let your servant leave in peace according to your word,
> since my eyes have seen your salvation which you prepared in
> front of all the people—a light to be revealed to the Gentiles and
> for your people Israel's glory. (2:29–32)

In this prayer Simeon reminded the reader that Jesus came for the righteous remnant, as well as those on the margins (including Gentiles). In addition Simeon reminded Mary that Jesus would face opposition and cause some to rise and others to fall. As Simeon shared his message another righteous woman, Anna, was led by the Spirit to tell others about Jesus.

In this section of Luke the two threads (the righteous remnant and marginalized) unite in Jesus. Outsiders or those on the margins, such as Joseph, Mary, and the shepherds, were given the opportunity to see Jesus and share him with others. Righteous Jews such as Zechariah, Elizabeth, Simeon, and Anna were also given the chance to see the Messiah and proclaim to others his grace.

United in Jesus

The section ended with Jesus at the temple. At age twelve he, like so many other Jewish males, went to Jerusalem for the first time at Passover. Passover was a yearly celebration of God's freeing the Jewish people from Egyptian bondage. As the family had made their annual trek, this year Jesus accompanied them. However, after his parents left he stayed behind and taught the religious leaders at the temple. When his parents had lost track of him, they returned to Jerusalem to find their son, there at the temple doing his father's business/affairs. This section ended where it began, at the temple, only this time the one standing and displaying tremendous knowledge and understanding of the Torah was Jesus. As the people were amazed that Zechariah was speechless, this crowd was amazed at Jesus's speech/teaching.

Luke introduces two threads that run throughout the Gospel. They involve the uniting of the righteous remnant with the marginalized of society. For Luke, Jesus came to call those who were seeking God and restoration, whether they were faithful Jews or humble people on the edges of society. Throughout Luke's writings there will be good, moral, God loving people who seek God and find peace in Jesus. We see these men and women in our communities today. Some were brought up in a Christian home, attended youth group, were baptized young, served in their church, and followed their parents' and their church community's faith. They may have never smoked a cigarette, drank a beer, or stayed out past their curfew. Their parents will say that they were/are great kids and know that they will grow to be a great reflection of the gospel. When they visit a church that's on fire for God, they get involved. They long to serve and grow closer to Jesus and other followers of Jesus. They are the righteous remnant. They are the ones who look for Jesus and seek God. Luke tells us that Jesus came for them.

There are others who live on the margins of life. Some live there because they grew up in a tough home, had parents who didn't care about them, or were dealt a bad hand in life. They try to do their best and they love

God. Others on the margins chose the dark side of life. Once they came to their senses they tried to turn around. They want to love God but wonder if they are loved. All look for Jesus, but some wonder if he will ever look for them. Luke tells us that Jesus came for them as well.

Then there is a third group. This group may have grown up with the righteous remnant or they may have lived with the marginalized. They have had opportunities to seek Jesus, but he is not their Lord. They don't care whether they are on the margins or with the remnant. The bottom line is that they don't care. Luke tells us that Jesus came for them as well. Unfortunately, they don't want him.

Jesus unites the righteous remnant and the marginalized who seek God. People may come from two different directions but in Jesus, they become one. For Luke, Jesus unites people. These two threads will cross often in the Gospel but they will always cross in Jesus. Neither is better than the other—both are in need of Jesus.

Luke seems to be writing to a church that has possibly forgotten those on the margins. They may be part of the righteous remnant or they may have themselves been on the margins. Luke suggests that Jesus unites all people.

First, *Luke tells many stories of Jesus's interaction with the marginalized, oppressed, poor, widows, and females.* Luke added these stories because the readers needed to hear them and embrace Jesus's ministry to the marginalized. *Second, Jesus was criticized by the religious leaders for associating with these people.* Luke indicated that Jesus intentionally associated with these men, women, and children. *Third, God was glorified when the marginalized experienced Jesus's presence through exorcisms, healing, or teaching.* In Luke's Gospel the honor of the empire of Jesus was manifested when the oppressed received blessings. *Finally, Jesus's sermon at the Nazareth synagogue suggested that his role as Messiah was to free the oppressed.* He later suggested to John the Baptist's disciples that, "the poor have good news preached to them . . . " (Luke 7:22). Luke portrayed Jesus's coming as one who freed those in captivity, or on the margins of society. For the Theophilus community, who may or may not have been marginalized, Jesus came to not only reach those who needed acceptance but called the the likes of Theophilus to do the same.

The cast of characters were reminders to Luke's recipients that they too were in the image of God and needed love and relationship within a faith community. As Luke introduced the cast, they very quickly fell silent behind the curtain. The cast illustrated that Jesus united the righteous remnant and the marginalized. Theophilus's audience, readers, and followers understood what "songs/themes were to come . . ."

4

Introducing Jesus
Luke 3–4

It was a cool fall morning in Portland and I was walking along Tom McCall Waterfront Park, which parallels the Willamette River and has a beautiful view of downtown. During the summer many of our outdoor guests (also known as the homeless) sleep on the grassy places or on the park bench to catch the morning sun. This October morning I had noticed that many of the people had already left the area, since the winter rains were beginning to become more frequent.

Morgan and Wendy had visited Agape two days before this and I told them I wanted to meet them for breakfast. I knew they were homeless as they had listed "Burnside Bridge" as their address on the visitor card I received that Sunday. I walked along the waterfront looking for them. There, on a grassy knoll, was a tarp, bicycle, and backpack surrounded by four people. Morgan looked at me, smiled, and said, "Hello pastor, I knew you'd come." I had to smile since it was cold and his smile brought a sense of warmth to the group.

Then he turned to Wendy and the two others near the tarp, as well as the four or five other people sleeping on the ground, and said, "Hey everyone, I want you to meet my pastor." It caught me off guard. He and Wendy visited church only once. I began to think of the few encounters I had with people when I was a younger preacher in a small rural Missouri church. I would argue with people who called me "my pastor" if they were not regular at church or involved with our faith community. I also made it clear that in the Churches of Christ we called our elders pastors and our ministers preachers or evangelists.[1] I felt it was important to correct them and to let them know that they were not "my people" nor was I responsible for them, unless they were willing to be baptized, place membership with us, and put money in the collection plate. As I thought about those conversations, all which had been hurtful to those people in my past, my face became very hot. Not the type of hot you get when you are mad. The type of hot you feel when you are embarrassed, ashamed, and remembering something bad you have done. As I stood there with my head down Morgan smiled, hugged me (almost as if he knew what I was thinking about), and said, "Yes, *my* pastor is here. Everybody, I want you to meet *my* pastor."

I had to smile again, said "Thanks," and hugged him back. He and Wendy introduced me to their group and I took them all to breakfast. They talked, I listened, we ate and prayed together, and we all enjoyed the morning. They told me they would see me Sunday. As I walked away I thought about my past "pastor" controversies. I realized that the gospel involves people, not associations. The gospel concerns crossing boundaries, not maintaining them. The gospel means embracing those for the faith, not distinguishing myself from them. The gospel provides words of life rather than words as ammunition. Morgan, like the people I encountered in my past, was proud to call me his pastor and I guess I should have felt welcome into his world as well as the worlds of others.

BEHOLD HE COMES

Luke has allowed an eighteen-year gap to grow between the story of Jesus at the temple, and John the Baptist's ministry. The boy Jesus was present at Jerusalem at the end of Luke 2, but we heard nothing of John. However, after eighteen years John entered the ministry during a time when Jerusalem was again under turmoil.

At the beginning of Luke 3 we read that the Israelite world had been divided into four sections. Rome controlled Jerusalem, through the governor Pilate, but allowed the Jews to lead the remaining three sections of the country with Herod Antipas, Philip, and Lysinias. Instead of one high priest, Herod and Rome had allowed two (Annas and Caiaphas) which was contrary to Yahweh's law. John's ministry began at a time when Israel was colonized by Rome, the leadership delegated to non-loyal Jews, and the religious instruction and form of worship contrary to God's plan for the nation. Judea was again under a foreign rule, which did not allow Judeans

---

1. Clark, *Emerging Elders*, 45–50.

to fully serve their God. They were again in captivity, but this time in their own land.

Captivities

Previously the Judeans experienced geographical captivity. In the Babylonian exile the Judean nation was scattered throughout parts of their empire. First, *they were in a foreign land separated from their home by land and water.* Those left in Jerusalem were living in the rubble of their former nation but under the control of Babylon and Persia. Others outside of Jerusalem were under the thumb of the Egyptian or Syrian nations. Geographical captivity provided a clear boundary that separated them from their land, home, and idea of safety. Secoond, *in addition to this, their temple, a representation of God's house, was destroyed.* Third, *those in a foreign land were immersed in an opposing culture.* The language, religious system, and social community were all foreign to the people of Yahweh. They were minorities in a strange land. Finally, *they had been punished by Yahweh for sin and were captive due to their own choices.* In the ancient world captivity sent a message to a nation that their punishment was both divine and human.[2] The only hope of reconciliation was to return to their homeland and rebuild their nation.

The Judeans during the time of Jesus experienced social captivity rather than a geographical one. Social captivity or marginalization is distinct from the previous captivity in four ways. First, *social captives live in their own community, land, and home yet face isolation and marginalization due to other circumstances.* Instead of having clear geographical boundaries they must interact with cultural, social, and taboo boundaries that separate others. Second, *Rome exhibited a powerful and oppressive presence in Judah, Jerusalem, and especially the temple, and further stimulated this marginalization.* The oppressor maintained this marginalization through the support of local entities that were loyal to their government. This reminded the Jewish nation that their belief system in Yahweh could be controlled by their corrupt leadership. Another point concerning social marginalization meant that *those in social captivity were immersed in their own culture, but quickly understood that their culture was losing power, control, or dominance.* Unlike Babylonian captivity, Roman social captivity oppressed the majority of people by becoming the dominant powerful culture, thereby colonizing the Judeans. Fourth, *the biblical texts suggest that Judea was being punished for unfaithfulness but the general theme was that corruption, Roman rule, and religious hypocrisy existed without an explanation of how the nation*

---

2. Nissinen, "The Exiled Gods of Babylon in Neo-Assyrian Prophecy," 34–35.

became captive. Luke introduced chapter three with a list of political rulers designed to express, to the reader, the level of oppression that existed. "The ubiquitous presence of Roman emperors, governors, tetrarchs, proconsuls, tribunes, centurions, and soldiers, along with the collaborating high priests, in Luke's narrative does not simply reflect the evangelist's interest in history. It also serves as a pervasive reminder that the Roman Empire and its agents dominated every aspect of the life of the people under its rule."[3]

Simeon and Zechariah looked for redemption but, unlike the prophets of exile, did not directly blame the leaders of their land. However, Jesus clearly placed blame on the corrupt religious leaders of his day. In Babylonian exile faithful leaders rose up through obedience and faithfulness to Yahweh. In Roman marginalization leaders were promoted through colluding with Roman and corrupt Jewish leaders. Corruption became the response to captivity rather than the major cause of it.

During the time of Jesus the Judean people were living in their own land but were socially marginalized. Since the Romans ruled Palestine the people were constantly under threat of violence, oppression, taxation, and injustice. The religious and political leaders were also forced to either collude with Roman authority or rebel (in which case they would lose). These leaders were expected to keep the masses in line and take the side of the Roman authorities. While Augustus had allowed the Jews freedom by replacing a ruler (ethnarch) with a council of elders, this freedom only lasted as long as the Jews cooperated with Rome. The removal of Archelaus, Herod Antipater's son, for brutality and incompetence as a ruler, created a level of anxiety among the people concerning the ability to follow their religious traditions.[4] Pontus Pilate had become the Roman governor of Jerusalem but created a stir by attempting to bring Roman images into the city.[5] The Jews resisted his advances and proved they would lose their lives before allowing Pilate to have his way in Jerusalem. This heightened the tension between Rome and the Jewish people.

However, those who were considered vulnerable (the poor, females, children, slaves, and dishonorable trades) or humble (humiliated) were susceptible to further oppression by their own leaders, who made decisions for the sake of unity and peace with the Romans. This created a large class of people who were considered a potential threat or unimportant in the daily activities of their community. The humble class was not only oppressed by their "captors," they were exploited by those God had called to lead them.

---

3. Reid, "Women Prophets," 47.
4. Tripolitis, *Religions of the Hellenistic-Roman Age*, 65.
5. Roetzel, *The World that Shaped the New Testament*, 27.

Social captivity or marginalization is distinct from geographical captivity in that people are separated by invisible boundaries. Unlike geography, which ends marginalization when people return home, social marginalization maintains this separation even in one's homeland.

Behold He Comes

Luke's story resumed with John the Baptist's ministry. John's preaching was a call to return from exile. While Matthew and Mark used Isaiah 40:3 and Malachi 4 to describe John and his preaching as a preparation for a visit from Yahweh, Luke used a longer Isaiah text (Isa 40:1–4). He will later discuss John as Elijah (Luke 7) but emphasized the return from Persian captivity.

> The voice of one crying in the wilderness: "Prepare the way of the Lord, straighten out his paths. Every valley will be filled in, and every mountain and hill made level. The crooked shall become straight, and the rough places shall become level roads, and all flesh/people shall see the salvation of God." (Luke 3:5–6)

This passage in Luke draws on the prophetic text of Isaiah, which was a call to the Judean people, who were in Babylonian/Persian captivity, that they would return home and receive comfort, "Comfort, comfort my people . . ." (Isa 40:1). The return from Babylonian captivity was a sign of restoration and salvation to a people transported to a foreign land or left in desolate Jerusalem. In the Lukan story John's message involved repentance and baptism for the forgiveness of sins. As the exilic prophets preached repentance and forgiveness, so John continued their message to a nation also in captivity.[6] However, John's preaching was a call for the nation to make a straight and sturdy highway for the Lord.

John's emphasis on social justice was also a theme found in the exilic prophets. Only Luke's Gospel directs John's comments to the crowd, while Matthew directed John's comments to the religious leaders.[7] The crowd of onlookers was called to repent by living as followers of God, their father. They were called to a life of justice and *shalom* through sharing with the poor, treating those dependant on them with value, and living honestly both in their financial and power relationships.

---

6. Clark, *The God of Second Chances*, 167–68.

7. Matthew's Gospel seems to use religious leaders to represent the corrupt followers while the disciples represented the open-hearted followers of Jesus. Wilkins, *Discipleship in the Ancient World and Matthew's Gospel*, 137–43. Matthew placed emphasis on this extreme comparison to call the reader to a choice, while Luke used the crowds to call the reader out of his or her complacency.

> The crowds asked him, "What shall we do?" He answered, "Whoever has two tunics is to share with the one who has none, and whoever has food is to do likewise." Tax collectors also came to be baptized and said, "Teacher, what shall we do?" He said, "Collect no more than you have permission to do." Soldiers also asked, "What shall we do?" and he said, "Do not extort money from anyone by threats or by false accusation, and be content with your salary." (Luke 3:10–14)

John's preaching and message carried such exilic implications that the people wondered if he were the Messiah, since the Messiah was to come and free the people from their captivity.

John made a distinction between himself and Jesus. First, *he claimed that he was not the Messiah, but one who prepared the way.* As a prophet he would only turn people to their Savior (Luke 1:17). John prepared the crowds by baptizing them in repentance for the forgiveness of sins. This form of baptism became important to Luke as the early church practiced this baptism of repentance. Second, *Jesus baptized with fire and the Holy Spirit.* These two terms were common in the exilic prophets where God punished the people with fire, wrath, anger, and violence. However, God also promised to restore the people into relationship through the Spirit, water, forgiveness, and healing (Isa 4:4–5; 42:1; Joel 2; Mic 3:8; Zech 12:10). The two terms suggested that not only would Jesus judge and reconcile God's people, but that Jesus was Yahweh, who came to restore the people in relationship. Luke set this theme in prophetic language as Jesus became the one who personally brought those on the margins of society into relationship with himself, since he was Yahweh in the flesh.

While Luke did not discuss John's resistance to baptize Jesus, as did Matthew, he did dismiss John from the narrative. John, like the prophets in the past, was a bold and courageous servant of God who confronted rulers and spoke a divine message of truth. Herod placed him in prison therefore removing him from the story, suggesting to the reader that his role was only preparatory.[8]

As Jesus was baptized an apocalyptic event occurred. Heaven was torn open, the Spirit descended, and God confirmed Jesus's deity. Luke wrote, "You are my loved son with whom I am pleased" (3:22). This scene introduced the genealogy of Jesus as the son of God. While Luke and Matthew have both similarities and differences in their genealogies, Luke's emphasis was upon Jesus "the son of Adam and son of God" (Luke 3:37). In Luke, John was the son of Zechariah (3:2) while Jesus was the son of God (3:22)

---

8. Juel, *Luke-Acts*, 17, 26.

and also the "supposed son of Joseph" (3:23). Luke's focus was on Jesus as prophet, divine Emperor, and ruler of God's people. He emerged on the scene as a ruler leading people home. This home was not geographical but social and spiritual.

Behold He Suffers

Jesus returned from the Jordan and was led into the wilderness. This story is common to Matthew, Luke, and Mark. Mark's Gospel simply stated that he was "driven by the Spirit into the wilderness and tempted by the devil." Then, the angels ministered to him. Matthew expanded on the story and used a model that would be quite familiar to the Jewish readers. Jesus wandered in the wilderness forty days and nights, as the Jews wandered forty years in the wilderness after the exodus. Jesus was tempted with three tests: bread, trusting/testing God, and worshiping something/one other than Yahweh. These three were tests that the nation of Israel failed during their wandering which is suggested by Jesus as he rebuked Satan with three quotes from Deuteronomy (Deut 6:13, 16, 8:3). Jesus, in Matthew's Gospel, proved to be faithful, unlike Israel, during his wandering in the wilderness.

Luke, however, slightly adapted the story to suggest that Jesus was part of his epic narrative. First, Luke differed from Matthew in the order of temptations. While Matthew's temptations ended with the worship of Satan, Luke's ended with the temple. Since his story moved from temple to house/family it emphasized that God's presence was both private and public. With both the destruction of the temple and Jerusalem the reality seemed clear that it would not be the place where God dwelt. In Luke's account of the temptation the temple was the final stand for Jesus, as it was at the end of the Gospel.

Second, the temptation to worship Satan included receiving authority, splendor, and delegation of authority, "I can give it to anyone I want . . ." (Luke 4:6). For Luke the temptation for Jesus was not only to test his faith in God, but a direct confrontation of the Roman rule of the world. Rome offered nations peace and glory, if they submitted to Caesar. Satan's authority was not just a form of evil, but one that was shared with the current empire.[9] The temptation requested a willingness to collude with a world power, as was being done by the religious leaders of the day. Luke seemed to suggest that Satan, the world power, ruled the temple as well as offered brokerage, and shared power and earthly authority in ruling the world. For

---

9. Grassi, *Peace on Earth*, 95.

Luke supporting or endorsing this view of world power was "putting God to the test . . ." (4:13).

In addition to this Luke couched the story in symbolism. Jesus proved faithful by resisting power, greed, and physical peace. While Matthew suggested that Jesus was Moses and the faithful Jewish nation, wandering in the wilderness and confronting Satan, Luke, however, suggested that Jesus was faithful by refusing to collude with a temporary empire. Satan as colonizer had corrupted social power (oppressing the hungry and poor), political power (colluding with Caesar), and religious power (corrupting house of God). In Luke's Gospel Jesus resisted these temptations by providing bread/status to the poor, giving authority to reach the marginalized to the apostles, confronting the temple authorities, and providing the Spirit (Acts 2). The early Christians would have been challenged by this story to choose their allegiance to Jesus, rather than the Roman Empire.

Behold the Man?

The temptation also launched Jesus's ministry to those in the dark regions of the community. In Matthew Jesus moved from the temptation to the "Sermon on the Mount," suggesting that he was the new Moses, again leading the nation out of the wilderness. In Mark Jesus continued to heal and work miracles after the temptation, supporting Mark's theme that Jesus was gathering his army for the new empire. Luke, however, told the story of Jesus the prophet/preacher in his hometown, proclaiming a message that provided both hope and resistance.

Luke wrote that Jesus "went to the synagogue on the Sabbath and, as was his custom, stood up to read . . ." Jesus was raised by an earthly father and mother who followed the laws and customs of Moses. Earlier Luke shared that this family attended the Passover feast each year, followed the child birth and tax laws, and attended synagogue each Sabbath. When people share with me that they don't need to go to church regularly I find it interesting to take them to this scripture and suggest that Jesus, the creator of the world, felt the need to attend a congregational worship each week. He even took his turn reading from the scrolls. Who are we to think this is not something we need to take seriously in our lives?

As Jesus read from the scroll Luke wrote that he found the place where this was written:

> The Spirit of the Lord is on me, because he has anointed me to preach good news to the poor. He has sent me to preach freedom/release to the captives and give sight to the blind, to free

> those who are oppressed, to preach the year of the Lord's favor. (Luke 4:18–19)

Jesus not only read the scripture, he intentionally found the text and either chose a different text from the weekly assigned synagogue text, or happened to read when this text was assigned for the day. Either way Jesus provided an interesting reading and application of the text found in Isaiah.

> The Spirit of Lord Yahweh is upon me, because Yahweh has anointed me to bring good news to the humiliated; to bind up the brokenhearted, to proclaim freedom to the captives, and open the prison for those who are bound; to proclaim the year of the Yahweh's favor, and the day of vengeance of our God; to comfort all who mourn. (Isa 61:1–2)

First, the text from Isaiah 61:1–2 in the Hebrew and the Greek (called the *Septuagint*) versions is in a different order than Luke's arrangement. Luke's text differs in that Jesus mentions the blind and the oppressed, while the original text only mentions freeing the captives and helping the broken hearted heal. Jesus's version included words that addressed the blind, suggesting that the poor were not just captives, but those marginalized from their society. These words were social justice terms that applied to the humiliated/marginalized, however, they were not in the original prophetic text. Luke's text also left out Isaiah's claim that he would bind the broken hearted. When Jesus read this scripture he was deviating from the standard received and approved text and reading, something practiced by rabbis and readers of his day.[10]

Second, Jesus read the text as if he was the anointed one. After his reading the others became silent, providing a time of reflection while waiting for the reader to interpret the scripture. In this case Jesus's deviation would have required an interpretation or explanation. However, Jesus claimed that "Today in your hearing this text has been completed." Luke placed Jesus's sermon in the synagogue between the stories of his miracles and healings, in some way emphasizing his mission. No doubt his reputation would have preceded this scripture reading and his claim to be the anointed one would have been met with opposition.

Finally, as the crowd began to grumble Jesus reminded them that God sought those who were in social captivity. He gave widows and a foreign leader (Naaman from Syria) as examples of those who experienced miracles by God's anointed ones. Jesus's criticism was that outsiders receive God's blessing when God's people rejected their Lord. This scathing comment was

---

10. Malina, "Reading Theory Perspective," 18.

met with anger and the crowd attempted to stone Jesus because he not only moved the scripture outside their comfort zones, but he claimed that God would choose Gentiles over them.

This supports a major theme throughout Luke's Gospel. In this narrative Jesus came to offer freedom and salvation. This freedom was not just for those who were holy, but for those who were captive, blind, sick, oppressed, and humiliated. Those on the margins of society who needed hope were among the targets of Jesus's ministry.

Behold Him?

If you were asked to summarize Jesus's ministry what would you write? That is a tough question and I feel that many of us would agree with John 20:30–31 in that there are too many stories of Jesus to limit his ministry to one theme. We might agree that each Gospel writer had presented a theological agenda and that each book had a different focus on Jesus. Others of us might find the actions and words of Jesus that were most appealing to us and suggest that these were the themes. Some might suggest that their church has distilled the stories of Jesus and produced a healthy view that addresses all major doctrinal concerns for Christians today.

No matter what our answer is, I find that few would hold to Luke's view of Jesus. For Luke, Jesus came to reach the people on the margins of society. By Jesus's expounding and applying the sacred text, Luke suggested that Jesus came to reach social captives rather than geographical ones. Jesus sought the poor, the oppressed, the humiliated, the blind, and the traumatized in our communities. While the Jews may have believed that they were in exile, Jesus claimed that salvation was for those who sought God. This sermon at the Nazareth synagogue was a launching point for Luke's Gospel.

A Marginalized Savior

As mentioned earlier, Luke retold the story of Jesus not only as a narrative of the creation of a new empire, but also to fill in the gaps of the Christian community. Theophilus and his community would have heard the gospel of Jesus, yet Luke shared unique stories and also added details to recurring stories in the other Gospels. These unique narratives and details overwhelmingly involved the poor, oppressed, handicapped, and others socially marginalized in society. For Luke, Jesus came to reach people shunned by their community. In addition to this, Jesus called the church to do the same.

The rejection of Jesus at the Nazareth synagogue was also the beginning of the theme of conflict that will continue throughout the Gospel. This conflict involved the community, corrupt religious leaders, as well as the disciples. The Theophilus community was being introduced to a new or possibly unexplored side of Jesus's ministry, and they were being pushed out of their comfort zones. Luke not only retold the story of Jesus and the founding of a new kingdom, the Gospel challenged the reader to embrace the ministry of Jesus.

JESUS TODAY

Today we as Christians struggle with many of the same issues that the Theophilus community faced. When I visit a Christian bookstore the majority of the items address current American cultural issues: getting out of debt, weight loss and appearance, personal self esteem, and praying with power. You will find few books on reaching the marginalized, accepting those who struggle with weight, and embracing those in debt. Unfortunately the concerns of Luke are many times not the concerns of many of our churches in North America.

For Luke, Jesus's ministry addressed those affected by social marginalization. Even more, the conflict Jesus faced originated from God's people who, for some reason, contributed to the marginalization of common or "unclean" people. I believe that the Gospel of Luke was written to challenge the church to have the same passion as Jesus. Rejecting this passion and choosing to embrace the opposite was a rejection of Jesus. To love Jesus meant that we must love his ministry.

When we were first preparing to launch Agape my coach, Larry Deal, and I met with a large area church to share with them a call to plant a new church. Larry worked with Kairos Church Planting, which trained and prepared us to develop our core team and launch this new congregation. Larry and I shared with the church leaders the vision to begin a new church in Portland, the need for more churches in one of the most unchurched cities in North America, and our goal to focus on social justice. "How is social justice part of the gospel and evangelism?" one of the leaders asked. I was surprised because I hadn't heard that before. The large church where I was preaching seemed to understand that reaching out to the poor was not only a form of service, but part of sharing the gospel of Jesus. After thinking a second I asked, "We are called to reach out to the poor and oppressed; how is it not part of the gospel or evangelistic?"

Since then I have observed the conflict that occurs in churches concerning outreach, evangelism, social justice, and community service. Those who engage their communities, reach out to the poor, become politically and socially active, and call for social change are sometimes accused of leaving the gospel. The Emerging and Emergent Church movements adopted the Missional Church language and suggested that the North American churches had become too comfortable with their position of privilege, which we were quickly losing as America became more and more critical of Christianity. The response was that Christianity needed to engage people and go to them (missional), rather than wait for them to come to their Sunday services (attractional). Christians and churches needed to rethink outreach and create a presence in our community. This involved connecting with people on the margins of society. However, as the decades passed, the new movements were evaluated by the old school models of measuring "church attendance" and "baptisms/conversions." What began as a movement to rekindle a positive view of the church and Christians quickly changed to one that adopted the old way of thinking. We were "too involved in social justice," or "we weren't converting enough people," according to some. In the end something that was good, true, and a reflection of the ministry of Jesus was considered a distraction from the true calling of the church.

Even more we forgot that we were reaching people who loved Jesus, not the church. To have them feel positive concerning Christians was a large step and one that takes a tremendous amount of energy. Conversion, therefore, becomes a process that takes time. Luke, however, seems to suggest that the true calling of the church is to follow the life of Jesus, who cared for those on the margins of society. For Luke social justice was a sign of the prophetic witness of Jesus, the church, and God's people.

> One of the invaluable roles that prophets can play within the church is to help it remain in touch with the margins. The church can, and does, become all too preoccupied with upkeep and maintenance, with keeping faith with tradition, with preserving the bounds of orthodoxy. These are legitimate and even necessary concerns. But they are also precisely the concerns of the Pharisees in Luke-Acts, and the lesson Luke teaches is that such preoccupation can hinder the perception of what new things God is doing in the world and block an openness to the work of the Holy Spirit in the actual lives of humans.[11]

---

11. Johnson, *Prophetic Jesus*, 186.

Over against all these admirable expressions of obedience to the prophetic vision, however, stands the unassailable fact that the church, as institution, has far more often through the centuries been a sign of wealth rather than of poverty and has aligned itself with the rich and powerful on earth more than the weak and lowly.[12]

The task of prophetic ministry is to nurture, nourish, and evoke a consciousness and perception alternative to the consciousness and perception of the dominant culture around us.[13]

I personally believe that what the church today most longs for are visionary leaders who speak to their people of an alternative future that can be believed and embraced and lived into. Like much of society around us the church can easily fall prey to its cynicism and despair. But the best antidote to such despair and cynicism is that alternate vision of God we glimpse the Gospel: a vision of a universe made new, whole, and fresh by a God who loves it inordinately and will not rest until that which is upside down is turned right side up—until the justice, righteousness, and *shalom* of God cover the earth as the waters cover the sea.[14]

My friends, who asked if social justice was evangelism, had missed a major theme in Luke's Gospel, as well as the other Gospels. In this they missed an important piece of Jesus's and God's life, heart, and passion. Evangelism is not baptisms and conversions only, it is the promotion of the *shalom* of God and the justice of a community that reflects God's glory. Jesus came to free those in oppression and wherever there are people who are oppressed, the gospel is absent. Therefore wherever it exists, there must be freedom, hope, and peace.

---

12. Ibid, 125.
13. Brueggemann, *The Prophetic Imagination*, 3.
14. Tisdale, *Prophetic Preaching*, 37.

SECTION 2
INTRODUCING THE JOURNEY

5

Reaching Those on the Margins
Luke 4:31—7:50

AFTER JESUS GAVE HIS Nazareth sermon, Luke's mantra for the epic story of Jesus, he left the synagogue and visited the city of Capernaum. Luke introduced the "rejection at Nazareth" as an inauguration of Jesus's ministry.[1] Capernaum was a small fishing village that had become his home. He immediately began fulfilling his synagogue sermon among the people by teaching in that city on the Sabbath. His authority amazed them, probably because they had not experienced the kind of power that Jesus was displaying. First, *his teaching had authority*. Jesus was different than many teachers of his day, who spent much time quoting the teachings of other rabbis. Jesus preached God's teachings and made application to their lives.

Second, *Jesus displayed authority over the dark world* as he healed a demon possessed man, Peter's mother-in-law's fever, and in other incidents where he confronted evil and sicknesses (Luke 4:31–43). He, as God, was not afraid to touch people, place his hands on them, and teach them. Jesus was invading planet earth and brought peace and healing to those who were suffering on the margins of society. He was going where few dared to go!

HEALING AND MINISTRY

The response was incredible. Demons were confessing his name, people were listening to him, crowds were pressing against him, and even Peter's mother-in-law served him after she was healed (4:33–37). People were

1. Brawley, *Luke-Acts and the Jews*, 11.

responding to this ministry and found *shalom* in Jesus. However, Jesus's focus was not healing but preaching the message of God to a people searching for hope.

> When it was day, he left and went to a deserted place. The people looked for him, came to him, and would have kept him from leaving them, but he said, "It is necessary for me to preach the good news of the empire of God to the other towns; since this is why I was sent." (4:42–43)

It must have been difficult to leave the crowds. There would have been many more people who were possessed, injured, sick, or desiring his touch. Yet Jesus knew that his main focus was to teach and preach good news to those who were hurting.

There are many healing stories in Luke 4–7. Jesus encountered demon possessed people (4:33–36, 41; 6:18), those who had illnesses (4:38–39; 6:18), those with skin diseases (leprosy 5:12–13), others who were crippled (5:17–25), and some who had loved ones terminally ill or who had passed away (7:1–17). Even though Jesus claimed that the focus of his ministry would be teaching, Luke described his ministry as one that addressed individual's physical and emotional needs. These stories indicate that God is a God who cares about suffering and desires physical peace. God's desire was so strong that Jesus and his followers were practicing a risky style of ministry.

Risky Business

Jesus broke conventional religious traditions and health codes in his ministry. Luke shared that Jesus became very close to people and would have been suspect in his community. First, he was working with highly communicable diseases which would have caused concern to those who were near him. Second, he worked with people who struggled with demonic possession, which was many times manifested by explosive episodes of mental illness. Finally, his presence in homes where death was present, or near, would have also brought suspicion as he may have been viewed as a carrier for death or unclean conditions. As a physician Luke would have viewed this as common work for a healer, even more the son of God who performed these miracles.

These individuals were excluded from their communities due to their sickness, contagions, or their inability to function safely in their surroundings. However, Jesus left the synagogue to develop a ministry and following from among these men, women, and children on the margins of society.

When we read these stories we should not see them as "wonderful miracles" that Jesus did to prove he was the son of God. We should understand them as stories where Jesus ventured into the areas that were abandoned, dark, and dreary to bring good news. One can imagine Jesus as God in flesh, sitting in a dark room surrounded by people who were hiding in a corner, while Jesus was smiling, eating with them, and telling them about the empire of God. Even more one must imagine groups of people standing outside waiting for him to emerge, hoping he would still be alive. By entering these homes he blessed those who were viewed as cursed. These miracle stories teach us that God is not afraid to be in the midst of darkness and seeks to bring light to every corner of the planet.

Lori and I love ministry. We both wouldn't be doing any other job. There has not been a day where I have not been eager to go to work. There have been times when both of us have been together in dark places. We have been in apartments or broken down homes crawling with cockroaches, rotten food, dark, smoky, and cold; we have been there because people we wanted to reach were there. Many times we have felt a cold chill of darkness, evil, and the demonic around us. We realized that if we felt uncomfortable how did those who lived there feel while trying to seek God? I know that we are not alone. There are countless Christian men and women of courage who have entered these places on the margins of society. Even more, I know many others who do not claim to be Christian who have visited the same areas in their communities. These areas are dark, scary, and depressing zones in our cities, communities, neighborhoods. However, many people call these places home.

Luke's Gospel suggested that God was not afraid to visit these homes, these neighborhoods, or these dark alleys in the city. Jesus came to reach people in these places, to touch them, hug them, bend over and talk to them, and drive out their demons. While the focus of his ministry was teaching, he knew that he needed to teach people where they lived. In addition to this, Jesus knew that he alone could not be the one to reach them.

Follow You Down?

The healing stories that follow were separated by stories that involved soliciting men and women to join Jesus. While it is amazing to imagine Jesus entering the darkest zones of our city, it is even more amazing that he asked for help.

Fishers of People

In Luke 5:1–11 Jesus called Peter to join his ministry. As mentioned earlier, Peter was a fishing partner with Jesus's cousins, James and John. Jesus was preaching by the lake of Galilee (a major body of water in that region) and used Peter's fishing boat. After a hard night of fishing, and catching very little, Jesus asked Peter to try fishing again. It may be that Peter was mocking Jesus by agreeing to this, as people knew that fishing had to be done at night, so the fish could not see the rope net. However, Jesus provided fish for Peter and Andrew, as well as their other partners in the fishing co-op. Jesus was helping them financially as they would have been struggling to survive if they missed a nightly fishing catch. The catch from Jesus would have provided enough that they could leave their business and follow him. Yet while Peter was humbled by Jesus's provision he was solicited to join the ministry and help restore others to the kingdom.

This would have been difficult. While Peter's mother-in-law had been healed, he would have known that the ministry Jesus was doing was not one people embraced. The call to follow Jesus came with a cost—you would have had to touch the very people you were taught to avoid.

The Tax Man Cometh

After filling their nets it would have been reasonable for Peter and his crew to pay their debts. One man who would have known about this catch, and any impending debt that all common people experienced in Galilee, would have been Levi (also known as Matthew). Jesus saw him in his portable office and called him to follow (5:27–32). It seems odd that Levi would have dropped his business, but knowing that he would have been fiscally responsible for Peter's great haul of fish would have given him good reason to follow Jesus and be part of his ministry. Even more, Levi wanted his friends to meet this financial wizard.

Tax collectors were not well respected by the common Jewish people. First, they worked for the local and Roman government and made sure people paid their taxes. Second, they many times stole from their community. There would have been nothing more frustrating than to make a large amount of money, or feel a sense of blessing by God, only to have a public official come and take a large percentage of that financial windfall. Tax collectors were viewed as traitors, thieves, and dishonest people. They weren't even good enough to be labeled sinners as in the phrase, "tax collectors and sinners." Yet Levi, as would any wealthy politician, invited his friends,

Jesus, and his disciples for a dinner. Levi's friends would have included business associates, family, crooked friends, and if it was similar to any Roman banquet/meal, possibly a few slave women or boys for sexual favors. For Jesus, and now his disciples, to attend this dinner would have required a trip to a very dark world. This world was so dark that he and his disciples were criticized.

> Levi made him a great feast in his home, and there was a group of many tax collectors and others reclining at table with them. The Pharisees and their scribes grumbled to his disciples, saying, "Why do you eat and drink with tax collectors and sinners?" Jesus answered, "Those who are healthy do not need a doctor, only those who are sick. I did not come to call the righteous but sinners to repentance." (5:29–31)

Jesus defended his actions with the religious leaders of his community. These leaders were men entrusted with the teachings of God and had the opportunity to bring God's message to all people. However, they had socially marginalized others in their community and labeled them unholy, unrighteous, or non-committed to God. In addition to this, they had worked so hard to avoid these people that they had driven them outside their community.

First, these leaders put the disciples on the spot by complaining to them concerning Jesus's behavior. Second, they blamed Jesus's disciples for not following the strict forms of religious observance through fasting.

> "The disciples of John fast often and practice praying, as do those of the Pharisees, but yours eat and drink." Jesus said to them, "The wedding guests are not able to fast while the bridegroom is with them. The days will come when the bridegroom is taken away from them, in those days they will fast." He also told them a parable: "No one tears a piece from a new garment and puts it on an old garment. If they do, the new will tear and the piece from the new will not match the old. No one puts new wine into old wineskins. If they do the new wine will burst the skins, will be spilled, and the skins will be destroyed. New wine must be put into fresh wineskins. No one after drinking old wine wants new, because they say, 'The old is good.'" (5:33–39)

The religious leaders not only had a problem with Jesus's associations, they were concerned that he didn't follow a common practice of fasting. Not only did the religious leaders periodically fast (some for two days each week), but John the Baptist's disciples did as well. Fasting was a form of self-denial and discipline that prepared an individual to grow spiritually through sacrifice, discomfort, and prayer.

However, Jesus believed that an age of celebration did not require fasting but feasting (joy). His story above seemed to refer to an event discussed in the prophet Zechariah. After the Jews returned from Persian captivity they began to rebuild Jerusalem. One of the common community practices, while in captivity, was fasting—a form of mourning over their sin. However, the spiritual leaders asked the prophet if they should continue this practice after returning to Jerusalem.

> The people of Bethel had sent Sharezer and Regem-Melek, together with their men, to offer a request to Yahweh by asking the priests of the house of Yahweh Almighty and the prophets, "Should I/we mourn and fast in the fifth month, as I/we have done for so many years?" (Zech 7:2–3)

Historically, God's people continued to worship, celebrate festivals, and observe fasting and prayer while living against their God. The leaders of the nation had been dishonest and unjust, yet they believed that they were to set an example by following the religious observances that God had required. However, God stated through the prophets that they were called to be just and righteous. "Administer true justice; show mercy and compassion to one another. Do not oppress the widow or the fatherless, the foreigner or the poor. Do not plot evil against each other" (Zech 7:9–10). They were expected to focus upon caring for people and treating others with respect, rather than the ritual of worship. While fasting was not bad, it should have been practiced with an honest heart and godly life. For Yahweh a pure heart was manifested by actions and social justice.

The Jews were challenged to care for others. Fasts were a time to humble themselves before their God. However, in the new kingdom God was calling for feasts rather than fasts.

> "Just as I had determined to bring disaster on you and showed no pity when your ancestors angered me," says Yahweh Almighty, "so now I have determined to do good again to Jerusalem and Judah. Do not be afraid. These are the things you are to do: Speak the truth to each other, and render true and sound judgment in your courts; do not plot evil against each other, and do not love to swear falsely. I hate all this," declares Yahweh. The word of Yahweh Almighty came to me. This is what Yahweh Almighty says: "The fasts of the fourth, fifth, seventh and tenth months will become joyful and glad occasions and happy festivals for Judah. Therefore love truth and peace." (Zech 8:14–19)

While fasting and humility were key elements in the Jewish faith, Yahweh encouraged them to feast, celebrate, and call all people (those unclean and Gentiles) to the table of fellowship. The new kingdom was not an empire of mourning and fasting. They had repented, they had been forgiven, and this was the time to feast and celebrate. When we are overcome with shame, we can find many reasons to punish ourselves. However, God wanted them to celebrate and feast so that they would forget their shame, guilt, and fear.

Jesus was confronted with this same issue in Luke's narrative. It would have seemed to be a logical question since Jesus was feasting in the dark places of society and not teaching his disciples to follow the religious customs of the community. It would also have been odd that in entering the dark locations of society, Jesus did not call the people there to repentance but acceptance. For Jesus there was no reason to fast and mourn. They were experiencing the return from exile and rather than mourning for sin, they were to celebrate the presence of Yahweh in the flesh. God was present in the dark regions of life. This called for joy rather than suffering and mourning.

Jesus also reminded them that a spiritual faith that focused on mourning could not embrace celebration, hope, and healing. This new drink would not only be too sweet for those who enjoyed sour wine, but its expansion could not be accommodated as the old religion had become rigid, negative, and contributed to the marginalization of people. "Slaves, children, and widows are improbably models that enable us to visualize the new landscape of the [kingdom of God], while familiar models of spirituality such as the religious elite are frequently exemplars of the old landscape."[2] An expanding empire receives criticism from those who refuse to embrace its mission and purpose.

Luke continued Jesus's thought in the next section as he suggested that the Sabbath was to be a day of rest, celebration, and joy (Luke 6:1–11). However, the religious leaders had made it a day of stress and anxiety. It had become a day when the disciples could not eat the food for the poor (leftovers in the field) nor could a person who was sick be healed. For Jesus the Sabbath was given to humans to rest and enjoy, but due to the religious leaders, it had become a day of slavery.

LEVELING THE PLAYING FIELD

Jesus then taught the disciples in the story known as "The Sermon on the Plain" (Luke 6:12–49). This section paralleled Matthew's "Sermon on the Mount" and is thought to be a reflection of both Matthew's and Luke's

2. Resseguie, *Spiritual Landscape*, 45.

common source (known as Q), which was adapted to their theological emphases in the story.³ One example is that Matthew's sermon described Jesus as ascending the mountain, followed by his disciples, and opening his mouth to speak (a literary construct suggesting that a rabbi was speaking something profound [Matt 5:1–2]). Jesus, in Matthew's account, was comparable to Moses and delivered the new law (Torah) of God for the people. His commentary and explanations created a sense of respect among the people: "When Jesus had finished saying these things, the crowds were amazed at his teaching, because he taught as one who had authority, not like their teachers of the law" (Matt 7:28–29). Matthew seemed to suggest that Jesus was the giver of a new law and new model for God's people. The mountaintop sermon was a sign of the divinity and authority of Jesus and his teachings.

Luke, however, shared his account in a different location. One suggestion has been that since ancient historians were less concerned with factual accuracy and more with narration and rhetoric both Matthew and Luke had permission to use the sermon, or collection of Jesus's teachings, and construct them in whatever story form they felt was necessary to communicate the theology of their Christian community. This is possible. Both Gospel writers would have been practicing a constructed theology in the story.

However, it is also possible that since Jesus was a traveling preacher, he would have given many of his lessons in different locations. He very likely would have given a sermon on a mountain/hillside as well as a sermon on the plain/plateau. Both Gospel writers would have selected whichever story they needed for their narrative.

One issue that I find unique to Luke is that the story, whether geographically accurate or adapted, has a powerful message for his audience. First, in Luke 6:12–16, *Jesus chose disciples and prepared them for the lesson on the plain*. Matthew located the choosing of the disciples before Jesus sent them out to preach and use divine authority (Matt 10:1–4); while Mark placed the choosing of the twelve in the midst of Jesus's encounters with sickness, evil, and disbelief from religious leaders. Luke is similar to Mark in that this story occurs in the midst of his section involving Jesus and evil/sickness, but the disciples were prepared to follow him to the next encounter with evil. For Luke the choosing of the apostles before the sermon on the plain again supported his theme of Jesus reaching the marginalized.

Next Jesus, in Luke, *chose the twelve on a mountain (common to all three writers) before descending to do ministry*. Luke's narrative suggested

---

3. Q is from the French word *Quelle*, meaning "what," and represents the material that biblical scholars believe comprised a collection of Jesus stories that pre-dated the Gospels.

that Jesus prayed "all night" and then called his disciples and chose twelve to be apostles (ones sent with authority). Prayer, in Luke, is a very common element and something powerful happened after each prayer. In this Gospel, and at this location in the text, what happened next is both powerful and unique—at least for Luke's readers.

> He came down with them and stood on a level place, with a great crowd of disciples and a gathering of people from all around Judea, Jerusalem, and the coast of Tyre and Sidon. They came to hear him and to be healed of their diseases. Those who were troubled with unclean spirits were cured. The crowd wanted to touch him, because power came out from him and healed them all. He lifted up his eyes to his disciples, and said . . . (Luke 6:17–20)

Jesus went down with the disciples and stood on a level place (he descended the mountain) after his prayer. In ancient literature, as well as the Bible, the mountaintop was the place to experience divinity, while the bottom of the mountain was the place to experience normal life as well as evil.[4] Jesus was in the midst of a crowd that was comparable to a mosh pit. A mosh pit is typically a group of people gathered in a group in a frenzy at a concert, sporting event, or large crowd of enthusiasts. The mosh pit is violent, energetic, and exciting. People typically get hurt in a mosh pit. Jesus, in Luke 6:17–19, was in a mosh pit. It was a swirling crowd of pain, suffering, emotion, fear, and evil. Most "gods" were too holy to be among the people. This God, Jesus, was in the middle of humanity. Power was emanating from him and people sensed its presence. The power was healing people rather than radiating violence. It would have been exciting, except for one group of people.

Luke 6:20 stated, "lifting his eyes to his disciples he said . . ." The English translations simply state that Jesus looked at them. However, in this story, where the crowds were at the bottom, and the disciples were descending from the mountain, the phrase seemed to be intentional. Jesus was below with the crowds while the disciples, including the newly appointed apostles, were separate. They were elevated, the crowds were below, and Jesus was at the bottom. The description smacks of irony. In Matthew the crowds waited below while the disciples ascended to Jesus as this select group heard Jesus's message. In Luke Jesus descended to the crowds while the disciples waited, in a slightly elevated portion of the hill. However everyone heard Jesus's message. Even more, the lesson, as in Matthew's Sermon on the Mount, targeted the disciples. I can imagine the disciples asking, "Should we go down

---

4. Resseguie, *Spiritual Landscape*, 5.

there to help him?" "No, he's doing just fine, and besides—I'm not going down there, those people are crazy."

> He lifted up his eyes to his disciples, and said: "Blessed are the poor, yours is the empire of God. Blessed are the ones who are currently hungry, you will be satisfied. Blessed are those currently weeping, you will laugh. Blessed are you when people hate you, exclude you, humiliate you, and consider you evil, because of the Son of Man. Rejoice in that day and leap for joy. Hey, your reward in heaven is great; this is what their fathers did to the prophets. Woe to you who are rich, you have received your comfort. Woe to you who are currently full, you will be hungry. Woe to you who currently laugh, you will mourn and weep. Woe to you, when all people speak well of you, this is what their fathers did to the false prophets. I tell you; love your enemies, do good to those who hate you, bless those who curse you, and pray for those who abuse you. The one who hits your cheek, offer the other, and the one who takes away your cloak [outer garment] do not withhold your tunic [underclothes] either. Give to everyone who begs from you, and do not demand your goods back if someone takes them away from you. Treat others as you want them to treat you. If you love those who love you, what benefit is that? Sinners love those who love them. If you do good to those who do good to you, what benefit is that? Sinners do the same. If you lend to those from whom you expect to receive, what credit is that? Sinners lend to sinners, to get back the same amount. Love your enemies, and do good, and lend, expecting nothing in return, and your reward will be great; and you will be sons of the Most High, who is kind to the ungrateful and the evil. Be merciful, even as your Father is merciful. (6:20–36)

Luke wrote that Jesus gave these lessons to the disciples directly while in the presence of the crowd. The lesson was powerful, but to the point. First, 6:20–26 was not the Beatitudes, as they are commonly known in Matthew. They were blunt challenges to the disciples—the poor, hungry, suffering, and marginalized will be blessed; the wealthy, well fed, happy, and socially acceptable already had their blessing. God did not need to give the honorable any blessing because they had already received this from people. However, the marginalized in their society needed God's blessing. There is no mistaking what the verses say for the modern reader. We may wrestle with Matthew's "poor in spirit," but Luke's "blessed are you who are poor," is very clear. Jesus called the disciples to follow him among the mosh pit of poverty, pain, and suffering. They needed to choose sides as representatives of the empire of God.

Second, Luke 6:27–36 reminded them what it meant to be in the mosh pit. When you are marginalized you can't demand justice, you can only offer to be different from your enemies. If you meet anger and violence with kindness and courage you would have been doing what every person on the margins of life had to do. There was little justice in the mosh pit and there people were faced with being either as mean as their oppressors, or patient and merciful. Jesus even ended the section with the statement, "Be merciful as your Father is merciful . . ." (6:36). Luke's readers knew that this sermon had come from a God who was humiliated throughout the prophets as well as the crucifixion. However, they also knew that God responded with mercy, and that Jesus's ministry offered this ministry to others—including those in the pit of evil.

Living at the bottom of a pit of evil offers very little hope. Hope comes from above and from within. In our work with people on the streets in Portland we find that there is a tremendous amount of generosity shared both among the homeless as well as those who own businesses and have compassion. Many times when I have offered to take someone who is spanging on the streets to lunch, I will go to a place where the servers know them and are nice to them. Sometimes I look around and others have invited someone to eat with them as well. It seems to be a small thing to buy lunch for a hungry person but it is powerful in that it offers hope for the recipients. In visiting with them I hear stories of other people who call them names, accuse them of being lazy, or stare at them (I have noticed this when I have sat on the streets and eaten with people). Our society is convinced that all they need to do is get a job and everything will be fine. Our society also is convinced that we have the right to label and criticize them, even to their face.

I have also witnessed their acts of compassion toward me, our church, and people we send to them who need help. Those in our churches who have lived the street life are the first to hug a person who publicly confesses sin and makes amends to our community at our public assembly. It is a powerful lesson that when you live on the margins of society, you realize that hope, mercy, and compassion are valuable commodities in life.

Jesus reminded the disciples, and the crowds, that judging (condemning people or communicating that they are hopeless), trying to "one up" others, and devaluing other humans serves very little purpose in the empire of Jesus. If people who live on the margins understand this, how much more should the disciples of Jesus? Goodness is something that should be viewed through actions, not words. Those who do good, do it because they have a good heart; those who do evil, do this from a corrupt heart.

> "Do not criticize, and you will not be criticized; do not condemn, and you will not be condemned; forgive, and you will be forgiven; give, and it will be given to you; a good amount will be pressed down, shaken together, running over, and set into your lap. You will be measured by the standard you use toward others." He also told them a parable: "Can a blind person lead the blind? They will both fall into a pit. A disciple is not above his/her teacher, but everyone when prepared will be like his/her teacher. Why do you see the speck that is in your brother's/sister's eye, but do not notice the log in your own? How can you say to your brother/sister, 'Let me take the speck out of your eye,' when you do not see the log in your own eye? You hypocrite, first take the log out of your own eye, and then you will see clearly to take the speck out of your brother's/sister's eye. A good tree does not produce bad fruit, nor does a bad tree produce good fruit. Each tree is known by its own fruit. Figs are not gathered from thorn bushes, nor are grapes picked from a thorn bush. The good person produces good from the treasure of his/her heart, and the evil person produces evil out of his/her evil treasure. The mouth speaks out of the abundance of the heart. (6:37–46)

Often I find that 6:37–42 and 6:43–45 are separate beliefs for many Christians today. Many of the younger Christians I would meet at church, or the Christian college where I had taught, were quick to proclaim that we should not be judgmental, criticize others, or point out areas that people needed to repent or improve upon. The rationale was that Jesus told us not to judge. While this is true they many times omitted Jesus's next statement that claimed that good trees produced good fruit, and bad trees produced bad fruit. He also claimed that you could tell a person's heart by their actions.

This is not a popular belief in our culture. Psychology, while an extremely valuable science that has helped us to understand people, has been misused in many of our faith and community circles. The common belief is that, "God knows my heart and does not judge me by my actions." This is also a common prayer for Christ followers. People have shared with me that those who have done bad things aren't really bad people, they are just misunderstood, or they have a good heart. However, this is contrary to what Jesus teaches in this section, as well as the other Gospels. As a minister who works with abuse, addictions, and controlling behaviors I have found this to be a common belief as well. A man can sexually molest his children, or other children, but we believe he is a good man because he meant well, said he had a good heart, or seems nice. A woman neglects her children's daily food, emotional needs, and right to live in a clean environment but through tears, in a courtroom testimony, convinces others that she meant well or has good intentions. Unfortunately we forget that their victims suffer greatly and have reaped the pain of bad fruit/actions/behavior. Even more, many of these victims leave the church because they believe that God/Jesus/Christians are unjust and ignore the suffering of the innocent. The sermon on the plain suggests that those who oppress others will face God's wrath, and that their actions/behaviors are a reflection of their hearts.

Jesus was speaking to and about people who lived on the margins of society. That society believed that if you were wealthy, had social honor, were male, and were educated you were assumed to be a moral and godly man. The society also believed that people's outward condition was a reflection of their moral values.[5] Therefore those on the margins of their communities were immediately assumed to be evil. In the sermon on the plain Jesus expressed a divine reversal where the marginalized were going to be cared for by God and the social elite cared for by their own people. Therefore, we should not judge/condemn others.

First, *judging meant labeling a person based on their status in society*. It also involved condemning others, which removes a person's hope for change or a better life. Second, *Jesus warned the disciples concerning leadership from a position of power*. Leaders were to examine themselves first (leveling the social status of themselves and others) and then, out of compassion and grace (that they themselves knew they needed), they could help others repent and change their lives. Finally, *morality was not based on outward appearances, social status, or finances; it was based on people's behavior, practice, and willingness to do good things for others*. A person's heart was manifested by what they did, not by what they wished they could do. A good person is one who does good things. A good person is one who hears Jesus's words and puts them to practice. A good person is one who endures throughout life as one who blesses others. While one might list many passages from the prophets suggesting that hypocrites acted religious outwardly (Amos 5:21–24; Matt 23), their actions were not from those who sought to do good for people. There are those who act "correctly" but are inwardly corrupt or dishonest. There are those who are moral and act "morally." There are those who behave badly because they love evil. *But there are never those who are good inwardly who do evil*. Outward actions/behaviors are important qualities of Jesus's disciples and a good method of determining someone's heart. At least the person who does good shows that they are open to righteousness, honesty, and good morals.

---

5. Parsons, *Body and Character*, 12, 15.

> Why do you call me "Lord, Lord," and not do what I say? Everyone who comes to me, hears my words, and does them; I will show you what they are like. They are like a person building a house, digging deep, and laying the foundation on rock. When a flood came, the river hit that house and could not shake it, because it had been well built. The one who hears and does not act/practice is like the one who built a house on the ground without a foundation. When the river came against it, it fell immediately, and the destruction of that house was great.

The sermon on the plain challenged the disciples and the reader to view the Christian faith socially as well as personally. While Matthew's sermon challenged the corrupt religious leaders in ancient Galilee, Luke's sermon challenged those who were part of the marginalization process of people, including the disciples who "looked down on others below them," where Jesus was. Today, the message is similar.

The empire of Jesus is unlike the empire of Rome/America/consumerism. In the United States we live in a country that is deeply embedded in the "American Dream." The American Dream is a belief system that developed in the late 1940s in post-WWII America. Through time this dream or lifestyle involved owning a home/land, having a steady job, and living in a nice neighborhood/city. This was not only a measure of success, it has become a measure of responsibility and social status. Morals are also attributed to those who fulfill the American Dream as they are viewed as hard working, successful, and responsible.

> In short, owning a home has been part of the American Dream and symbolizes freedom, security, mobility, and community. Despite a lack of evidence, we equate the behavior of buying a home with a number of positive behaviors and values, and the behavior of losing a place to live with negative behaviors and values.[6]

Christianity has embraced this viewpoint especially through the emphasis on churches being successful once they become financially independent, own or build a building, and have members who are good financial contributors. One measure of discipleship today is the "giving" of disciples.

The negative aspect of the American Dream, as Laura Stivers illustrates, is that those who don't own property (a high majority of Americans rent or live with another family) do not carry the same level of respect or authority in our communities. In addition to this, those who don't own a home may be considered deviant, lazy, immoral, or irresponsible. Homelessness

---

6. Stivers, *Disrupting Homelessness*, 46.

becomes linked to sin, rebellion, and worthlessness in our society. Stivers has written well concerning the Union Gospel movement and it's labeling homelessness as a sin and moral evil in society today.[7]

With the turn in the economy and new research, it has become clear that the American Dream is unrealistic and highly judgmental. First, people in America financially struggle to change the status in which they were born. If they were born to a family in poverty, the statistics claim that they will stay at that level. People in the United States can no longer claim to pull themselves up by their bootstraps. Second, with affordable housing increasing at a much higher rate than salaries, more and more people will choose to rent and thereby become "homeless." Agape has continued to work with the city of Portland's various homeless initiatives, which have produced compelling evidence that those in transitional housing, in Portland, spend 60 percent of their income on rent, with 30 percent being considered an adequate percentage for survival.[8] Finally, homelessness exists not because people are lazy but because there is a large financial gap in affordable housing, resources, and an opportunity to have a "good chance" to succeed and provide for one's self and family.

I am amazed at the number of times I have heard Christians remark that poverty is a chosen lifestyle. We base this on the mythical stories that some spangers/beggars live in mansions, that jobs and transportation are available for all, that it is easy to find a place to live, that racial and gender prejudice do not exist, and that we have the security that we would not ever become homeless. I know this because I hear many Christians talk, even to Lori and I, concerning the people we help in Portland. I also know this because I am seeing an increasing number of young Christians who want to do this type of ministry but hear from their parents that social justice is a worthless cause.

Yet in the sermon on the plain Jesus reversed the American Dream and claimed that God will bless those who cannot afford or choose not to buy into this emptiness and false sense of security. Jesus tells us today that the only way to really know mercy and love is to embrace those in the mosh pit. The newer research on church growth suggests that growing churches are focused on social justice.[9] The Christian church is also growing rapidly in third world countries and areas where Christians are persecuted. Why? Because there has been a return to the Gospels and the ministry of Jesus.

---

7. Ibid., 65.

8. Multnomah County, *2013 Point in Time*.

9. Rainer, *Effective Evangelistic Churches*, 135–36; Stetzer, *Planting New Churches in a Postmodern Age*, 158.

Jesus constantly encounters marginalized men, women, and children. "The margin is not a place of deficiency but teems with possibilities of re-forming life no longer as determined by the alleged unified center . . . Rather the margin is a place of creative, critical engagement with hegemony. . . Luke-Acts often deals with the reintegration of marginalized people to the social order . . . which is a restoration of Israel's social order."[10]

Today the message is still as powerful as ever. Jesus called his disciples to join him in the mosh pit and love people who were on the margins of society. There, on the margins of life, we learn that we must offer hope and grace for there to be change both in our lives and the lives of others.

ARE YOU OFFENDED WITH MY MINISTRY?

One day John the Baptist's followers came to Jesus to see if he was the Messiah. John was in prison and sent them to talk to his cousin. Much has been written as to why John did this. Was he expressing a level of faithlessness concerning Jesus? Did he truly know who Jesus was? One explanation might be that even though John knew that Jesus was the Messiah, he wanted his disciples to ask him in person. When comparing this story with Matthew's account Luke had the disciples repeat the question to Jesus. This repeated question, for Luke, somehow suggested that it was to be their question, not John's. Another possibility was that John had lost faith in his mission. His imprisonment and impending death may have shaken this courageous prophet. He, like many others in the Bible, would have experienced doubt and wondered if Jesus was the right one.

> The disciples of John reported all these things to him. John, calling two of his disciples, sent them to the Lord, saying, "Are you the one who is to come, or do we wait for another?" When the men had come to him, they said, "John the Baptist has sent us to you, saying, "Are you the one who is to come, or do we wait for another?" In that hour he healed many people of diseases, afflictions, evil spirits, and many who were blind were given sight. He answered them, "Go and report to John what you have seen and heard: the blind see, the crippled walk, the lepers are cleansed, the deaf hear, the dead are brought back to life, the poor have good news preached to them, and blessed is the one who is not offended by me." (Luke 7:20–23)

---

10. Lee, "Pilate and the Crucifixion of Jesus," 89–90.

I also believe it is possible that John was concerned about his own death. The Greek phrase, "Are you the one coming or is it possible that another may come," suggests not doubt, but concern about the future.[11] John knew that death was on the horizon, yet he seemed concerned whether or not he was finished with this role in preparing the way for the Lord.

Luke's repetition of the disciples' question also suggested its absurdity. Luke wrote, immediately following the question, "At that hour he healed many from sickness . . . " It is almost comical to imagine Jesus busy with people, touching them, healing them, listening, and standing amidst cheers and "Hallel lu Yah"—while John's disciples were interrupting him to ask this question. Imagine them saying, "Excuse me, Jesus? John has a question. Are you the one coming or do we look for someone else?" Imagine Jesus looking them straight in the eyes as if to say, "Really—you have got to be kidding me?"

Jesus responded with, "Tell John what you see and hear . . ." This response suggested first that Jesus was doing what he was sent to do and what he had preached while at the Nazareth synagogue (4:16–19). He was not a dreamer or visionary but an activist. Luke stressed that Jesus was fulfilling his mission as the Anointed One. The list Jesus gave to these disciples involved the personal healing of those who were vulnerable, handicapped, and on the margins of life (notice that poverty was in the list of disabilities rather than sin).

A second point Luke stressed concerned his statement, "Blessed are those who are not offended by me." The question that the disciples of John asked seems somewhat insulting: "Is this it? Are *you* the guy?" The question may have been more a reflection of the reader's perspective as well. "You mean that Jesus came to help social outcasts? That's it. That's the ministry we are supposed to follow? Is that all there is to Christianity?" Jesus's response would have been, "Blessed is the one who is not offended by my ministry."

Jesus defended John by discussing his ministry and character. John was a prophet like Elijah, who was sent to prepare the way for Jesus's/Yahweh's visit and ministry. He was a man of courage and one who was truly prophetic. The reader would remember Zechariah's promise and song and know that John, like Jesus, was fulfilling his God-given ministries (Luke 1:15–17). John's ministry ended in a prison, with an executioner and neurotic King. Jesus's ministry was among people who suffered from the same neurotic king and lived in a spiritual prison. Yet Jesus stated that John's ministry was secondary to his. Jesus's mission was not flashy but simple. He

---

11. Martínez, *The Question of John the Baptist*, 106–7.

lived, taught, and worked among the oppressed. If this offended the reader, hearer, or believer today—then they should rethink becoming his disciple.

> To what can I compare the people of this generation—what are they like? They are like children sitting in the marketplace and calling to each another, "We played the flute for you, and you did not dance; we sang a lament, and you did not weep." John the Baptist came without eating bread or drinking wine, and you say, "He has a demon." The Son of Man came eating and drinking, and you say, "Hey, a glutton and a drunkard, a friend of tax collectors and sinners!" Even wisdom is justified by all of her children. (Luke 7:31–35)

The opponents of both Jesus and John were inconsistent in their rejection of either. John was willing to observe strict religious and dietary regulations in worship and his walk with God. Jesus, however, was much more lax. He ate with sinners, yet this referred not just to the act of consuming food with strangers, but talking, listening, and associating with sinful people in an intimate way. People accused him of excess because he viewed food and drink as opportunities to engage people rather than shun them. While "glutton" has been a traditional translation, the Greek verb only states that Jesus was an "eater" as opposed to John who abstained from foods for periods of time. This accusation was not a criticism of Jesus's appearance or food consumption, but his social and religious actions. Jesus was criticized not by *what* he ate, but *with whom he ate*.

Luke's epic narrative of Jesus in 4:31—7:35, involved stories of Jesus's interaction with those on the margins of society mixed with Jesus's call to his disciples to join him on this mission. Luke's early audience was challenged to complete their portrait of the Messiah as one who came to free the oppressed and called them to do the same. This Gospel included stories unique to Luke and more directly emphasized Jesus's ministry to the poor and those who were marginalized by their communities. It seems that Luke was calling the early Christian community (at least Theolphilus's group) to understand that the empire of Jesus is a community restored from spiritual exile. For Luke, Jesus brought freedom by calling his listeners to alter their view of people, their status/honor, and their place in community. This is very apparent by the final story of this section.

VIEWING WOMEN DIFFERENTLY

Jade was a woman who had been attending our church for a few months. She was invited to Agape by a former "street kid" who met her in a drug treatment program in Portland. She had been active in prostitution and had lost her children to the system. Jade and my wife Lori met often and she was baptized that Christmas. We had worked with her to stay in the system, complete her treatment program, and work to get her children back. She had done well but once she was on her own, the lure of the sex industry was back in her life. She had been somewhat distant over the weeks and Lori and I finally found a time to meet her for lunch.

I made it to Gravy, a popular diner, located in Portland's eclectic Mississippi district, in time to meet Jade. Lori had texted me to tell me she was running late from her study/meeting with another woman with issues similar to Jade. "Oh, great," I thought. "I will be meeting Jade alone." I don't know why I was uncomfortable but knew it was important to visit with her. Jade met me at the door. I gave her a hug and told her we had missed her. "I hope you like this place," she said enthusiastically. "I just live right around the corner." I looked at my phone and there was the text from Lori, "Running thirty minutes late—go ahead and talk to Jade without me."

Over the years many male ministers have told me that they would not meet with women in public alone. While we as men set boundaries and try to be professional in our meetings with females, it amazes me that most males worry, not about themselves, but the woman. When did meeting with a woman in public become unsafe for the man? The research suggests that males are exploiting, abusing, objectifying, and raping females. It also tells us that male clergy continue to be inappropriate with congregants and community members at alarming rates, even more so that other healing professionals. Marie Fortune and James Poling in 1994 cite research from the mid 1980's claiming that 12.6 percent of surveyed clergy report having sexual intimacy with their congregants. This figure is much higher than the 5.5 percent of counselors/psychologists who claim to be guilty of the same conduct. There are also extremely high percentages of female clergy who are harassed by senior ministers.[12] How have those from the vulnerable population become the ones we should suspect of indecency?

We sat down at the table and talked. We always loved Jade and worried about her. We loved her children and wanted the best for her. I could tell that things were getting tense for her, especially as she worked two phones during our conversation, which said to me she was "working" again in the sex industry. Sometimes success is scary to people. She had a tough life attending two support groups, taking care of her children, staying clean, and avoiding the financial lure of prostitution. She was also an attractive woman

---

12. Fortune and Poling, *Sexual Abuse by Clergy*, 5.

and had men, who knew what she had done, offering to care for her. Selling sex pays well and covers a multitude of bills.

We talked about the kids, how she was doing, and how she was struggling. She was currently having a relationship with a married man and cared for him. However, I could tell that she felt guilty. "How do you think his wife feels about this?" I asked. "I dunno," she replied, "I guess I hadn't thought about that. But, I have needs, I am lonely. His wife is a bitch, and he has sexual needs. He needs me." I shared with her what it was to be a real man. Men are capable of relationships, men are more than sex-crazed animals, men can have self-control, and men are able to be loyal to their commitments and vows. "I was always taught that men weren't that way," she questioned. "Men are supposed to be strong, tough, and sexual." I knew that she saw vulnerability as weakness. I guess that this was how she survived. However, unless vulnerability and openness are embraced, we cannot love, live in community, or develop healthy relationships.

We live in a world that has given us a warped definition of masculinity. This has been going on since the foundation of time. The ancient Babylonian text *The Epic of Gilgamesh* suggested that a man-beast became civilized when Gilgamesh, the demigod, introduced him to a prostitute. This story has existed for centuries. Prostitution is not the oldest profession; exploitation is.

I guess Jade obtained her view of males from pimps, Johns, her father, and cultural masculinity. She is a product of her environment. Irresponsible and immature males have taught her about masculinity; however, it is a pseudo-masculinity. I kept texting Lori at times, "Where are you . . ." to which she would reply, "On my way . . ." or "got hung up here but really needed to talk to this person." However, she would always reply, "Keep talking to Jade, she needs to hear from a man, you're doing fine." It's not that either of us worries that I will cross the line. We worry that we will not be strong enough to break through the stereotypes that will keep us from loving Jade like we believe Jesus loves her, and fail to make the choice to help her. In some way I saw this as Jesus's way of pushing me out of my comfort zones as a man.

> He was asked by one of the Pharisees to eat with him, and he went into the Pharisee's house and reclined at the table. A woman, who was of/in the city and a sinner, learned that he was reclining at table in the Pharisee's house. She brought an alabaster flask of ointment, and standing behind him by his feet, weeping, her tears fell on his feet so she wiped them with the hair of her head, kissed his feet, and anointed them with the myrrh. Seeing this the Pharisee, who had invited him, said to himself, "If this

man were a prophet, he would know what kind of woman is touching him, because she is a sinner." Jesus answered him, "Simon, I have something to say to you." He said, "Say it, Teacher." (Luke 7:36–40)

When I watch movies or hear lessons concerning the life of Jesus, this seems to be a popular story. We typically hear the story as if Jesus was sitting in a house with religious leaders, cheerfully eating a meal when suddenly a woman bursts into the dinner.[13] The emphasis of the moviemakers is that this woman has faithfully pushed through the guards or servants and interrupted the Jesus meal. The guests are disturbed but the woman goes to Jesus and begins to kiss his feet and shed tears. The hosts are judgmental and seem to express a show of disgust for the presence of this female. She is a "sinful woman" seeking repentance and expressing gratitude. The lesson of the story expresses Jesus' love for the sinner and the humiliation of the arrogant and self righteous.

While this view provides a wonderful story and lesson concerning grace, love, and forgiveness, Luke's text gives us indications that the dinner hosts would not have been as righteous or surprised by the event. First, *in the ancient world Greco-Roman meals involved women or young boys whose role was to offer sexual favors for the guests.* Proper women were usually not allowed in the presence of males and typically ate in a separate room. Since this was a Jewish meal hosted by a Pharisee, one might expect that this form of immorality would not be present, but Luke has indicated that many religious leaders were corrupt (Luke 11:37–52; 16:14). Second, *the story tells us that a woman leading a sinful life (probably a prostitute/sex worker) knew that Jesus was there and brought oil to the dinner.*[14] Jesus also mentions

13. Arlandson, *Women, Class, and Society in Early Christianity*, 160; Fitzmeyer, *The Gospel According to Luke I-IX)*, 684. Van Til states that she "bursts on the scene" ("Three Anointings and One Offering," 75). Cosgrove indicates that the woman walks to where Jesus was reclining at the table ("A Woman's Unbound Hair in the Greco-Roman World," 675). Osiek suggests that the open door of the house made it possible for her to "drop in" unannounced ("Archaeological and Architectural Issues," 97). Bailey also indicates that the woman would have been able to freely enter from the street (*Poet and Peasant*, 6–9).

14. There is a good amount of debate concerning whether the woman was a prostitute or just a woman labeled "a sinner," but there is good evidence to suggest she was in prostitution. First, she was "of the city" which is a common term for woman of the street (the adulteress was confined to the "house" in her judgments by the biblical authors; Prov 7:8). Secondly, the term used for her was common in ancient Judaism to refer to a prostitute. Finally, Averen Ipsen's work with the biblical texts and sex workers suggests that the components of foot massage, oil, kissing the feet, and loosening her hair were all actions practiced by women in prostitution and viewed as inappropriate for those considered to be modest women. Ipsen, *Sex Working and the Bible*, 141.

that the woman had been kissing his feet since he entered Simon's home for the dinner party (7:45), suggesting that she was at the meal before Jesus came. This indicates that the woman was present at the meal, rather than bursting on the scene after the meal had begun. It also may suggest that she was a welcomed guest, whom Simon had allowed to be present. Simon the Pharisee did not object to her presence and yet he, as the dinner host, had the responsibility to provide a safe environment for his guests. Did he intentionally position her at the dinner to trap Jesus, or offer sexual favors? While some may have difficulty believing that a religious leader would allow such behavior, one only need to read the history books or current news to realize that this is possible behavior—even for clergy.

The implications of this story, and the actions of the woman, would be quite shocking to the modern reader. We have been conditioned to read the story concerning a repentant woman who offered a show of gratitude and thanks to Jesus, who must have somehow forgiven her in an earlier encounter. However, I am suggesting that there are deeper implications to this story.

First, *the woman was forgiven in her encounter of Jesus*. The show of tears may be an act of repentance, but not necessarily. It is possible that the woman knew she could be forgiven and was expressing faith. It is also possible that they were tears of sadness at the realization that she was again expected to perform sex for money. The tears could have also reflected her realization, in the presence of the Lord, of her sinfulness and shame. Whether or not she had a repentant heart would not have been important to Luke, as we will later discuss in the parable of the prodigal son. The issue was not her repentance but her actions in the presence of the self-righteous host. She showed faith by her actions to Jesus.

Second, *the actions of the host indicate that Jesus was being set up*. Simon was inappropriate in how he treated (or neglected to treat) Jesus. Jesus in turn broke etiquette by personally criticizing his host, but the woman honored Jesus by her service and display of affection. The host acted as many males do today—he exploited the woman. Her emotional outburst did not cause sympathy in him, only judgment. He criticized Jesus for not condemning her. He also criticized Jesus for allowing her to touch his "shame zones." In the ancient world the head was an honorable body part but the feet were shameful parts. She invaded Jesus's space and he allowed her to do this. This would have been extremely dangerous socially for any male.

The actions of Jesus seem to be Luke's focus in this story. Jesus models a healthy view of women for all men. Even though the woman may have been preparing to "service Jesus," he treated her with love and respect. I can imagine the apostles who were present thinking, "Does he know what she is doing to him?" yet Jesus modeled for them how men were to respond to all women. Jesus's story of the forgiveness of debts was aimed at Simon, who felt that he was better than the woman, and because of his self righteousness, felt he could exploit the woman, use her, and send her out the door. She was on the margins of life trying to survive. Simon was part of the culture that put her there, and as long as he could keep her there he could exploit her.

If we follow this thought and suggest that the woman was an invited prostitute the story can take a different turn from the more common interpretation. First, the assumption that she experienced forgiveness in a previous encounter and therefore burst on the scene to express this does not fit into the story. We are assuming too much if we suggest something that the text does not tell us.[15]

However, her actions and motives are not the main focus of the story, as they might have been with the story (different or similar) in the other three Gospels. While she may have been propositioning Jesus, the response of the Lord is the focus of Luke's story.

"If this man were a prophet he would know who was touching him." This comment by the Pharisee, while to some suggesting that Jesus should be able to know her hidden life, may also support Luke's theme of exile and restoration. The common metaphor for Israel was the *zonah* (prostitute), as Yahweh through the prophets condemned the nation for adultery and prostitution, and this term was used often in the prophetic texts. Jesus, as a prophet, according to Simon, should understand that this woman represents the very metaphor used to condemn the nation. However, Jesus, as Yahweh in the flesh, accepts the *zonah*. Once again the captives were being freed, embraced, and accepted by their God. Jesus's behavior not only displayed the grace and mercy of Yahweh, rather than the faithfulness of the marginalized *zonah*, but the willingness to welcome sinners even though the Lord's host failed to offer proper hospitality.

"This woman accepted me, you did not . . ." seems to be the stronger theme of the text. Whether the woman was inappropriate with Jesus or sincerely repentant does not seem to be the issue. Her tears may have shown remorse, may have reflected sadness for Jesus's humiliation, or they could have been tears of sadness for her role in the dinner and its ceremonies. However, her motive doesn't seem to be the issue. She treated Jesus with more honor than Simon, reflecting the previous condemnation that the leaders had rejected John's baptism while the people had embraced it (Luke 7:29–30).

---

15. Bailey, *Poet and Peasant*, 242.

Luke offered many stories that suggest forgiveness, healing, and salvation without judging the motives of the recipient. This is clear by the characters in the Gospel of Luke who seem to suggest selfishness rather than genuine concerns for honoring God. The Prodigal Son (Luke 15:17–20) sought safety because he was without. The Rich Fool/Farmer sought to build bigger barns (12:16). The unrighteous judge offered justice because he did not want to be shamed or bothered (18:14). The unjust steward used favors to gain friends and avoid living on the street (16:3). Whatever their selfish motives, these characters (excluding the rich farmer) become models for God's people. In many places Luke only focused on doing the right thing in spite of one's motives. This seems to suggest that salvation is dependent on God, not people. God/Jesus come to free the oppressed not because of their morality, but because of who Yahweh is.

Jesus provided a model for manhood in the ancient world. His embrace of females in his ministry suggest that he practices acceptance without sexual manipulation (8:1–3). While he may have been accused of inappropriateness with females in his ministry, stories such as "Simon and the Sinful Woman" reflect his relationship and boundaries. As mentioned earlier the woman in the story is not the main focus. The issue involved Jesus and his host. She was simply one who, like many of Luke's victims, had been oppressed and manipulated by males. Her presence at the meal and Simon's lack of preventing her from being close to Jesus, suggest that suspicion must rest on the host, not the guest (whether welcome or unwelcome). If she was a prostitute then the message is clear—Simon was trying to entrap Jesus by using people. This theme should not surprise us as Luke's Gospel, and the other Gospel writers, clearly suggest that the corrupt religious and political leaders desired to destroy Jesus.

Jesus's response, however, was not only to offer forgiveness, but safety. He would not further oppress, dishonor, or reject her. While her advances may not have seemed appropriate, his response was. While the Pharisee may have been providing inappropriate entertainment, he was also neglecting to fulfill his cultural role as host. Simon's greed and control prevented his relationship with Jesus/God from being a blessing, but the woman was able to receive blessing because she only did what she could.

Today little has changed. In our work with women in prostitution I find that the story still resonates with our current context. In working with men it is also clear that we objectify women and disrespect what we label as "feminine." As with current sex workers the females (victims) are visible while the males stand in the shadows. We want to know the motives of the women, their lifestyle, and their sins. However, we don't ask why the men still have them present, why men buy women and children, or how men can live in harmony with females while this oppression exists. We assume that these women boldly invade our safety and sexuality by "bursting on the scene," but we forget that they have always been there—because men wanted them readily available and accessible. We assume that they must express tears of remorse rather than ourselves acknowledging our own shame for failing to honor them as victims and accept them. We forget that offering honor to all guests includes them. Even more we become uncomfortable that the creator of the universe allows them in the divine presence, while we shun them and label them as deviant.

The statement that Simon made to himself calls us to understand what it means to be prophetic. "If this man were a prophet . . ." For some today to be a prophet means to know people's hearts, their sins, and the things they hide from us and from God. However, with prostitution nothing is hidden. Even more, because it is in the open and exists we stand condemned. As Phyllis Bird wrote, "Prostitution was not supposed to exist in ancient Israel but it did. They were 'legal outlaws.'"[16] In fact, it existed as a necessary evil. Roth suggested that people believed that men needed it to avoid adultery and continue as law-abiding citizens.[17] Prostitution exists not because of "sinful women" but because of men who lack the ability to have healthy relationships with their fellow humans. To be a prophet in Luke 7:36–50 meant that we see people and those who exploit them. Today it means that we embrace the marginalized and offer mercy. "This man was a prophet and received the true sinner."

Borders for the Marginalized

Luke's readers would have been challenged in this section. Jesus was culturally inappropriate, at least according to the mores of his time. He moved close to people in their sin and shame and visited the dark areas of life and his community. He boldly went where no respectful, honorable, or spiritual male could acceptably go. Jesus expressed courage and love as he not only came to free the oppressed but give them hope, good news, mercy, and acceptance. He too became an outcast.

He also called his followers to join him. To follow Jesus means to go where he went, to love those he loved, and to show mercy to all. To follow Jesus is risky, not just physically but socially. To follow Jesus to the margins means we ourselves become marginalized. If our society shuns people on

16. Bird, "Prostitution in the Social World," 42.
17. Roth, "Marriage, Divorce, and the Prostitute," 29.

the edges of acceptance, then Christians must be there as well. Our new community will be those needing hope rather than judgment; justice instead of oppression; and love in place of neglect.

Evangelism will once again become, "Your faith has saved you—*shalom!*" It will happen to the most unlikely individuals. It will produce unusual results.

6

Mentoring on the Margins
Luke 8—9:50

JESUS AGAIN WENT ON the move as a traveling preacher/teacher, and was accompanied by his disciples as well as a group of women. Luke indicated that some of the women had been cured of evil spirits.[1] These women would have joined the team during the earlier ministry in Luke 4–7. Not only had these women joined Jesus, they supported his ministry financially. Jesus not only called people to wholeness, he called them to embrace a ministry that many societies would consider suspicious.

Jesus taught the disciples a story concerning the power of God's word to transform people. We commonly know this as "The Parable of the Sower." In the ancient world people spoke in complex riddles, memorized large quantities of material, and worked to decipher and decode stories. However, to speak in a parable or common story was a very simple task. The word *parable* meant something exaggerated, suggesting that these stories were not meant to reflect an exact account of reality. The meaning was obvious to the listener as the teacher used common stories to connect with them and in the case of exaggeration, emphasized the major point of message. In addition, the teacher provided the deeper meaning or interpretation of the story to his or her audience. Jesus told common stories to common people and gave them an application that they could embrace. Some teachers would offer a story including a list of other rabbis' and past scholars' thoughts on the matter. This was designed to either prove their point or discredit the other teacher. However, Jesus's parables were simple to understand and grasp, unless you were someone who was used to complexity in your teaching.

1. Schaberg, "How Mary Magdalene Became a Whore," 31–37.

Therefore, because it was too simple or too common, an elite person might not listen to or take the story to heart.

The Parable of the Sower was one example of this type of story (Luke 8:4–15). It would be clear to any person working the soil or living off of the land that seed would grow and mature based on the type of soil where it was planted. Some seed would be taken by the birds because the seed could not penetrate the hard soil from the path surrounding the garden. Seed growing on rocky soil would sprout in the thin layer of dirt, grow quickly due to the warmth of the dirt, and then quickly wither since the rocks prevented the roots from growing deeper. Seeds among thorns or other weeds would not grow to maturity because the other plants would grow beside them and compete for sunlight and moisture. Finally, the seeds in good soil would flourish and produce fruit depending on the genetics of the plant. This was common knowledge to the hearer. Who would understand that Jesus was referring to a matter of one's heart and acceptance for God's word. His disciples would have accompanied him enough to know that the motive of his teaching was to persuade people to love and follow God.

LISTENING THROUGH FAITH AND COMMITMENT

However, when the apostles asked Jesus for the meaning of this story his response was that they had access to the message while others could not understand its meaning.

> He said, "You are given knowledge of the secrets of the empire of God, but for others they are in parables, so that 'seeing they may not see, and hearing they may not understand.' This is the parable: The seed is the word of God. The ones along the path are those who have heard; but the devil comes and keeps the word from their hearts, so they may not believe and be saved. The ones on the rock, when they hear the word, receive it with joy. But they have no roots, believe for awhile, and in time of testing fall away. The ones that fell among the thorns are those who hear, are choked by the cares, riches, and pleasures of life. Their fruit does not mature. Those in the good soil are those who, hearing the word, hold it fast in an honest and good heart, and produce fruit with patience. No one lights a lamp and covers it with a jar or puts it under a bed. They put it on a stand so that those who enter may see the light. Nothing is hidden that will not be shown, nor is anything secret that will not come to light. Be careful what you listen to, for to the one who has, more

> will be given, and from the one who does not have, even what he thinks that he has will be taken away." (Luke 8:9–18)

The reason some would not understand the stories was not because they were too complicated—people would not understand them due to a lack of faith. They may also have chosen to ignore the meaning as it would cut many to the heart. The stories would have been too simple, common, or plain. They would have been beneath a trained teacher or rabbi. Jesus shared that understanding was an issue of faith.

While this parable is mentioned in Matthew and Mark, Luke shared that the plants/faith died because "they believe for a short time," "they cannot believe and be saved," or "they do not mature." For Luke, Jesus claimed that spiritual growth was a matter of faith and obedience. In addition to this, the disciples were cautioned to "be careful how you listen . . ." In the story following the interpretation of the seeds and plants, he mentioned that light was meant to be shared with others. The disciple's life and faith would be observed by others and would become helpful for their salvation. The parables were not complex stories that couldn't be understood, they were simple common stories that called people to a life-change that many would have resisted. Jesus claimed that the value in these stories would be shown by the faith of the hearer.

This faith and belief would create a community that not only understood the truths of God's empire, but the value of Jesus's family.

> Then his mother and his brothers came to him, but they could not get near him because of the crowd. He was told, "Your mother and your brothers are standing outside, wanting to see you." But he answered them, "My mother and my brothers are the ones who hear the word of God and do it." (Luke 8:19–21)

Luke again emphasized Jesus's focus on listening by suggesting that the family of God would be those who heard and practiced what was taught. As mentioned earlier, Jesus was culturally suspect in his relationship with his family and his role as an older son (most likely taking the leadership role since Joseph must have died), causing his family to want to meet with him. Whether they wanted to be part of his ministry or were coming to take him away is not clear from this story, yet in other locations of the Gospel we understand that Jesus's family didn't believe much of what he was teaching. Jesus not only called his disciples to faith and commitment, but his mother, brothers, and sisters as well. For Jesus, blood was not stronger than faith and the new family or household of God's empire involved loyalty to the Father.

These stories are part of Luke's narrative explaining Jesus invasion of the dark corners of the marginalized world, and his call to the disciples to follow and manifest a life of faith and courage. The miracles that Jesus performed in the next few verses demanded courage from the disciples as well as the reader. First, *even though Jesus calmed the waves at Lake Galilee, he questioned the disciples concerning their faith* (Luke 8:22–25). While popular Jesus movies depict this story as occurring during a hurricane, thunderstorm, or storm at sea, the truth is that those on Lake Galilee can experience quick windstorms that produce white-capped waves. While it would have seemed scary to be on a boat in the middle of the lake, the storm was not as violent as the cinema wants us to believe. In any event, Jesus continued to sleep during this storm. One can speculate what he was trying to teach the disciples, but it is obvious that he was tired. The disciples, unfortunately responded by waking him. There are many texts in the ancient world which suggest that prayer, petition, and loud cries will "wake the gods" into action. This story is similar, only Jesus claimed that their actions showed a lack of faith. The story expressed a high level of fear or anxiety in the apostles, but also the lesson that while God is many times silent, we are not neglected by our Lord.

In the second story, Jesus encountered a demoniac residing on the margins (tombs) of his community. A demoniac was a person who was acting violent, mentally ill and unable to care for themselves. In the ancient world these people were believed to be under the influence of evil spirits. This man, named Legion, obviously had a multitude of evil spirits. Luke only focused on the man's self injury. The demons caused him to injure himself as well as his community. For the town's convenience he was driven out of the city and therefore civilization. He was mentally ill and dangerous. Jesus displayed complete power over his form of evil and sent the demons into the pigs (this is the first incidence of deviled ham). As the people in the community came to the location and noticed that their pigs had drowned, they were afraid. "All the people of the region of the Gerasenes asked him to leave them because they were overcome with fear" (8:37). Notice that the people were afraid not only because of what happened to the pigs, but because they saw the man clothed, sane, and sitting at Jesus's feet. They asked this healer to leave them. Instead of asking him to stay, as so many in Luke's Gospel had done, they sent him away. Having a demoniac outside of your city walls was convenient. It kept evil outside your city, and it provided a scapegoat for the community. With the death of the pigs and healing of their "scapegoat" they now had a bigger problem—the demons were in the water. Luke suggested that Jesus's presence created change and unbalanced their well-ordered lives, as it does ours today. The Gerasene community now had to deal with mobile evil; however, the former scapegoat was now a messenger for Jesus. He would show his repentance by facing the same people he had hurt, telling them about Jesus, and—it would be assumed—making amends to them.

Jesus's next miracles concerned the female with hemophilia and the synagogue ruler's daughter; both involved faith, persistence, and courage. The woman with a flow of blood pressed through the crowd to touch Jesus. Since women in menstruation were considered unclean this woman may have been perpetually unclean and not able to visit the temple. Because of her faith (as shown by her desire to touch Jesus) she experienced some of Jesus's power, which he felt leave him when she touched him. Jairus, the synagogue ruler, was encouraged to believe and trust that even in death God was active. He showed compassion on Jairus's sick daughter who died while Jesus and the band of disciples were headed to the home to heal her. Jesus touched her and raised her back to life.

Jesus continued to lead his disciples to the margins of life. From the dark corners of a graveyard with a howling demoniac, to the streets of the city with an unclean, bleeding woman (a hemophiliac female would be susceptive to massive blood loss during her menstrual cycles), to the home that smelled of death—he showed his disciples his mission. Marginalized people who were separated from their city, their right to worship, and their families were restored to peace. He had prepared his disciples by mentoring them in the mission of God. He was God in the flesh who had come to reach the captives, the oppressed, the blind, the poor, and those on the margins of their society. The disciples were encouraged to join him in this ministry, observe him, and imitate him. Any skilled mentor would suggest that one cannot train students and then expect them to practice what they have learned without guidance and slowly taking ownership of ministry. Jesus, at this stage of his ministry, next began to delegate and slowly involve the disciples in his mission.

THE MENTOR SENDS OUT THE STUDENTS

> He called the twelve together, gave them power and authority over all demons and to cure afflictions, and sent them out to proclaim the empire of God and to heal sicknesses. He said to them, "Take nothing for your journey, no staff, bag, bread, nor money; and do not have two tunics. Whatever house you enter, stay there, and depart from there. Wherever they do not receive you, shake off the dust from your feet as a testimony against them when you leave that town." They left and went through the

> villages, preaching the gospel and healing everywhere. (Luke 9:1–6)

As Jesus has mentored and modeled God's mission for his disciples he next began to delegate his authority to these followers. First, *he gave them authority and power over evil so that they could carry out his message.* While his main focus was preaching, he did equip his followers to not only preach and teach, but to heal those in the community. The apostles, like Jesus, were to be itinerant and receive support from people who wished to give, even if they were females (8:1–2). Their focus was ministry, rather than being comfortable and successful. Second, *their ministry caught the attention of King Herod, who began to see similarities between Jesus's and John's ministry.* Because the apostles were faithful with Jesus's mission the neurotic king Herod had heard of his ministry. In addition to this, as with any apprentice who gets their taste of this new task, the apostles were both overjoyed and amazed at the experiences that they had with their newly appointed mission.

As Jesus attempted to regroup with his disciples and spend time with them, a crowd followed them. Again, Jesus found an opportunity to delegate and involve his students in his mission.

> As the day began to end/decline, the twelve came and said to him, "Dismiss the crowd in order that they may go into the surrounding villages and countryside to find lodging and get food, since we are in a deserted place." He said to them, "You give them something to eat." They said, "We do not have much, five loaves of bread and two fish—unless we go and buy food for these people." There were about five thousand men. He said to his disciples, "Have them recline in groups of about fifty each." They did this and had them all sit down. Taking the five loaves and the two fish, he looked up to heaven, said a blessing over them, then broke the loaves and gave them to the disciples to set before the crowd. They all ate and were satisfied. What remained was gathered; twelve baskets of broken pieces. (9:12–17)

This story occurs in all four Gospels with Jesus asking the disciples to give food to the people. The disciples were confused since there were over 5,000 people present. Jesus delegated this task by having them connect with the people, gather the baskets, and distribute the blessings. This story again reflects Jesus's patient guidance and mentoring to the apostles as well as his willingness to pass on ministry, chores, and duties. The disciples broke the crowd into groups of fifty (typically this would be fifty men, not including women and children). Imagine looking out over the one hundred groups of people and wondering if the food was enough. In the end the apostles were reminded that this was a God of order and loyalty in that there were twelve baskets left over, the number of Jewish tribes and apostles. Jesus was again the mentor who was in charge.

Who Do You Say I Am

> It happened that as he was praying alone, that the disciples were with him. He asked them, "Who do the crowds say that I am?" They answered, "John the Baptist, others say, Elijah, and others that one of the prophets of old has resurrected." Then he said to them, "But who do you say that I am?" Peter answered, "The Christ of God." He strictly charged (rebuked them) and commanded them to tell this to no one, saying, "The Son of Man must suffer many things, be rejected by the elders, chief priests, and scribes, be killed, and on the third day be raised." He said to all of them, "If anyone wants to come with me they must deny themselves, take up their cross daily, and follow me. For whoever wants to save their lives will destroy them, but whoever destroys their life for my sake will save it. For what value is it if a person gains the whole world and loses or destroys themselves? For whoever is ashamed of me and of my words, the Son of Man will be ashamed of them when he comes in his glory and that of the Father and of the holy angels. But I tell you the truth, there are some standing here who will not taste death until they see the empire of God." (Luke 9:18–27)

This passage is common to the synoptic Gospels. When this passage occurs in Matthew and Mark the setting described by the authors is the area known as Caesarea Philippi, an area known for idolatry, where statutes to divine beings were present. One can imagine Jesus standing in front of the idols asking the disciples who they believed him to be. In Luke the story happened when Jesus was praying after the feeding of the more than 5,000 people. Luke seems more concerned with who Jesus was to the disciples now that they have been active in ministry and taken leadership seriously. The preceding miracles would have challenged their perception of the Messiah and suggested he was very powerful. Jesus wondered what the people they served were saying about him, and the response from the disciples was that they believed he was one of the heroes of the Bible. Earlier in the chapter king Herod had taken notice as well. Jesus's reputation had spread and the disciples heard directly what people thought of Jesus. Yet, Jesus was unconcerned with what the people thought about him as was evident by his next question, "What about you?"

Peter was the first to confirm what the apostles thought—Jesus was the Messiah of God. What is interesting is that Luke does not record Peter's questioning Jesus's prediction of death and suffering, as did Matthew and Mark, nor does he include Jesus's famous rebuke of Peter, "Get behind me Satan . . ." Luke did not seem to be concerned with this fact. The disciples, in this section, were simply followers who experienced their first ministry experience and were reflecting on the focus of this work. While they had served and helped people this was now a time to reevaluate the mission. First, Jesus shared with them that his mission was to suffer. As it was in the past, so it would be again—God will open arms of love and compassion and be rejected by the very people who need salvation. Second, this death will not be his end because there would be a resurrection proving that life emerges out of sacrifice and death. Third, in order to follow Jesus one must do the same and be willing to suffer, die, or be sacrificed. Jesus called it carrying the cross. Luke used this suffering theme more than any other writer (2:34–35; 9:20–27, 31, 44; 13:34; 18:31–33; 20:17). Luke also inserted that this be "daily." He reminded the reader that to be ashamed of Jesus, his words, and his ministry was not the way to eternal life. Finally, Jesus claimed that this empire, this mission, and this call to commitment were present and the apostles as well as the Theophilus community needed to make their choice. Luke will repeatedly remind the readers that the ministry of Jesus involves sacrifice and obedience. To embrace this shameful ministry and venture toward those on the margins required courage and faith.

This time of reflection was important as the apostles had experienced Jesus's conflict with those who resisted his association with the marginalized and those in the dark recesses of Galilee. As the twelve began to embrace ministry and witness its power, Jesus gave a sober reminder that the mission of God, his mission, involved sacrifice and humility. To be successful one must never outgrow or be too good for those with whom Jesus associated. If his critics called him a "friend of sinners and tax collectors," then the same should be true of his followers. Luke does not record Peter's objections to Jesus's death, not because it was contrary to the mission, but because Peter's objection was not the focus of Luke's narrative. Luke may have been more concerned with the reader's objection to Jesus's call to follow him, carry a cross daily, and be a friend of sinners and tax collectors.

Who Did God Say He Was

Eight days later, eight being a resurrection number in the ancient world, Jesus took his three closest apostles to a mountain to pray. Peter, James, and

John, who would become strong pillars in the early church, were those to which he must have been closest. In the previous story his prayer involved a time of reflection and confession for the apostles. This time while he was praying the three friends saw something miraculous. Jesus radiated light, as did Yahweh in the prophets and presence of Moses. These three, like Moses, had the opportunity to witness this manifestation. In addition to this they saw Jesus talking with Moses and Elijah (representing the law and prophets) concerning his death/departure (exodus in the Greek language) that he would face at Jerusalem. Jesus had just shared with the apostles that he would be killed, but now the story was becoming clearer. His death would happen at Jerusalem, the place where God was supposed to live. The followers had experienced Jesus's ministry and now they were being called to reflect that this ministry was to involve death, sacrifice, faith, and courage.

The three were sleepy (they always tended to sleep when Jesus took them to pray) and would have been startled by what they saw. Peter offered to take care of Elijah and Moses, however they experienced a greater manifestation of Jesus on this mountain.

> As he was saying these things, a cloud came and overshadowed them, and they were afraid as they entered the cloud. A voice came out of the cloud, saying, "This is my Son, my chosen one; listen to him." When the voice had spoken, Jesus was found alone. They kept silent and told no one in those days what they had seen. (Luke 9:34–36)

Luke is the only writer to describe entering the cloud. The language here echoes the language of the Hebrew Bible describing Yahweh filling the temple/tabernacle with a cloud/smoke and the people experiencing fear. Peter, James, and John were experiencing the presence of Yahweh/Jesus and had been more concerned with speaking than listening and observing. However, they did something most would not—they entered the cloud. Even though they were overcome with fear they came into the presence of God. A voice testified that Jesus was God's son and the authority to be heard. They, like Moses, were able to eenter the presence of God, and there they witnessed Jesus' divinity.

Reflection, Faithlessness, and Humiliation

As this section ends the apostles were challenged by Jesus concerning their lack of faith to heal a sick child (they been able to do this earlier), arrogance concerning who was the greatest, and their unwillingness to delegate Jesus's ministry to other people (Luke 9:37–50). While Luke wrote that Jesus sent out the disciples and then brought them back to reflect on their ministry, they, like so many in the past two millennia, had forgotten the mission of God and the purpose of Jesus. Jesus's patience was shown as he gathered his followers and took the time to teach them. He had given them power and they had used it well, yet they still struggled with the mission. The mission was to go to the captives and set them free. This called for courage, faith, humility, and love. The apostles, like any of us, were learning and needed guidance. Luke focused these past nine chapters on Jesus's Galilean mission and prepared the reader for the next phase, the trip to Jerusalem. In this next section the disciples will experience ministry at greater levels than before.

Jesus predicted his death and suffering at Jerusalem. However, before he could go there he needed his followers to have engaged in ministry so that they might fulfill God's mission after his death. He mentored these men and women by having them accompany him to the people imprisoned in darkness and on the margins of society. He also gave them tasks, power, authority, and responsibilities. They did well, but Jesus knew that they needed to be grounded in the work. To have a teacher who was a friend of outcasts might have been noble, but it needed to be a way of life. Luke described it as carrying a cross daily. For Jesus, if you were ashamed of his words, his message, his companions, and his ministry, you were ashamed of him. He was only looking for people who would embrace his style of ministry and whom he would therefore accept.

WHAT ARE WE ASHAMED OF?

Today American Christianity has struggled to find an identity. While we heap praise on those who work with the marginalized, our budgets, our time, our presence, and our passion suggest that it is empty praise. We state, "I don't know how you can do that . . ." or "Bless you for that work—it is good for you to do it . . ." Yet it is something we would never choose to do. We have redefined carrying our cross as to living with inconvenience. We smile that Jesus was the friend of sinners, but work hard to avoid "those people." If Jesus did ministry in our communities would we join him? Would we be proud if our ministers were friends with sinners and tax collectors? Do we believe that ministry involves going to the marginalized, or do we use religion to keep people outside our boundaries?

Practicing Incarnation

I have heard ministers talk about needing a break. I have always wondered if Jesus took a break from people. While I know that any ministry is exhausting and that we need those times to escape and have alone time, personal *shalom*, and family time, being on mission for Jesus doesn't always stop. I firmly believe that we in full-time ministry need boundaries and must work hard to set those boundaries. But I don't believe that we should ever be rude to people. Being nice, friendly, and listening are not roles in ministry—they are common courtesies that we as humans must teach our children, congregations, and practice ourselves. This is what it means to be human.

Many ministers have shared that when they are in public they don't want to talk to people. I understand, but don't agree. When I go to the gym I am not interested in having theological discussions, arguing ministry tactics, or counseling people. However, when I go to the gym I am a person engaging other people, as we encourage our congregations to do. The incarnation doesn't start at 9 a.m. and end when I leave the spiritual community. The incarnation is to be who we are.

One day at the gym Karen came to me and spoke, as she and others have done often. I go to the gym to work out, blow off steam, and visit with the people whom God places in my path. I typically talked to Karen and others while there but the previous night Karen had come to a class I was asked to teach at her church. The class concerned sexual assault and the church. This morning she began with, "Dr. Clark, I didn't know you were a minister. Thanks for the class." We visited awhile and she left to finish her workout.

A few months later she asked me how to help a friend who was in a bad marriage situation. I listened to her and shared with her that Lori and I would be glad to help her friend, help her help her friend, or be a resource. The situation was not good nor was it healthy for any woman to be in. As we suspected, the next day she came to Lori and I at the gym and said that she was the friend needing help. Lori began to work with her and we supported her. We talked with her church leaders, had some come to one of our abuse trainings, and gave her resources, support, and a listening ear at the gym or when she met for coffee. In addition to this we were amazed at how many people at the gym supported her, invited her to stay in their home, and confronted her husband, who also came to the gym. Because the husband saw no need to change she left the relationship, is supported by her church leaders, and always brings a sense of warmth to people at the gym. We have also met many others at the gym and developed relationships as well. It didn't matter what anyone believed, what mattered was that someone needed help.

I wonder what would have happened had I put in my earphones, shut people at the gym out of my mind while working out, and viewed the workouts as something to do, rather than viewing the gym as a place to practice incarnation.

As Luke prepared the reader to join Jesus at Jerusalem he also reminded the early Christian community that Jesus modeled God's mission so that we could join him, be like him, and experience joy in the lives of others. The journey in Galilee was ending but it was a time of reflection. Jesus calls us to mission but sometimes in the midst of mission asks, "Who do you think I am?" or "Are you willing to follow?" Sometimes he declares, "Come with me and stay awake . . ." Jesus continues to mentor his followers but reminds us that if we are doing his work we will see change not in the heart of the city, but in the heart of those who truly want Jesus in their lives.

SECTION 3
Joining Jesus on the Journey to Jerusalem

7

Joining Jesus on the Margins
Luke 9:51—11:54

THIS NEXT SECTION OF Luke involves Jesus's journey to Jerusalem (9:51—19:27). Luke used a common theme in Greek and Roman classics that employed a *journey*. The hero, in epic stories, typically embarked on a journey, faced obstacles, excitement, and returned home. The journey theme flushed out important concepts for the author. The actions of the hero display courage, wisdom, manliness, and integrity. The the journey offered a view into the theme of the book, skill of the writer, and the audience reading/hearing this work.

Luke uses this same theme for Jesus. For Luke, the journey was not only a major theme, it expressed the spiritual development of the disciples and reader.

> Luke's journey to Jerusalem is nearly seven times longer than Mark's and nearly six times longer than Matthew's. Four hundred and twenty-three verses in the United Bible Societies' text are devoted to Jesus' pilgrimage to Jerusalem in Luke 9:51—19:44, while Matthew has seventy-five verses, and Mark, only sixty-two.[1]

The first few chapters of Luke provided an introduction to Jesus's ministry/mission, his interactions with people, and his call for the audience to follow the Lord. This next section portrayed the journey of Jesus and his disciples offering wonderful teaching moments for them. In addition to this James Resseguie suggests that spiritual formation during the journey included the

1. Resseguie, *Spiritual Landscape*, 29.

hard road to the suffering and death of Jesus, the way of brokenness for the disciples, and the self-indulgent path that the disciples were to avoid.[2]

The beginning phrase, "As the time approached for him to be taken up he set his face toward Jerusalem . . ." involved "setting the face forward," common in Ezekiel and Jeremiah (Luke 9:51). The phrase suggested that Jesus was focused or determined to go to the city and fulfill his mission. Luke began this next section referring to what will happened by the end of the Gospel. First, he mentioned *Jesus's being taken up*. The phrase refers to his death, resurrection, and ascension that will happen at Jerusalem (Luke 24:51; Acts 1:2). This also referred to his discussion concerning his "exodus," which occurred on the mountain where he was transfigured with Elijah and Moses present (9:28–36). Luke and the Theophilus community knew that Jesus would face suffering at Jerusalem. Jesus was portrayed as one who willingly chose the journey to the city, knowing its outcome.

Luke also mentioned that Jesus set his face toward the city. This was another method of claiming that his death and crucifixion were no accident. Jesus was willingly choosing to go to this city, even though he knew it would be the place of ultimate rejection, and he was asking the disciples to join him on this journey. He had shared with them earlier that he would suffer (9:22) but that he would also expect them to join him on this journey of suffering, called *carrying the cross*. While they may have struggled with understanding what it mean to carry a cross, by joining Jesus on the journey they would see firsthand what a life of faith offered. In addition to this Luke's readers would also be challenged to follow Jesus both in the text and in their own ministry.

The cost of following Jesus required the courage to practice patience. In 9:52–56, the disciples were angry with the Samaritan people since they did not accept Jesus. Because he was headed to Jerusalem, and therefore was a committed Jew, the Samaritans would have resented his presence. As mentioned earlier, some from the Jewish nation believed the Samaritans to be of racially mixed blood and not pure Jews. The Samaritans, on the other hand, had developed a hatred for the Jews, who seemed to be judgmental. It is interesting that while this community rejected Jesus they would later become a powerful group in the expansion of the new Christian community (Acts 8). While the disciples felt angry at this decision, Jesus called them to ignore the rejection and move on. Even though refusing hospitality or not properly welcoming a king brought judgment in the Hebrew Bible and in ancient Near Eastern culture, Jesus indicated that the way of God involved forgiveness and mercy.[3]

---

2. Ibid., 37.
3. Allison, "Rejecting Violent Judgment," 459, 479.

Second, the cost of following Jesus required making sacrifices. In Luke 9:57–62 three people asked to join him on this journey. Jesus told them that his ministry was homeless, one that left family, and one that must not regret any decision that required following him. To be homeless was a sign of irresponsibility in the ancient world. While there were Roman cynics and philosophers who boasted that they lived out in the open, without any debt or obligation, Jewish people believed that a responsible male, like Jesus, must carry a trade, care for his family, and live in community. Jesus, as an older son of a construction worker, was obviously not fulfilling his cultural responsibility as a son. His call to follow this ministry was a sacrifice of honor.

Children were expected to honor their parents and families with a proper burial. While many have worked to soften Jesus's call to the second and third individual's request to abandon their family, what he said was culturally dishonorable (9:59–62). Jesus had clearly shown that he was countercultural by his rejection of the builder trade, claiming that his disciples were more family than Mary and her children (Luke 8:19–21), and the gathering of disciples for a wandering ministry. Even more, his challenge to the three people who requested to join the journey was radical. Luke's message was clear—following Jesus on his journey to Jerusalem was a sacrifice and a call to be dishonored in a culture valuing stability and safety.

SENDING OUT THE TEAM

As Jesus continued the journey toward Jerusalem, he also continued to delegate his ministry mission to his followers.

> After this the Lord appointed seventy-two [people] and sent them on ahead of him, two by two, into every town and place where he was to go. He said to them, "The harvest is plentiful, but there are only a few workers. You must pray to the Lord of the harvest to cast out (kick out) workers into his harvest. Go, I am sending you out like lambs in the midst of wolves. Do not carry a moneybag, backpack, or sandals, and don't stop for an extended greeting with anyone on the road. When you enter a home, first say, '*Shalom* to this home/family.' If a peaceful person is there, your *shalom* will rest upon them. If not, it will return to you. Remain in the same home, eating and drinking what they provide. The worker deserves his or her pay; do not go from family to family. Whenever you enter a town and they receive you, eat what they set before you. Heal the sick there and say to them, 'The empire of God has come near to you.' But whenever

you enter a town and they do not receive you, go into its street and say, 'The dust of your town that sticks to our feet we wipe off as a sign against you. Be advised, the empire of God has come near.' I am telling you that it will be more tolerable on that day for Sodom than for that town." (Luke 10:1–12)

This text is unique to Luke in that this is the second occurrence of Jesus's sending out the disciples with a mission. In Luke 10:3 he used the word for "cast out" instead of sending out the disciples. Throughout the Bible God's people needed to be "shoved" into mission. In Genesis the people of God were told to scatter and fill the earth (Gen 1:28; 8:17; 9:1, 7) yet by chapter eleven, they decided to gather together and build a tower. God again scattered them through disparate languages (Gen 11:9) so that they would fulfill God's original plan to fill the earth. Throughout the Hebrew Bible God dispersed the people, causing the Jewish nation to reach other countries and have influence on other faiths. In the Book of Acts, the early Christians gathered at Jerusalem until Stephen was martyred and Saul began to persecute the church (Acts 7). Through this violence the scattered church began to grow in other parts of the Roman Empire (Acts 8:1–2; 11:19–21). Historically God's people have sought comfort over mission. Jesus not only sent out his disciples but he asked them to pray that God would "kick them out" into the field. For Jesus, the work of God was already done. His disciples still need to go, or be shoved, out of our comfortable environments to advance the story of Jesus and his empire.

This mission would again take faith, courage, and patience. The disciples were to become very vulnerable and trust other people for food, clothing, and lodging. Those who were generous were to be blessed, while those who were rude and unwelcoming were to be avoided. The disciples were to be honorable and serve those who cared for them. They were given authority to bless others, preach the good news of Jesus, and heal the pain of the people in the town.

Jesus also reminded them that they were his representatives. "The one who listens to you listens to me, the one who rejects you rejects me, and the one who rejects me rejects the one who sent me [the Father]" (Luke 10:16). The disciples, who had not previously been religious teachers and were intimidated by them, were now given authority to teach and heal. They were also told that how people treated them was a direct reflection of how people treated Jesus. On the one hand this was a reminder that they too would suffer as Jesus did. On the other hand it was a reminder that Jesus would take care of those who preach his message.

After returning, the disciples were excited at both the power they experienced and the healing of people found through Jesus's ministry. Like many young interns and ministers we have had at Agape, the disciples were "fired up" at what they experienced. Jesus likewise shared their joy by offering a prayer of praise (Luke 10:21–22) and reminding them that Satan is defeated when God's people fulfill their mission and role for the kingdom of Jesus.

REFUELING FOR THE MISSION

Teach Us to Have Mercy

Luke included another unique parable in the journey to Jerusalem that called the disciples to prepare for ministry by addressing compassion. This parable has been commonly called the "Parable of the Good Samaritan." However, the adjective good is not used in this story. In addition it is helpful to realize that Jesus's audience would not have seen a Samaritan as a good person. The story would have been odd in that the villain became a hero.

> A certain lawyer stood up to test him, saying, "Teacher, what shall I do to inherit eternal life?" He [Jesus] said, "What is written in the Law? How do you read/understand it?" He answered, "You will love the Lord your God with all your heart, soul, and strength (and mind),[4] and your neighbor as yourself." He said to him, "You have answered correctly; do this, and you will live." But he wanted to justify himself and said to Jesus, "Who is my neighbor?" Jesus replied with a parable: "A man was going down from Jerusalem to Jericho, and he fell in the midst of robbers, who stripped him, beat him, and departed, leaving him almost dead. By coincidence a priest was going down that road, saw him, and passed by on the other side. Also a Levite came to the place, saw him, and passed by on the other side. But a Samaritan, as he traveled, came to where he was, saw him, and had compassion. He went to him, bound up his wounds pouring oil and wine on them, set him on his own animal, brought him to an inn, and cared for him. The next day he took out two denarii and gave them to the innkeeper, saying, 'Take care of him, and whatever more you spend, I will repay you when I return.' Which of these three, do you think, was a neighbor (neighborly) to the

---

4. "Mind" is found in some of the earlier manuscripts suggesting that this last word may not be part of the text. I have included it here since there are valid arguments on both sides of the discussion concerning its place or absence in the text. In addition, omitting or keeping the phrase does not change the point of Luke's story.

man who in the midst of the robbers?" He said, "The one who practiced mercy." Jesus said, "Go, and do the same." (10:25–37)

In this well-known story, Jesus was being tested in his knowledge of the Torah (law) of God and the goal of receiving salvation. However, Jesus focused on two commands—love God and love your neighbor. Unfortunately the problem that many of the religious leaders and teachers faced was not loving God—but loving others. The lawyer even went to the extreme to clarify whom he should love.

The story of the man who fell among the robbers would have been a common event. The road from Jerusalem to Jericho was downhill and even to this day is dangerous both in terrain and criminals who attack travelers.[5] Jesus would have been telling a story with which his audience, and Luke's readers, would have identified. In many cities the value of having Rome as your ally meant that a police force of Roman soldiers would be present to offer safety and protection. However, when one walked to Jericho, few soldiers were present to protect others. Typically people travelled in groups (Luke 2:44). The man in the story was obviously alone and therefore vulnerable. He became more vulnerable as the gang physically assaulted him, took his clothes and money, and left him physically at risk. This story would have evoked sympathy from many readers and listeners concerning the plight of this victim.

However, the interesting point in the story was that the priest and Levite (priestly servants) should have stopped to help the man. Instead they walked by on the other side of the road. God's leaders ignored the cries of the vulnerable and oppressed and acted without compassion. Fortunately, a Samaritan (who would have been viewed by the listener to be as corrupt as the gang members) saw the man and had compassion on him. Through his compassion he cared for the victim, took him to a hotel, and offered money to the innkeeper—even offering to pay more if needed. He, according to Jesus, acted as a man who cared for the vulnerable. Jesus also asked which person proved to be a neighbor to the vulnerable man.

The interesting response of the lawyer illustrated the problem that the disciples were facing during the time of Jesus. The lawyer, when asked who proved to be a neighbor, could not bring himself to say "the Samaritan," but instead stated, "the one who showed him mercy." Jesus response for the listener was to go and do the same as the Samaritan (who showed compassion) had done.

While the disciples were preparing for their next ministry mission, Luke challenged his reader through this unique parable. First, *discipleship*

---

5. Bailey, *Poet and Peasant and Through Peasant Eyes*, 40–42.

involves compassion and mercy. I have found that in our work with domestic violence, abuse, prostitution, sexual assault, and pornography one of the main ingredients missing from males who are involved in these sins is compassion and empathy.[6] Men who do these things lack compassion; or at least they may struggle to show it. How else can men embrace such behavior and images that degrade our sisters? Often when I ask groups of men, when I am speaking, to describe current terms for "having sex with a woman" they use violent terms such as "tap that," "hit that," "bang her," or other phrases. For males, violence and sex seem to go together, creating an environment where compassion and empathy become unwelcome. Rites of manhood among American males try to crush these emotions and ethical values. If males model these values we are labeled feminine, gay, or childish. Yet Jesus clearly states in this parable that compassion and mercy are not only his qualities, they are to be major qualities of the disciple.

Second, *Luke suggested that faith development requires practicing compassion and mercy*. Jesus did not tell the lawyer to "Go and think like this man . . ." he told him to "Go and do . . ." Spiritual formation must involve acts of love and sacrifice for those who are vulnerable in our communities. As a minister I have people suggest to me that their spiritual formation will occur during a retreat, when we are alone, or in isolation of others. This can be true. Yet it is also true that, as Jesus said, spiritual formation can happen during acts of compassion, outreach, love, and service. Unfortunately the research on American churches is that we have focused more on individual spiritual formation than with serving in community. We have separated "works" from "spiritual growth." However, Jesus claimed that loving God and neighbors is displayed through actions rather than contemplation. In the story of the Samaritan and the robbery victim the point is clear—even when a wicked person acts like Jesus they reflect salvation. The American churches must embrace the challenge to "go and do likewise . . ." for our own salvation and the salvation of our communities.

Finally, *this story is a challenge to develop relationships with and aid vulnerable people in their healing as an offer of mercy even when there is great risk*. Most inns in the ancient world were run by corrupt individuals. The Samaritan gave the owner of the inn money and offered to pay more if needed. This showed tremendous faith, courage, and risk from the Samaritan as he offered to help his neighbor. He took great risks to help this man, even if it cost him his life, money, and time. Unfortunately, the Levite and priest were unwilling to cross the boundaries of safety and mercy to help their fallen brother. They, like many of God's people throughout the Bible, were not

---

6. Clark, *Am I Sleeping With the Enemy?*, 76–79.

willing to let compassion lead them. Therefore, they missed the idea of what it meant to not only love a neighbor, but to truly love God.

Teach Us to Listen

After this parable Luke shared another unique story on the road to Jerusalem. The characters in this story are also found in John's Gospel, which involve the death and resurrection of Lazarus as well as Jesus's conversation with his sisters Mary and Martha (John 11:1–37). Martha was portrayed as a strong woman who seemed to be critical of Jesus's delay to attend to her brother (Jesus was sent word that Lazarus was sick and when he arrived the man had already been dead for four days). She reminded Jesus that he could have prevented Lazarus's death (John 11:21). Mary, on the other hand, was the one who reminded Jesus that he could have prevented death, but did so with tears. Jesus, because of her tears and the tears of others, also wept (John 11:34). John also wrote that Mary had anointed Jesus's head with oil when they were at Bethany (11:2; 12:3–4). Luke's audience would have known of this family as they were very close to Jesus and, if Mary is the same woman mentioned in the anointing in Matthew 26:6–13 and Mark 14:1–9, the churches would have heard about her act of compassion toward Jesus. "I tell you the truth, wherever the gospel is preached throughout the world, what she has done will be told in memory of her" (Mark 14:9).

Luke's audience would have been familiar with the stories of Mary, Martha, and Lazarus. It would not have been surprising for them to be familiar with a sense the tension that existed between these two sisters.

> As they went on their way, Jesus entered a village. A certain woman named Martha welcomed him into her home. Her sister Mary sat at the Lord's feet and listened to his teaching/words. Martha was distracted with much ministry and confronted him saying, "Lord, don't you care that my sister has left me to minister alone? Tell her to help me." The Lord answered her, "Martha, Martha, you are worried and bothered about many things, but one thing is necessary. Mary has chosen the good helping, which will not be taken away from her."

In this story Martha seemed to be a hard working woman who felt compelled to provide hospitality toward Jesus (unlike Simon the Pharisee in Luke 7:36–37). She was "distracted with much ministry . . ." would be a literal translation of Luke's Greek.[7] However, Martha was fulfilling the ap-

---

7. Carter, "Getting Martha Out of the Kitchen," 268.

propriate role of both host and female in the ancient world. Luke does not tell us the location of the home, or whether Martha was married or acting as a single woman. He simply states that on the journey, someone invited Jesus and his disciples into their home. This is a common theme for Luke in both his Gospel and Acts. For Luke, hospitality toward Jesus and the disciples was noteworthy and a sign of a Christian heart.

Mary, however, took the traditional role of male student by listening to Jesus, as he had encouraged people to do (Luke 8:15, 21). However, this was not appropriate for a female in the ancient world and it seemed that Martha was not only scolding Mary, but Jesus as well. Her statement "don't you care . . ." was critical of Jesus's failure to practice common customs as well as her work load: "my sister has left me to do the work by myself . . ." If Mary was willing to listen, then Jesus should have been telling her to go and serve.

Jesus's response would have been controversial for Luke's audience. First, his reminder that Mary had chosen what was important was true: he used "portion" or "helping" possibly in response to her business to prepare "helpings" for the group. Jesus challenged Martha over her focus on traditions, work, and cultural expectations. This, coming from one who fed over 5,000 in the wilderness, was unimportant. To be at his feet and in the presence of God was what mattered. Second, he mentioned that the helping Mary had or had experienced could not be taken away. The experience of being in the presence of God would be a driving force in the preaching of the apostles and life of the early church later in the Book of Acts. This will also be seen in the ministry of the Apostle Paul who, after his experience of Jesus on the road to Damascus, had a thriving ministry in a world hostile to a resurrected God. Mary's experience would be more stable than Martha's desire to serve, do ministry, or fulfill cultural customs. This story again reinforced for the disciples and early readers that "doing ministry" can many times distract us from an experience of Jesus in the lives of others.

Teach Us to Pray

Luke next moved to a scene in which a disciple asked for guidance in prayer. The Jews prayed three times each day and had set regulations for prayer before eating, washing, traveling, and other important times. From reading the writings of the Jewish rabbis it seems that Jewish people in the ancient world prayed often. If this were the case the disciple's request for help may have reflected a desire for relationship rather than repeating memorized formulas of prayers.

Even though religious texts suggest that the Jews prayed often, this may only reflect the habits of religious leaders, teachers, and the highly educated who could read and memorize biblical and other authoritative texts. It may be that most people in ancient Judea did not pray. This seems more likely to me after reading material concerning magical texts, incantations, texts of other religions, and history of common cultures in the ancient world. First, *many people in the ancient world could not read or write (estimates suggest 90 to 95 percent) and would therefore have little access to texts or prayers.* The role of priests in the ancient world was to bridge the gap between gods and humans and therefore become interpreters, mediums, prophets, and oracles between the two groups. Those priests who were educated and knew magic, spells, and incantations could communicate on behalf of the god, usually for a price. Even in Judea the religious leaders fulfilled the role of intermediary between Yahweh and the people. While magic and idolatry influenced some of the ancient Jewish writings, the leaders fulfilled the role of helping the people talk to God. Politically, they also became part of the retainer class, those who mediated between leaders and the people.[8] Unfortunately for the poor and uneducated, God was distant and someone who could only be approached through a religious leader. If the leader was corrupt, then God was even further from their understanding.

Second, *this distance prevented them from viewing God relationally.* Therefore, God, like many other deities in the ancient world, would need to be manipulated through correct language, words, or rituals. In Jesus's discussion of prayer in Matthew 6:7–8, he reminded the disciples that they did not need to manipulate God with phrases and words; their Lord knew what they needed and would care for them. However, manipulative language was common in ancient magical, pagan, and some biblical texts, especially the term "rise up" or "wake up." Repetitious language was used to rouse the divinity to action. When the prophet Elijah had a showdown with Baal's prophets, the pagan priests cried out, cut themselves, and prayed for their god to act (1 Kgs 18:16–40). These actions were designed to get the attention of their gods, so that they could respond. In the ancient world the belief was that prayer "moved the divinities to act." Those who were powerful in words, actions, or knew the correct formulas got results. Those who relied on holy men and women to intercede for them either put their hopes on the humans, or themselves found methods to communicate to their god. Unfortunately, these prayers did not involve relationship but manipulation. It may be that the disciple asking for help wanted power and the key to getting God to help.

---

8. Saldarini, *Pharisees, Scribes, and Sadducees*, 41.

Finally, *prayer or communicating to the divine became less about enhancing relationship and involved control, manipulation, and getting results.* Jesus modeled relationship and communication with God in his prayers. He spoke of his relationship with his father and God's desire to bless people. Luke's text became a powerful teaching tool to those who not only may not have prayed, but also to those who used prayer for results. Either group would have found that these styles of prayer were ineffective.

> Jesus was praying in a certain place, and when he finished, a certain one of his disciples said to him, "Lord, teach us to pray, as John taught his disciples." He said, "When you pray, say: 'Father, your name is to be made holy. Your kingdom is to come. Give us each day our daily bread, and forgive our sins, as we will forgive those who owe us. Do not lead us into temptation.'" He then said, "Which of you who has a friend will go to them at midnight and say, 'Friend, lend me three loaves of bread, because my friend has arrived from a journey, and I have nothing to give them'; and he will answer from inside, 'Do not bother me; the door is shut, and my children are with me in bed. I cannot get up and give you anything'? I tell you, though he will not get up and give him anything because he is his friend, yet because of his shamelessness/honor he will rise and give him whatever he needs. I tell you, ask, and it will be given to you; seek, and you will find; knock, and it will be opened to you. For everyone who asks receives, the one who seeks finds, and the one who knocks has it opened for them. What father among you, if his son asks for a fish, will instead of a fish give him a snake; or if he asks for an egg, will give him a scorpion? If you, who are evil, know how to give good gifts to your children, how much more will the father, who is in heaven, give the Holy Spirit to those who ask?" (Luke 11:1–12)

Jesus offered a very simple prayer for the disciples both in the story and those reading Luke's narrative. The prayer was not meant to be something recited each week in church (although it is not wrong to do so) but a mantra for the early Christians. The disciples honor God, represent the empire of Jesus, request food and spiritual forgiveness, and offer to extend that mercy and forgiveness to others. The petitioner continues to be vulnerable, dependent, and countercultural. This formula was simple. Even more, it was a challenge to the first-century Christian.

For those who used prayer to manipulate or guarantee results, it is worthless. The prayer offers hope for the basic necessities of life and is a commitment for the Christian to extend mercy to others. The petitioner continues to be vulnerable, dependent, and countercultural. The prayer asks God for spiritual protection as the disciple faces evil in a world struggling to find God. Jesus's story of the father and child indicated that God would provide for the disciples if they cried out for the Holy Spirit. Notice, the cry was not for power, possessions, or status. The cry was for a relationship with the Father.

The source of God's generosity would not be found in the skill of the prayer nor would it happen through the correct formula or words by a disciple. The story of the family man who provided bread for his friend suggested that he did so due to the man's *honor or shamelessness* (11:8). Some interpret the phrase "because of the man's boldness he will get up and give him what he needs" to suggest that because the man boldly bothered his friend he received food. However, the text also can suggest that because of the man's honor, he will rise up and give his friend food, since his friend would be dishonored by not having enough food for his guests.[9] This understanding of the verse suggests that God will respond to the needs of the disciples not because we can harass our Lord into action, through prayer, but because we serve a God of honor. Because our Lord is honorable, we will be cared for.

This understanding of prayer is not one of using a correct pattern to get results, it is one of trusting God to respond because of who God is. It is the belief that the disciples offer prayers while doing ministry and trust that God will equip us to fulfill the will of the Father. As with Jesus in his final hours in human form in the Garden of Gethsemane, God's will was accepted and prayer is a means to enter into and listen to God's passion, desires, and love.

I remember one year preaching this text in a church where I ministered. I had noticed many of our youth talking about P.U.S.H. bracelets. These letters were an acronym for *Pray Until Something Happens*. I had mentioned that sometimes this belief caused us as Christians to view prayer as a way of getting results. While the kids may not all have agreed with what I said, it opened a door for a lot of conversations. However, much of the prayer logic I experience in Christian churches today borders on this concept of moving God to action to get an intended result.

- I often hear lessons concerning church growth and prayer. The key to growth in our churches is more prayer!
- I hear sermons from evangelists that suggest we pray for financial security, wealth, health, and safety. I guess that those of us who are poor, sick, unhealthy, and victims of crimes need to pray more, or we're not getting through to God.

9. Snodgrass, "*Anaideia* and the Friend at Midnight," 507–8.

- I hear prayer testimonies that describe perseverance in prayer which produces the desired results. I guess I need to pray more and keep telling God to give me what I want.

- I listen to speakers at prayer conferences who remind me I need to spend more time in prayer and isolation with God. I agree, but I also wonder how I am going to get the massive work God placed on me done and still be there for my family. I feel guilty because I should pray more.

- I grew up with a dad who didn't talk to me a lot. I found myself becoming a man who bothered him as little as I could. I do the same with God. I am a father who loves talking with my sons, but know that sometimes they say a lot, other times they don't. Being a dad means taking advantage of the times when they can talk. I am beginning to wonder if that is how God wants our relationship to be.

Jesus's teaching on prayer was simple. The disciples were not given a formula to be repeated, a written text to be copied, nor powerful words to move and manipulate God to actions. For Jesus, God would care for the children because of honor. God is a Father who provides and a friend who cares. This relationship in prayer and mission would have been somewhat foreign to the common disciple of Jesus, however it was a side of God that Jesus manifested to those hearing his messages and reading Luke's text.

CONFRONTING CORRUPT MINISTRY

Confronting Evil

For those who may have viewed a relationship with Jesus/God or prayer as a tool to manipulate the forces of nature or evil, Luke suggested that this was not so.

> Every empire that is not united becomes a wilderness, and a divided home/family falls apart. If Satan is not united how will his empire stand? You say that I cast out demons by Beelzebul, but if I cast out demons by Beelzebul, by whom do your sons cast them out? Therefore they are your criteria. But if it is by the finger of God that I cast out demons, then the empire of God is upon you. When a strong man, fully battle ready, guards his courtyard [the front of his house], his possessions are safe; but when one stronger than he attacks him and overcomes him, he takes away his armor, in which he had confidence, and divides

his spoil. Whoever is not with me is against me, and whoever does not gather with me scatters. (Luke 11:17–23)

Luke continued to discuss the confrontation between Jesus and the religious leaders of the nation through this story. The story seems humorous in that the response of the leaders to Jesus's work to help people heal and cast out evil was that Jesus himself was evil. Jesus's rejoinder was well presented—armies and families divided against themselves are ineffective. Fighting Satan demands unity, courage, and strength.

Jesus also asked the question concerning the leaders, "If I drive out demons by the Beelzebub how do you do it? If I drive them out by the finger of God then God's empire is here . . ." The question challenged the religious leaders because they were not driving out demons and were not healing people. They criticized Jesus's power because they themselves were not getting results, yet Jesus indicated that they were the ones who were ineffective.

Jesus also challenged them to make a decision to follow him or let him alone. This may seem arrogant to the modern reader but his call was an acceptance of reality. The power of God against evil in society is undeniable. Regardless of who we are or what we experience one has a difficult time refusing to acknowledge that religion and faith can have a positive impact in community, culture, and our social world. No matter what people have tried to do to religions, they continue to exist, morph, and provide hope and courage for people under persecution. For Jesus, evil must continually be confronted and the disciple must be on guard against Satan and his demonic angels. As a woman offered a blessing to Jesus's mother Mary, his response was that the blessing would be to those who hear God's word and obey it (Luke 11:28). Obedience, for the disciple, would be the key to spiritual battles with evil and communities that reject the hope that Jesus can heal others.

Confronting Morality

Luke suggested that those hearing Jesus's message began to grow. As the disciples accompanied him and witnessed his power Jesus offered the challenge for moral purity. First, *he confronted those basing their faith in the miraculous and needed evidence of his power.* "This is a wicked generation, it asks for a miraculous sign . . ." (11:29). For Luke, even Gentiles who responded to God deserved salvation, as opposed to the children of Israel who disregarded their loyalty to Yahweh. God's people wanted signs not because they had relationship with their Lord, but because they needed convincing. Jonah convinced the people of Nineveh with a sermon that was only five words in the Hebrew language, while the Queen of the South (Egypt), gave Yahweh glory by recognizing Solomon's wisdom from God. God's people would be held to a higher standard as those who see Jesus's glory and have the responsibility to reflect it to others.

Second, *Jesus called the crowds to understand that their morality would be key to their salvation and role in ministry.* In the ancient world the eye was considered a window to a soul.

> No one after lighting a lamp places something to hide it, or puts it under a basket. They put it on a stand, so that those who enter may see the light. Your eye is the lamp of your body. When your eye is healthy/good/honest, your whole body shines, but when it is bad, your body is dark. Be careful that the light in you is not darkness/evil. If your whole body shines, and you do not have a part of darkness, it will shine like a lamp which, like a star, gives you light. (Luke 11:33–36)

It is possible to interpret the eye being a lamp that projects light, but the reverse was actually true in the ancient world. The eye lights the soul and reflects one's inner life. The eyes were also considered reflections of one's inner moral character.[10] The "evil eye" was a common word used for a curse or stare from an individual. To stare someone down today makes a recipient feel uncomfortable. In the ancient world this was a form of cursing or placing a spell on another person. A good eye was one that brought joy to the recipient. In this text Jesus indicated that how people looked/viewed or treated others was a reflection of one's heart, morality, and spirituality. The disciples who are truly good can bring about joy and peace in the lives of others by how we treat them.

Confronting Corruption

Jesus's teachings had become powerful enough that a Pharisee invited into his home for dinner. Previously Jesus had experienced dishonor and shame in the home of Simon the Pharisee (Luke 7:36), an invitation which he received after the criticism that he had associated with sinners. This second invitation from a Pharisee came after he was criticized for casting out demons. Before both meals, Jesus set the tone by publicly rebuking the religious leaders. The meal at Simon's home resulted in Jesus breaking cultural traditions by criticizing his host for neglecting to show hospitality (7:44–47). At this

---

10. Turan, "A Neglected Rabbinic Parallel," 85.

next dinner, Jesus criticized his host and his guests for their lack of morals and their corruption as God's leaders.

> While Jesus was speaking, a Pharisee asked him to dine with him, so he went in and reclined at table. The Pharisee was amazed that he did not first wash before dinner. The Lord said to him, "You Pharisees cleanse the outside of the cup and of the dish, but inside you are greedy and wicked. Fools/Morons! Did not the one who made the outside make the inside also? But give alms/charity to those things that are within, and everything will be clean for you. Shame on you Pharisees! For you tithe mint, spice, and every herb, and neglect justice and the love of God. These you should have done, without neglecting the others. Shame on you Pharisees! For you love the best seat in the synagogues and greetings in the marketplaces. Shame on you! You are like unmarked graves, and people walk over them without knowing it." A certain one of the lawyers answered him, "Teacher, in saying these things you insult us too." He said, "Shame on you lawyers. You place unrealistic burdens on people, and you yourselves do not touch them with one of your fingers. Shame on you! . . . Woe to you lawyers! For you have taken away the key of knowledge. You did not enter yourselves, and you hindered those who were entering." As he went away from there, the scribes and the Pharisees began to press him hard and to provoke him with questions to catch him in what he said. (Luke 11:34–54)

Jesus's criticism became shameful enough that a lawyer tried to interrupt, to which Jesus turned on the lawyers and rebuked them. In the ancient world it was inappropriate to criticize one's host. However, Jesus violated the cultural norms because the sin of those in leadership was so prevalent that they were flagrant in their ungodly behavior.

This Jesus seems contrary to the modern Jesus who is viewed as being non-judgmental, nice to all people, and winking at sin. This Jesus also seems contrary to the Jesus who is viewed as condemning others, ignoring those in the community, and espousing hatred and venom. Jesus was not a wild-eyed radical who stood outside of the funerals of people and held up protest signs. He was not a pot smoking, beer guzzling, laid back Messiah who just wished everyone would join his crew. He was a Savior who hated corruption, oppression, and exploitation. He was a Savior who sat in a very intimate room, eating and associating with a different type of sinner, and who taught the ways of the empire of God. Jesus may have raised his voice, or he may have been very blunt. Regardless of the volume the narrative tone is one that was common in the prophets. The issue was not *how* he said what he did, but *that* he said what he did. This story suggested that Jesus was honest. He treated the Pharisees no different than any other sinner. They needed to be confronted with their sin and this was the place to do it.

Confronting Oppression

"You really screwed up, Cassy. You just rolled over and let them stick it to you in the behind," Bob said. I was sitting with the couple in the waiting room of the hospital. Cassy had been coming to Agape for years. I had first met her on the street and she and Bob continued to connect with me as we tried to reach out to them. When Bob returned home from prison he, Cassy, and their first-born child tried to rebuild a family. They had become disconnected from Agape for a few months when Cassie returned eight months pregnant. It was evident she was using heroin again and we had to make the hard phone call to Child Protective Services. However, Cassy was ahead of us and went to the hospital to deliver the baby, which alerted family services. She had called us after the baby was delivered and Lori and I knew that the baby would be taken from her.

Fortunately the hospital nurses had already worked up a plan to keep mom and her baby together as long as possible. I have always taught my students that nurses are a Godsend in any hospital: they have the best intentions, bridge ministers with patients, and make decisions to support moms in the toughest of times. This was one of those situations. When Lori and I arrived at the hospital and shared who we were, they began to share the plan with us and we agreed to work with them to help mom, baby, and the system run smoothly.

Unfortunately Bob was not as cooperative. He was aggressive, and emotionally harassing Cassy. The nurses were frustrated with him and left him alone in the waiting room with Cassy and their baby. I came in to talk with them. Bob continually blamed Cassy, criticized her, and kept repeating over and over again, "You screwed up Cassy," and used even stronger expletives each time.

As I sat there listening and trying to interject I realized that I had a problem. My stomach was hurting, but not the pain that comes with sickness, something bad that one eats, or eating spicy food. I realized that my right fist had been clenched tightly for ten minutes. My jaw was tight. My heart was pounding. Bob was half my size, was extremely skinny (addict skinny), and I was getting tired of his mouth. I could very easily have put him through the wall. Lori and I were extremely close to Cassy and her child and had worked hard to help her, but in a very short time Bob returned from prison and led their family back into addiction. I had talked with Bob when he came out of prison concerning his role as a man, father, and friend. He assured me that he would never use drugs again and that his family would be safe. Now, he was wrecking his own life as well as the lives of other vulnerable people. Even more, he was ticking me off.

I have three sons. While we would have loved to have daughters God never gave us that chance. But at that moment I understood what it was like to be a father of a daughter. It would have been easy to call security, have Bob escorted out of the hospital, taken him behind the hospital and physically taught him to be respectful and shut his mouth, and then escorted him to the bus station, bought him a one-way ticket, and told him if I ever saw him back in Portland I would physically beat him to a pulp. That would have been easy. Or, I could have talked to a couple of the guys at Agape who would have done it for me.

I'm not proud of how I felt. I'm not saying I acted on those feelings. I'm not saying that I have a pure heart and never think of violence. I'm saying that I was that angry and found myself in a situation where I had to do something, I had to intervene, and I had to get involved even though I was emotionally invested. I am sure that many people who I have talked with concerning Christianity would say that my feelings were wrong or that I was being judgmental. Unfortunately none of those people in my past would have become involved in the discussion between Bob and Cassy. It is easy to wash our hands, say we don't want to get involved, and call those who do judgmental. It's harder to become emotionally, mentally, and physically involved to stop someone's humiliation and call another to repentance.

Instead of physical violence I told Bob to stop. I told him that I wouldn't allow him to talk to my friend that way anymore. I took them to the cafeteria for lunch and as Cassy took her daughter out for a walk I shared with Bob that a man doesn't treat his partner, child, or others the way he was treating them. We had a good talk and it seemed like he listened. The nurses thanked me. Cassy thanked me. Bob thanked me.

When I got home Lori and I had a long talk. I shared my frustration and Lori laughed about the texts I sent her. I shared how exhausted I was and that I was ashamed I had felt so angry. She said, "Maybe it's good that you became that emotionally invested. Sometimes you suppress your feelings when you try to help people; maybe today you realized you're human." She was right. It is exhausting to care, but it's the right thing to do.

Jesus was passionate about social justice. First, Luke and Matthew both include Jesus's discourse with the religious leaders, however Luke alone includes the phrase, "Give what is inside the dish to the poor and everything will be clean for you" (11:41). For Luke, Jesus directly addressed the social corruption of the religious leaders. They had failed to represent God and the people because they were concerned with looking spiritual rather than practicing true spirituality. This practice involved caring for the poor, practicing justice, and love. Jesus's challenge for these leaders was that they cared for themselves more than they cared for God's people. This was a similar charge from the prophet Ezekiel, who said that the shepherds cared for themselves and neglected the sheep (Ezek 34). For Luke, Jesus's challenge to the religious leaders of his day, as well as Christian leaders in the early church, was that spiritual leadership is condemned when leaders fail to provide justice and peace for the followers of Jesus. Even more, it is condemned when we fail to name the injustices in our past and, instead of building monuments to our corrupt father, build bridges to a community too afraid to seek God for salvation.

This section ended with the religious leaders displaying anger and provoking Jesus to do something illegal. Jesus had once again stirred up trouble and a tense environment existed around him and his ministry. No doubt his disciples sensed this and would have felt the pressure from the crowds as well as the leaders. In the coming chapters on the journey to Jerusalem, Luke will illustrate that this tension builds and climaxes in the death of Jesus. As in the past, corrupt leaders oppose God, yet God spoke through the prophets and other men and women devoted to their Lord. The Bible is filled with tension, yet in the end God's will is done.

Jesus called the disciples to join him on the journey to Jerusalem. As the disciples followed him they were given ministry and then called to reflect on this mission in a current context. Then as today, the church practices ministry in a world emerging from chaos and seeking salvation. The disciples emerge toward faithfulness in an attempt to find a ministry that is loyal to Jesus, reflects the good eye, and avoids the injustices so prevalent with the corruption of the past.

8

Repentance and Healing in the Margins

Luke 12:1—13:22

I HAD BEEN COUNSELING THIS couple for many weeks. While I understand that ministers should not counsel couples or individuals for extended periods of time, this couple had become active at our church in this small Missouri town. Typically, I encourage my seminary students to refer couples or individuals to professional counselors within a few pastoral counseling sessions, but this couple had been doing well in the sessions we had experienced. This was the second marriage for both and the husban had shared with me that he felt that his wife was neglecting his needs for her high school aged daughter. The couple was fifteen years older than me and, as a younger minister, I felt somewhat intimidated trying to help them. At times he would mention, in our sessions, that I was younger and less experienced at marriage, and was not an official counselor. At times I wanted to mention, "At least I am not in counseling for my marriage," but that would have been inappropriate. God's leaders must display compassion and understanding, which includes ignoring insults.

Things had been going well for the past two months until Cheryl called and asked to meet. This night the couple sat in my office and an awkward silence filled the room. Someone was ashamed to talk and I had to begin with twenty minutes of surface chitchat to find out what happened. Cheryl finally blurted out, "Mike left our session last month early." I said, "Yes, I remember." Cheryl reminded me that she and her daughter stayed and the three of us talked more about her tension with Mike, his actions toward her daughter, and the tension that had filled the house the past two weeks. Then Cheryl said something that completely caught me off guard. "Tell him, Mike. Tell him what happened." Mike just sat there with his head down. "Tell me what?" I asked. Mike said nothing. I could feel the tension, but he was refusing to talk. I kept trying to encourage him to say something but he continued to stare at the floor. "Tell him what you did," she said louder. Mike still kept his head down.

She finally shared the story. While Cheryl, her daughter, and I were meeting, Mike had walked to his car, took his keys, and scraped both sides of Cheryl's daughter's car. We knew who had done this and even worse, he just sat there staring at the floor. Suddenly, the man who reminded me that I was young, inexperienced, and not qualified had nothing to say.

When they returned home he exploded, emotionally blew up, and smashed items in the house. Cheryl left with her daughter and moved to another state. Our elders stood by her, helped her rent and load a moving truck, and supported her in leaving Mike. I never saw him or her again. He would not return my calls or respond to my invitation to meet again. It was over. A man who had never raised a hand to his wife and step daughter had wrecked his marriage. I have often heard that there is two sides to every story. I am not sure that is true. Here is one story where an individual single-handedly destroyed a relationship but also shut people out and refused help. Guilt, shame, anger, and pride stood in the way of him accepting help. I wouldn't say he was possessed but I would say he was under the influence.

In one short incident he changed his family's future. I thought he was doing well, I felt he had been working hard, and I assumed that they were healing. Unfortunately he lied, he hid things from me, and even worse, he refused to open up. My heart broke for that family, but even more for Mike. If he didn't repent he would do the same to another family and in the end, face a God who expects men to reflect Jesus as fathers and husbands.

After Jesus's confrontation with his Pharisee friends the crowd of followers that had developed pushed to be in his presence. However, Jesus took the time to stop and teach his disciples. While the crowd would have included his disciples, it would also have had people who were coming to see Jesus for the first time. Luke grouped the next section of parables/teachings together as teachings specifically for his disciples. For those who were journeying with Jesus to Jerusalem, he had a special message.

WATCH OUT FOR CORRUPT LEADERS: DON'T EAT WHERE I JUST ATE

While Yelp (an application for smart phones that offers information concerning restaurants) may not have existed in Jesus's day, he clearly left a negative review of his meal with the Pharisees. Jesus warned the disciples from associating with the leaders' sinfulness and hypocrisy. Their sin would be made known to their people and God.

I find it interesting that when we meet with those who live on the streets, those in the sex industry, or people working closely with these individuals it is apparent which police officers are corrupt and which are viewed as good. Typically people dismiss what they hear from vulnerable individuals or potential victims. The little people have an interesting view of justice, hypocrisy, and integrity. While this does not suggest that these individuals may always have accurate information, I find it interesting that we typically ignore vulnerable people in our society. Females aged eleven to fourteen comprise the largest group of sexual assault victims. Why? We have deemed girls this age to be untruthful, confused, or inaccurate in their perception of the truth. Those with physical or mental challenges are also vulnerable and susceptible to oppression. Unfortunately we dismiss their cries because we deem them "needy." Children are major victims of violence and sexual abuse in our society because we believe that they cannot speak the truth. Those who victimize these groups know that others view them as unbelievable and therefore have access to oppress these vulnerable ones. Those who live on the street are also seen as untrustworthy and therefore easy to oppress. Religious leaders, as in the days of old, also know who is believable and who is accessible to oppression.

In Jesus's day it was the same. Those on the margins of society knew the good leaders and they knew who the ungodly ones were. The Pharisees had not only committed hidden sins, they had boldly proclaimed their beliefs to be above the law. For Jesus, *their sin* was to be proclaimed. Instead of keeping secrets the disciples, like their master, were to bring them out into the open. Jesus was not only stating that God would one day bring behavior to judgment, he was asking his disciples to speak out.

> During this time many thousands of the people had gathered and were trampling one another. He began to speak to his disciples first, "Beware of the yeast of the Pharisees, which is hypocrisy. Nothing is covered up that will not be revealed, or hidden that will not be made known. Whatever you have said in the dark will be heard in the light, and what you have spoken in secret will be proclaimed on the rooftops. I tell you, my friends, do not

be afraid of those who kill the body and can't do anymore. I will show you whom to fear: fear the one who, after death, has authority to cast into hell. Everyone who acknowledges me before people, the Son of Man also will acknowledge before the angels of God, but the one who denies me before others will be denied before the angels of God. Everyone who speaks a word against the Son of Man will be forgiven, but the one who blasphemes against the Holy Spirit will not be forgiven. When they bring you before the synagogues and the rulers and the authorities, do not be anxious about how you should defend yourself or what you should say, for the Holy Spirit will teach you in that very hour what you ought to say." (Luke 12:2-12)

The call to the disciples was for them to boldly speak out concerning injustice in their communities. This boldness would bring persecution, yet Jesus warned them that disobeying God was worse than fearing the leaders of the nation. Peter later faithfully stood his ground when the Jewish leaders threatened he and the other apostles: "Judge for yourselves whether it is right in God's sight to obey you rather than God. We cannot help speaking about what we have seen and heard" (Acts 4:19-20). Jesus's message reminded the reader that God's people needed to fear God enough to stand for the truth.

I once had a young man ask me what my responsibility would be if someone told me they had been molested. He asked if I was legally required as a minister to report the event. I said, "Yes. But I also believe that whether or not I am legally mandated I am spiritually mandated by God to do something or face Jesus in judgment." He looked confused, then said, "Wow, that is a heavy responsibility, you really think Jesus would send you to hell for not doing anything about it?" I understood his point but responded with, "Hell is not the issue—he stands *for* victims and *against* oppressors. Turning my head away from the cries of victims is as much a sin as oppressing them myself. I am either going to be with him or against him when it comes to helping victims." I suspect that something had happened to this young man. We had dinner together and talked. I don't know if he felt judged but I do know he felt I would help him if anything had ever happened. This may be why he chose to say nothing since help can invite persecution and rejection from those we confront. Yet, it is what we are called to do. In this section Luke challenged the early reader of his Gospel to see discipleship as a call to justice and a stand against oppressors and oppression.

Watch Out for Riches

The parable of the Rich Fool is another story unique to Luke. A man asked Jesus to fulfill the role of providing justice with his brother in an inheritance dispute. Luke didn't indicate if the offending brother was legally within the law or if he was withholding from his brother. Jesus's response suggested that the one asking for justice may have been acting out of greed.

> A certain person in the crowd said to him, "Teacher, tell my brother to divide the inheritance with me." He said to him, "Man, who made me a judge or representative for you?" He then said, "Be careful and on your guard against all greed, because one's life does not consist of an abundance of possessions." He then told them a parable, "The land of a certain rich man was very fruitful and he thought to himself, 'What shall I do, for I have nowhere to store my crops? I will do this: I will tear down my barns and build larger ones, and there I will store all my grain and my good things. I will say to my soul, "Soul, you have a lot of good things put away for many years; relax, eat, drink, and be merry."' But God said to him, 'Fool, this night your life is taken from you, and the things you have prepared, who will they belong to?' So it is for those who save treasure for themselves and are not rich toward God." (Luke 12:13-21)

In this parable the farmer was greedy. First, when farmers had an abundant harvest they were to give back to God. In addition to this in order to remain in good standing with their community they needed to share the abundance with their community. People in the ancient world believed in *limited goods*. Because resources were limited the assumption was that those who had money and power tended to control the amount of limited goods. Therefore the wealthy were assumed to have the power to bless or withhold (as did God). Those who hoarded the resources were viewed as evil. Those who shared these goods were believed to be good. Instead of sharing the abundance of his crop, thereby indicating that God blessed him and that he, like God, was good, the farmer hoarded his crops by building bigger storehouses. For the modern reader he may seem to be wise, storing for the future. However, in the ancient world he was foolish not only because he would not share with his community, but because in his retirement plan he showed a lack of faith. If he would have blessed his community then he would, once again, plant in the spring, live by faith, and trust that God would bless him.

This parable was a reminder that life is uncertain. While it is not meant to teach that Christians should not have a retirement plan, or save for their future, it does suggest that disciples view their lives as under the grace of God, and that sharing and blessing others should be a response in our life.

My first full-time preaching position at a church was in a small Missouri town. Bonne Terre was an old lead mining town that sat forty miles south of St. Louis. Many of the residents were either retired from the lead company, or drove to St. Louis to work each day. The community, along with the five area towns in this "Lead Belt" of Missouri, was mostly people who were either retired or worked hard to save up to retire. The church was very small and comprised of mostly older Christians. While we were there the church grew and became a good resource for the community.

Within my first year one of the women was diagnosed with cancer. She and her husband were active members, related to many of the families in the area churches, and were wonderful to us. Lori and I visited Irma and Wayne often and listened to them tease each other and then grieve at her condition. One day when Irma was very sick I was talking and praying with her. She stopped after the prayer and turned to me, with very tired eyes, and said, "Son, I want you to listen to what I am going to say. Wayne and I worked hard all of our life and saved for retirement. We looked forward to the day when we could take our RV and travel wherever we wanted. We talked about that day and became very excited the older we got. Now I have cancer and I am going to die. I will never enjoy what we worked so hard to have. In fact, I love Wayne and he loves me—but I know some other woman will enjoy this retirement, and I'm okay with that."

I was twenty-six years old. I had never had anyone share something like this with me. I didn't know how to respond. I couldn't think of anything "pastorally" to share. All I could say was, "Yes m'am." She then said, "You and Lori enjoy your life now. When you have kids spend money on them and enjoy your time in the present. Give to God now and don't wait until you get older. You don't know if you will be around when you are old." These were sobering words. I know she wasn't telling me to avoid saving for retirement, have insurance, or putting aside money for college funds. She was talking about an attitude. She was telling me as a husband, father, man, and minister to value the present.

Irma died a year later. I spoke at her funeral and shared this story. I hugged her sons, daughters-in-law, and grandkids. I hugged her husband and her good friend who later became Wayne's wife. I hugged Lori. Irma, like many people in our lives, realized what Jesus meant when he shared this parable. What she said has meant much to me. As a minister it has never bothered me that I represent a profession that will always be middle to lower class on the economic scale worldwide. It has reminded me that living by faith not only means trusting God to provide, it means enjoying who and what Jesus has given to us today.

Watch Out for Fear and Anxiety

Jesus's challenge to the disciples also included anxiety and fear. Obviously speaking against the corruption of the Pharisees coupled with the anxieties of daily life would create a tension in the lives of these early followers. Scholars estimate that fifty percent of a person's income went to pay rent while the rest went for food, taxes, and day to day necessities.[1] Those who were poor, stayed poor. Those who were born wealthy stayed wealthy. While Corinth professed to be a city where individuals could climb the economic scale, occupied Palestine (especially Galilee) was not so fortunate. Theophilus may have been a wealthy individual but most of his congregation would not have been. Steven Freisen has done extensive research on the economics in the ancient Christian world and found that only a small number, 1 percent, of people were wealthy while a similar percentage made enough money to have a small excess, 5 percent.[2] This suggests that the high majority of the population, including the church, was comprised of those in poverty. Friesen also indicates that those Christians who were well off would have been barely above the poverty line.[3] Those in the early churches who finally made enough money to live comfortably would have been asked to give to, care for, and share with those without in the churches. It seems that Christianity removed people's ability to live comfortably and prepare to retire.

> Don't be afraid little sheep; it is your Father's good pleasure to give you the empire. Sell your possessions, and give to the needy (alms). Make for yourselves moneybags that do not grow old, with a treasure in the heavens that does not fail, where no thief approaches and will not be destroyed. Your heart is where your treasure is. (Luke 12:32–34)

Jesus's parable and teachings in this section were spoken (and written) to people who had a legitimate reason to worry concerning their day to day lives. As a colonized people they would have constantly lived under the threat of Roman oppression. Yet, Jesus told them that their role in the kingdom was not to horde, but to share. This text is similar to Matthew's text in Jesus' Sermon on the Mount (Matt 6:25–34), yet one difference is

---

1. De Vos, *Church and Community Conflicts*, 97.
2. Friesen, "Prospects for a Demography of the Pauline Mission," 365.
3. Ibid., 367

that Luke inserted Jesus's call to sell and give to the poor (Luke 12:33). For Luke's audience, few may have been individuals with some wealth, and the challenge was for them to use their resources to care for the poor. This again promoted a sense of equality among the Christian church as was practiced in Acts 2:42–47 and 4:32–37. For Luke, Jesus not only called the poor to trust God and not be afraid, but he encouraged those with resources to live by faith as they cared for the needy among them.

Watch Out for Apathy

> The Lord said, "Who is the faithful and wise manager, whom his master sets over his household/family to treat them and give them their food at the proper time? Blessed is that servant whose master finds him fulfilling his responsibilities when he comes. I tell you the truth; he will set him over all his possessions. But if that servant says to himself, 'My master is delayed in coming,' and begins to beat the male and female servants, and to eat, drink, and get drunk, the master of that servant will come on a day when he is not prepared and at an hour he does not know, and will cut him in pieces and put him with the unfaithful." (Luke 12:42–46)

This parable suggested to the disciples, who had experienced corrupt and abusive leadership from their religious teachers (12:1–11), that they be faithful and merciful with those they will lead in the church. The master in this parable may seem abusive and violent to the modern reader, but to those who were (and have been) victims of oppressive leadership the point was clear. The God of mercy and forgiveness is also righteous. Those who hurt and abuse others will be dealt with. This does not suggest that there is a different type of final judgment from God or that there are different levels of hell (to be beaten with fewer or many blows), or that God demands us all to give an account of our actions on earth. The parable would have been understood by the ancient follower of Jesus to suggest that God is a master who expects people to treat each other fairly, respectfully, and honorably.

In the story the servant who was in charge of the master's household was called a manager or steward. The Greek word for this is a term that suggests leadership over a business or home. Christian leaders would be those who were expected to fulfill this role. The abuses of the slave/manager would not only remind the disciples and Gospel reader of the corrupt leadership in pre-exilic Judea, it would remind them of the corrupt leadership they were currently experiencing. However, Jesus was reminding his disciples that they needed to be leaders with integrity, honor, and mercy. How they treated others in the church, especially those vulnerable and marginalized by their communities, would affect their salvation. Jesus had already warned the disciples that they must stand against corrupt leadership, avoid greed, not live by fear/anxiety, and now be honorable leaders with the church of God.

REPENTANCE IS NECESSARY FOR THE KINGDOM

Jesus switched his lesson from his disciples to a broader group, the crowd. In this next section (12:54—13:9) Jesus challenged the crowd concerning repentance. After he finished calling his disciples to be aware of corrupt leadership, even among themselves, he next challenged the crowd concerning concerning their view of salvation, peace, and the empire of God. People in the crowd knew how to watch the skies and observe the condition of the weather but they unfortunately did not know or understand relationships with others. First, Jesus called people to reconcile with their enemies (more pointedly those they had wronged) rather than wait until a judge sentenced them for their crimes (12:54–59). Indirectly this would have referred to God as judge. Many in the crowd, most likely the religious leaders as well as some of the zealots/terrorists who would have been listening to see if Jesus would support their cause, would have been challenged. For Jesus and the disciples, reconciliation with all people, especially those we have wronged, was key to life in the empire of God. Luke's reader would also understand this challenge to reconciliation as an act of making amends or repentance.

Repentance is a word that is missing from much of our religious language. We may use it to criticize people or label them deviant ("this person needs to repent," or, "repent you sinful being") but we many times fail to understand what repentance is in the Christian life. In our work with domestic abuse we find that many victims are pressed by clergy to "forgive and forget" in dealing with their abuser. Children who have suffered horrible experiences at the hands of their parents, caregivers, or others present in the home may struggle with anger and rage. Unfortunately many are told that they must forgive or that they have to do the hard work to forgive. If the church works with abusers we tend to spend less time with them and only require an, "I'm sorry," or public confession of guilt. Then we return to the long task of convincing (or manipulating) the victim to forgive.

This is not repentance. Repentance, in the words of the many people I know in recovery communities, involves making amends. Repentance suggests that I allow those whom I have hurt to vent, name my sin, and express their feelings while I listen and learn to hurt as they have been hurt. Making amends in repentance means that I take responsibility for all my sins and actions, name them to the victim, and tell them I was wrong. This, for many, is a long process. However, it is necessary so that victims can completely forgive. Victims need validation and it must come from those who oppress them.

The Greek word for repentance meant a "change of mind/thought." This did not capture the true meaning of the word found in the Hebrew, "turning around," which suggested a change of life and conduct. Too often the modern church has viewed repentance as admitting or confessing guilt, yet the true word involves a more complicated modification of behavior.[4] Repentance for the disciple involves confession, making amends, and hearing the pain of those we victimized (this includes God/Jesus). As Jesus told the crowd, repentance involves making the first move to reconcile with my adversary (those I have hurt). It also involves changing behavior. Saying "I'm sorry" or "Forgive me" is not repentance. It may be an expression of sorrow or guilt and may be a first step toward repentance, but it is only a small piece of the puzzle. In Luke 13:1–5 some in the crowd must have asked what Jesus thought about Pilate's slaughter of a group of Galileans. A group of protesters gathered together to resist Roman occupation of their part of the country. Pilate was a ruthless leader and sent a detachment of Romans that killed protestors not only as a sign that Rome would not be disrespected, but as a sign that Judea needed to keep their rebels in line. Jesus's response was that those who were living a life contrary to God would also experience the same judgment. The parables of the master who came home and found his servant abusing others, the rich farmer, and the adversary in court all suggested that God was just and would deal with others as they deserved.

Repentance, for the disciple, is the process of change. Jesus called the listeners to repent and change their direction. The nation of Judea, while in social exile, needed to repent and reach those on the margins. God, as a farmer, was not interested in working with or blessing a nation that produced bad fruit. Nations, like trees, existed for a purpose; to reach people and fulfill God's mission.

> A man had a fig tree planted in his vineyard, and he came to get fruit but found none. He said to the farm hand, "Hey, I have been coming for three years to get fruit from this fig tree, and I find none. Cut it down. Why should it use up the ground?" He (the farm hand) replied, "Master, let it go this year, until I dig

---

4. Grassi, *Peace on Earth*, 91.

around it and put on manure. Then if it produces fruit next year, good; but if not, you can cut it down." (Luke 13:6–9)

This is a hard parable. The tree seemed to be the nation of Judea, or its people. Since the tree produced no fruit (which is why fruit trees are planted), the owner of the vineyard wanted it removed. He was well within his rights. The tree was taking up space, soil, nutrients, and sunlight. He could easily plant another that would bear fruit.

However the caretaker of the vineyard offered another solution. Repentance! Give the tree a chance, put strong nutrients (manure) around it, and give it another year. If that doesn't work then the tree can be destroyed. This is repentance. Repentance offers another chance. Repentance offers hope. Repentance sometimes can produce change. However, not all trees grow with the extra boost of nutrients.

Many years ago I had a friend who was fired from ministry in a small church near us. I was upset since this church had lost members due to the way other ministers were treated in the past. The church had been declining for years and was known as a problem community. My friend and his family were their most recent victims. A few months later, at an area preachers meeting, one of the older ministers mentioned that we needed to take turns preaching at the church, have college students rotate through the pulpit, and do what we could to help the church. I had heard these stories and pleas over the years, and it always irritated me. A church was known for crucifying ministers and we seemed to keep sending them more flesh. Even worse, my friend was at the meeting. I spoke up at the meeting and said, "No, I don't think we need to do that. I'm tired of watching good men and their families suffer, and then trying to rescue this congregation. I believe we need to step back and let them die, or let God deal with them." Younger ministers nodded their heads in agreement and some of the older ones looked a little hurt at what I had said. I was young but not idealistic. I probably spoke out of turn then, but today would do it again. I was fortunate enough to serve in churches that took very good care of Lori and me, but I personally knew that not many were that way.

A week later the older minster who had suggested helping the church came to my office. He had brought an older man with him who was a leader in that church. I had known both of these men for years and knew they were good, compassionate men. The older gentleman mentioned he had heard what I said, in fact the minister had gone to that church the next Sunday and told them what I had said. He said, that their church has said with one voice that they would not close the doors. He was visibly upset. We just need another minister to help us out. "How many ministers have you had in the past ten years?" I asked. He told me and admitted that what happened to them was not good. "We just can't seem to grow," he lamented. "We have been having this problem for decades." I had him open his Bible and turn to Luke 13:6–9 and read the parable. After he finished he nodded his head yes. I asked, "How many chances is God going to give the tree before he cuts it down?" The older minister said, "As many as it takes," but the other gentleman said, "I don't know but the parable is right. I see your point." We talked about the difficulties they faced as a church but the parable somehow gave us all a sobering reality concerning what Jesus said about church growth.

We prayed together and they left. I hadn't made any friends in that discussion and probably made more adversaries after he shared with the church what I said. I guess in some ways I was more prophetic than pastoral. However, the parable challenges the church today. God expects growth and fruit. We have allowed apathy and mediocrity to fill our ministries to the point that we become comfortable in our churches without affecting our world. We blame others for our decline and lack of growth rather than taking a good hard look at ourselves. Sometimes Jesus says, I need fruit or the tree is going to be replaced. Fortunately we have that second chance, but again, it is with a condition, that we repent and bear fruit as a people.

Growth in the Kingdom

An Empire that Makes Straight

Repentance produces growth and the kingdom of Jesus needed repentance. As Jesus warned the disciples to avoid fear, corruption, and oppression in their leadership, he also called the nation to renew its relationship with God. This became clearer as Jesus went to a synagogue service.

> He was teaching in one of the synagogues on the Sabbath. There was a woman who had had a spirit of disability for eighteen years. She was bent over and was not able to straighten herself. When Jesus saw her, he called her over and said, "Woman, you are freed from your disability." He laid his hands on her, and immediately she became straight, and she glorified God. The ruler of the synagogue, irritated because Jesus had healed on the Sabbath, said to the people, "There are six days to work, come on those days and be healed. Not on the Sabbath day." The Lord said, "You hypocrites, each of you on the Sabbath unties his ox or donkey from the feed trough and leads it to water. Shouldn't this woman, a daughter of Abraham whom Satan bound for eighteen years, be freed from this bond on the Sabbath day?" As

he said these things, all his adversaries were put to shame, and all the people rejoiced at all the glorious things that were done by him. (13:10–17)

The synagogue ruler was the man who was in charge of the order of worship, assigning the readings and songs, and making sure that the attendant and other servants would be present to make sure the service ran smoothly. Imagine him sitting in the front row at the synagogue reading the order of worship in his bulletin when he notices Jesus healing a woman who had been in the synagogue. Obviously this woman had been part of that community and came to worship with the group. The woman was a Jewish woman who had a crippling form of arthritis or scoliosis. Luke, the only writer using this story, indicated that she had an evil spirit as well. Her eighteen-year ailment was obvious to those in the synagogue yet they functioned normally as she attended, they prayed, and she returned home in pain.

This day the woman came to Jesus and he placed his hands on her back. Suddenly she straightened up and the congregation began to clap. The synagogue ruler, scanning down the order of worship did not see "A Time for Healing" in the bulletin. He did what any good congregational manager did in those days. He stood up, somewhat angry, and stated that this was a day of worship not healing. "Healing is a work, so let's make sure this doesn't get out of hand and take over the worship. Maybe tomorrow we will have time to heal people." Imagine the response of the synagogue. "Maybe this guy is right, should we have clapped for her healing?" Others might have thought, "She is healed, I knew it would happen one day."

Jesus responded claiming that hypocrisy showed more care for an animal on this Sabbath day than a woman who, like them, was a Jew (daughter of Abraham) and had suffered for almost two decades. He rebuked those who questioned the healing because they continued to marginalize people like this woman. Luke wrote that his opponents (religious leaders and those questioning the healing) were humiliated/shamed but others gave glory at what was done. It is likely that most Jews would have agreed with Jesus, but some of the corrupt leaders would have been dishonored. In this story the people of God were taught that repentance and reconciliation with God meant that they needed to show mercy to those who were captives, suffering, and on the margins of life.

The Empire of Scoundrels

This section ended with two very small parables, the mustard seed and yeast. Luke did something interesting with these parables that I believe challenges the ancient and modern reader of the Gospel to a greater faith and outreach to those on the margins.

> He said, "What is God's empire like? To what shall I compare it? It is like a mustard seed that a man took and scattered in his garden. It grew and became a bush, and the birds of the air made nests in its branches." Then he said "To what shall I compare the kingdom of God's empire? It is like yeast that a woman took and hid in three measures of flour, until it was all leavened." (13:18–21)

Matthew, Mark, and Luke use the mustard seed parable in their Gospels. They agree that the growth of this seed represented God's empire. Matthew and Luke both mention that the mustard plant grew to a large tree. The mustard seed was tiny and does produce a very large plant with a strong odor. However, Luke suggested that a person took the seed and planted it in their garden. This is odd. First, mustard could be bought at the market and there was little need for persons to plant it in their garden. Second, the plant was a weed, grew quickly, and could overshadow other plants in the garden that needed light. Third, as a weed it would attract nasty animals, including birds, that would be detrimental to a garden. It would not make sense for a person to plant mustard in their garden.

However, there was not an explanation why this person planted a mustard weed in their garden. Nor was there an explanation why a person put yeast in the bread dough. The point with both parables was that the empire of God grew rapidly, infected its host quickly, and attracted something seen as a negative (the Jews typically ate unleavened bread). I believe that if Jesus modernized this parable today he might suggest that the empire of God is like a cancer cell. Nothing would strike fear in the hearts of people today than to hear about a cell that, because of its DNA, grows, multiplies, and attacks rapidly. However, this is to be the nature of Jesus's empire.

These parables were not meant to give a pretty story of the empire as a place for singing birds and warm bread to brighten our day. They suggested that Jesus's church grew rapidly, infected the earth, and attracted those undesirables and scoundrels that might make the holy seem profane, the sacred seem common, and the powerful seem weak. I am reminded of the Apostle Paul's comments to the early Corinthian Christians that God chose the dishonorable to shame the honored.

> For consider your calling, brothers: not many of you were wise according to worldly standards, not many were powerful, and not many were of noble birth. But God chose what is foolish in the world to shame the wise; God chose what is weak in the

world to shame the strong; God chose what is low and despised in the world, even things that are not, to bring to nothing things that are, so that no human being might boast in the presence of God. (1 Cor 1:26–29)

The early Christians had to learn, from their leaders, that the empire of Jesus did not involve power, oppression, corruption, greed, and fear. It required courage, mercy, faith, love, and trust. Luke's readers needed to know that there was more to the story, which involved practicing mercy, compassion, and repentance among a people struggling to see their God.

9

Undesirables on the Margins of the Empire

Luke 13:22—17:10

As Jesus was journeying to Jerusalem the disciples were not only walking with him, they were learning the heart of his ministry, mission, and passion. The disciples were called to repentance and a life that honored God, rather than one which sought honor from people. In this section Luke arranged stories that addressed the struggle to become and continue as a disciple of Jesus. For Luke's readers this struggle was not simply physical, it was cultural.

Scholars have called the ancient world an agonistic world, meaning that life involved a constant struggle for honor, value, and resources (agonistic is from the Greek word *agon*, meaning contest, sport, or fight). In order to be at the top of the social ladder, and stay there, one had to constantly manipulate, confront, and invade space for peace and freedom.[1] Masculinity in this world also involved struggle. Men were assigned masculinity at birth and based on their parent's status in society. However, throughout life manhood was to be defended and proven. Gender slippage was the term used for those males who through contest, honor/shame, or reputation lost their ability to be considered a cultural "man."[2] Struggle was a constant for many people in the ancient world. Even if you were at the bottom of society, you struggled to find a way to move further in life so that you, and possibly your children, could have a better standard of living.

1. Clark, *The Better Way*, xvii.
2. Conway, *Behold the Man*, 18.

STRUGGLE TO GET IN

My first trip to Albania was very interesting. In 1999 I accompanied one of our elders at church, Dr. Richard Ady, who founded an organization that taught Bible and English to Albanians, especially after the country found freedom. Albania was one of the few atheist countries and one of the poorest Eastern Block countries under communism. Enver Hoxha, the dictator in the 1960s, removed all religion and committed horrible acts of violence toward imams, rabbis, priests, nuns, and other leaders of faith communities. Because this country was poor, people learned that what was important was pushing to the front and getting all the resources you could so that you and your family survived. Unlike in the United States, people did not form straight lines, wait their turn, or observe an orderly single-file line. They shoved and pushed their way to the front.

My second day in Tiranë, the capitol city, one of the college students from Oklahoma, who was interning with the missionaries for the summer, took me to get ice cream. I stood in a crowd for ten minutes waiting and noticing there was no line. An older lady grabbed my shirt, pointed her finger at me, shook it, and talked loudly in Albanian. Then she looked at the ice cream vendor and yelled at him, to which he yelled back. She shoved me to the front and kept speaking loudly at me. My anxiety level was rising and I turned around to yell at the intern who was sitting with some Albanians outside the circle. They were all laughing. He said, "Hey Ron Koke Mushkë (mule head) she's telling you to get up front or you'll never get any ice cream." I got my ice cream and said thank you in Albanian (the only words I knew at the time) ducked my head and headed to the intern.

Struggle to Overcome Your Culture

> A certain person said to him, "Lord, will a few be saved?" He said to them, "Struggle to enter through the narrow door. For many, I tell you, will want to enter but will not be strong enough. When the house manager has risen and shut the door, and you stand outside knocking on the door, saying, 'Lord, open it for us,' but he will answer, 'I do not know where you come from.' Then you will say, 'We ate and drank in your presence, and you taught in our streets.' But he will say, 'I tell you, I do not know where you come from. Go away from me, all you who do evil.' . . . The last will be first, and the first will be last." (Luke 13:23–30)

In the past when I read these verses I thought that Jesus was talking about striving as a general attitude of trying to get to heaven. However, after my experience in other countries I believe that Jesus told the disciples to shove their way into the empire of God. In the ancient world only those invited to dinner were allowed to attend. Narrow doors were typically the back doors and only a few servants and uninvited guests were given the option to enter and eat at a back room. Those who did not make it would stand outside and watch others eat, or leave hungry. This story was a challenge to the disciples to struggle (*agon*) to enter God's presence.

The journey to Jerusalem would have been difficult for the disciples both in terrain and the issues that Jesus faced. Luke included stories in which the disciples were not only pushed out of their comfort zones, but experienced Jesus's critique of their spiritual leaders. Luke's account indicated that the disciples were to view their spiritual journey as an aggressive pursuit of a relationship with God. This aggression was not one that "pushed people out of the way," but one that "pushed oneself to experience God."

Unfortunately not all who wanted to enter God's empire would. Jesus's comments concerning Jerusalem indicated that the city that rejected him would not be welcomed by their Lord.

> At that time certain Pharisees came and said to him, "Go away—leave, Herod wants to kill you." He said to them, "Go and tell that fox, 'Hey, I cast out demons and heal today and tomorrow, and finish on the third day. However, it is necessary for me to go today, tomorrow, and the next day because it is not possible that a prophet be destroyed outside of Jerusalem. Jerusalem, Jerusalem, who kills the prophets and stones those who are sent to it. How I wanted to gather your children together as a hen gathers her chicks under her wings—but you were unwilling. Look, your house is abandoned and I tell you, you will not see me until you say, 'Blessed is he who comes in the name of the Lord.'" (Luke 13:31–35)

While the disciples were encouraged to struggle to enter God's realm, so Jesus struggled to reach the goal of Jerusalem. But Jerusalem, as in the days of Babylonian captivity, was destined to be destroyed. This, because they did not know that Jesus struggled to be their God.

Jesus's plea reflected his love and mercy over the city. While some might suggest that the destruction of Jerusalem by the Romans, 70 CE, was a cruel act of vengeance, Jesus indicated that the city had another option. Jesus, using the language of Yahweh, reminded the disciples that as always Jerusalem rejected God's initiating relationship. God offered protection, hope, love, and peace, yet those corrupt leaders of the day rejected this love. Like the fruitless tree that was given another chance, Jerusalem again proved to reject their maker, their Lord, and their creator.

STRUGGLE TO FOLLOW JESUS

Swimming Against the Current

Treating People Better than Our Traditions

Jesus was again invited to the home of a Pharisee on a Sabbath. As usual the leaders were watching Jesus, trying to trap him. By this time it became clear that Jesus was not interested in playing the corrupt games of the leaders, nor were many of them willing to follow his teachings. This Sabbath day, and Sabbath day meal, was a holy time and one filled with manipulation, exploitation, and judgment. However, the victim was a man who was marginalized, suffering from gout. Jesus healed this man and found an opportunity to teach. As he had done with the woman in Luke 13, so he challenged the leaders that they were more concerned about an animal than a human on the Sabbath. In Luke 13 it was the synagogue ruler and congregation who were offended by his mercy on the Sabbath. In this story it was the Pharisees who were the source of the hypocrisy. However, they could not answer Jesus because they knew that they had been loyal to a system rather than relationships.

Ignoring Customs

In the ancient world table etiquette was very important. Many things changed over time but the dinner or *Symposium* had a traditional standard that seemed common. First, respectable women were not to be present with the males. Unlike women in prostitution or boy/girl slaves, honorable women were not welcome at the table. While they may have had a separate dining room with the slaves and children, they were expected to be apart from the men; and if they were present they were to be silent. Second, the dinner courses followed a system and pattern (much like our holiday dinners in America). Third, the dinner invitation was key to the success of the meal. If you were invited you accepted and went to the meal (even if you didn't want to go). You were either invited to make the host look good or to make business or social contacts for the host. The dinner was designed to benefit the host, rather than the guests. Finally, guests did not complain to the host.

This was an offer of hospitality and it was expected that the guest one day return the favor. The host may one day need the guest's services, children for marriage, a favor, or contact with their friends and other associates.

Jesus, however, challenged the common meal etiquette of his day. First, *he suggested that the guests not choose the best seat (next to the person of honor) but instead choose the worst seat (14:10).*

> He said to the man who had invited him, "When you give a dinner or a banquet, do not invite your friends, brothers, relatives, or rich neighbors, lest they also invite you in return and you be repaid. But when you give a feast, invite the poor, the crippled, the lame, the blind, and you will be blessed, because they cannot repay you. For you will be repaid at the resurrection of the righteous." (Luke 14:12–14)

Second, *Jesus reversed the idea of the dinner blessing the host and suggested that the host bless those who could not repay him.* Here Jesus called the early Christian to be countercultural and offer favors freely and without expectation or exploitation. His idea of hospitality being an open door for the marginalized (those who would understand striving to get in the door) was explained further in the next parable concerning the generous host. "For Luke this is a radically inclusive community, comprised not only of sinners and social outcasts but also of the physically disabled and disfigured who, on the basis of the appearance of their physical body, have been ostracized as misfits from the body politic (or religious). Much of the prejudice and bias of Luke's day was grounded in this pervasive physiognomic consciousness that presumed one's outer appearance determined one's moral character."[3]

When people rejected the invitation to come to dinner with the generous host, he became angry and opened the door to those living on the streets. Even more he ordered his servants to compel the poor to join them, "The master said to the servant, 'Go out to the highways and hedges and compel people to come in, that my house may be filled. For I tell you, none of those men who were invited shall taste my banquet'" (Luke 14:23). Jesus's call to discipleship was not only a struggle against the cultural current, it was a personal struggle. God's people were called to urge and encourage others to embrace.

---

3. Parsons, *Body and Character*, 15.

Ignoring Family

As the crowds followed Jesus and listened to his messages the disciples were with him on his journey. Luke's arrangement of the material illustrated to the early reader that the journey to Jerusalem was hazardous and required devotion and commitment. In this section Jesus gave an extremely hard and controversial requirement to continue to follow and be his disciple.

> If any come to me and doesn't hate their father, mother, wife, children, brothers, sisters, and their own lives, they are not able to be my disciple. Those who do not bear/carry their cross and come behind me are not able to be my disciples . . . Everyone who does not dismiss all of their possessions is not able to be my disciples. (Luke 14:25–27, 33)

This text provides fond memories for me. It was a text I read often before I was baptized into Jesus. The college student who studied with me had me read this and pray about my commitment to Christ before taking this step of obedience and faith. For me, the cost did not remove me from my family; however in the ancient world this was much different. The parable is both powerful and challenging. In the ancient world family was important and it was one's job to provide for them. However, in this text Jesus called the disciples to challenging, radical commitment.

First, the disciple was to love Jesus more than his or her family. While Jesus used the term "hate" in this text, the context suggests that one have such a strong affinity for Christ, that their family (if they reject Jesus) comes second to Jesus. Over the years I have witnessed young people who made the decision to follow Jesus in baptism become isolated from their families, threatened with death from "honor killings," kicked out of their homes, and many times shunned emotionally and physically.

While it is hard to comprehend parents treating their children this way, the biblical texts teach that this might happen. However, Jesus didn't allow this excuse to keep people from him. The call to be a disciple of Jesus was a call to face rejection even from our families.

Second, the disciple was to love Jesus more than his or her self. As in Luke 9:27 disciples were once again called to carry the cross, suffer shame, and follow Jesus to the dark places of life. Their lives were to be an offering to Jesus as they followed him to Jerusalem, death, and resurrection.

Finally, the disciple was to love Jesus more than possessions and status. In 14:33 Jesus told them to renounce all their possessions. While some would suggest that this meant that Christians should get rid of their possessions, this is not what Jesus said. Renouncing possessions in the ancient world referred to status, property, rights, and honor in the community. To renounce one's possessions meant being willing to freely give to others, without expecting favors and honor in return. This referred to the earlier section concerning the dinner guest inviting those who could not pay them back.

One might read this sermon and wonder why Jesus was so hard. Our picture of Jesus is changing as he moves closer to Jerusalem but one view we struggle with concerns a Savior who demands allegiance. Why? Jesus referred to "counting the cost" in his lesson. The disciple who follows Jesus will be faced with commitment, devotion, faith, trust, and many times discouragement. Even more the journey to Jerusalem was a trip to death. There was a cost involved. Even today there is still a cost. Jesus wanted the disciples to reflect and take inventory on their spiritual lives as they proceeded to Jerusalem. In addition to this lesson from Jesus, Luke's account of the parable of the sower (8:11–15) indicated that one third of those who follow Jesus will produce spiritual fruit. Discipleship is difficult and over my twenty-seven years as a Christian I will admit that a third of the Christians I have known are still faithful and active in God's empire. A seminary in Portland tells its first-year students that one out of three ministers will stay in ministry more than ten years. From personal experience I agree, yet the challenge is still there. Not all make the long journey from conversion, discipleship, to death in Jesus. The Christian journey is difficult and one must count the cost before joining.

In times of persecution the Christian journey is not only difficult, it is hazardous. When pressure is exerted on the church some Christians will quit. They will back out due to fear, anxiety, or guilt. Jesus knew that the disciples would face struggles, critique, and physical torture for Jesus's name. Disciples must count the cost if they plan to follow him.

I have used these verses in my studies with people for many years. No matter if one is a teenager, young adult, retired, or person in jail. I believe that this verse gets to the root of discipleship. It is overwhelming at times but a valuable teaching from the Messiah. For those who wish to follow Jesus they must count the cost. Do we love Jesus above our families, ourselves, and our possessions? While some might suggest that this causes disciples to mistreat their families I would suggest the opposite. We may believe that we live in a world that glorifies the family but the research doesn't suggest this. The United States is still a country where our children are at risk physically, emotionally, and economically. We are also a country that doesn't compare with others when it comes to women's health and safety. Our soldiers suffer from trauma and struggle to be healthy models for their families. We as a country do not overindulge families. However, disciples have the opportunity to be countercultural and be dynamic spouses, parents, and role models for their families and those needing spiritual guidance. We can do this because Jesus called his disciples to be good fathers, wives, and children. He called his disciples to value people over possessions. He called his disciples to value his mission more than their lives. In every way, the disciple becomes not only a witness of Jesus, but a model of humanity.

I ONCE WAS LOST . . .

After Jesus proclaimed a hard and powerful message it was amazing who responded. One can imagine Jesus at a large tent revival sharing his message in Luke 14:25–34 and a crowd responding during the invitation. This crowd included sinners, tax collectors, and other marginalized people. The ones considered "unholy" by the Pharisees were coming forward and responding to an altar call. However, instead of cheering for God, the Pharisees and religious leaders complained, "This man welcomes sinners and eats with them" (Luke 15:2). This has been the constant complaint against Jesus. Yet in this text, the sinners responded to him. Even when Jesus gave one of his hardest lessons, those who would have been challenged the most responded. Those who felt that they had not sinned smirked at Jesus's love and mercy for "those people."

Luke, in turn, arranged three parables concerning things *found*. First, a shepherd left ninety-nine sheep to search and find a lost lamb. When he found it, instead of kicking it back to the pen, he lifted this fifty- to seventy-pound animal upon his shoulders and went home happy. He then called his friends and had a party to celebrate the return of the one sheep. An interesting point would be that he might have had lamb for his guests—which he probably got from one of the sheep he had left behind. This, for any shepherd, was not only risky, it was a tremendous amount of work.

Second, a woman lost her coin and searched the dirt floor of her house to find it. She lit her lamp, swept the floor, and persisted until she found the coin. Then she gathered her friends and celebrated her find. Another interesting point would be that she would have entertained her friends during the celebration with money that may have cost more than the coin. However, while this was risky, she enjoyed finding something more than she lamented losing what she had.

Finally, a father lost his son to greed, the world, and shame. Luke arranged Jesus's story of the "Prodigal Son" (Lost Son) as one of three unique Lukan parables in his Gospel. Because these are only found in Luke, they support his theme of Jesus on the margins as well as his embracing outsiders. Many know the story of the lost son and his return to the father. In the story the son prematurely takes his inheritance from his father, goes to a far-off land, and spends the inheritance on rough living, friends, and pleasure. After days of famine, poverty, joblessness, and homelessness he found himself feeding pigs for another individual. Jews are not allowed to eat pork, so feeding pigs was low status. Now this young man had become so poor that he could only think of returning home. He realized that life with his father was better than where he was because the father provided for the servants, his family, and his people. It made sense for him to return home and become a hired slave (since he had spent all of his inheritance and therefore was no longer part of the family). He made the long journey home.

Upon his arrival his father ran to him, embraced him, was filled with compassion, and clothed him. He was again part of the family. The reunion was one that brings tears to the eyes of those who not only hear the story, but have lived it. For parents the story reminds them never to give up, even though a son or daugther seems no longer part of the family. For children the story reminds us that God is always waiting.

However, the story was not about the lost son. It was about the people who weren't shedding a tear over the reunion. It was about the people who grumbled that Jesus ate with sinners. It was about the people who resented staying faithful to God. It was about those who refused to run when the son came home. It was about those who watched Jesus, in the figure of the father, run to the sinners and embrace them with love and joy.

> His older son was in the field. As he came closer to the house he heard music and dancing. He called one of the servants and asked what was happening. He [the servant] said, "Your brother is here and your father killed the grain-fed calf because he came back safely (healthy)." He [the brother] was furious and did not want to come inside. But his father went out to encourage him. He said to his father, "Hey, these years I worked like a slave and did not slight your commands, yet you did not give me a goat so that I could party with my friends. Instead this son of yours who chewed up your savings with prostitutes came back and you killed the grain-fed calf." He [the father] said, "Child, you are always with me and what I have is yours. It is necessary for us to celebrate and rejoice because your brother was dead and is now alive. He had perished but has been found/saved." (Luke 15:25–32)

Over the years that I have preached this text many have told me that they had not heard the part about the older son, or at least they had forgotten about it. We become wrapped up in the drama of the love and forgiveness that we want from God that we don't notice the resentment and resistance we have had for the lost children in our communities.

The older son was hurt. He had worked hard, been loyal, and stayed faithful to his dad. Clearly what the younger brother did was inexcusable, dishonorable, and shameful. The younger brother had spit on his dad and counted him as dead. He had given his family the "finger" and headed out of town. The younger brother, according to the father, was not only lost ("my son was dead") but he was cut off from the family. The text doesn't tell us that he repented, only that he realized it was impractical for him to starve when his dad cared for is servants. He did confess his sin to his dad but we have little clue that he was sincere. The younger brother talks to himself about returning to his home. This is one of five of Luke's characters who talk to themselves (Luke 7:39; 12:17; 16:3; 18:4), the texts reserve that language for those who are not necessarily acting honorably. There is little indication that the returning son was honestly showing repentance. However, it didn't matter. The father accepted him without question.

One can understand why the older son was hurt. His father was acting inappropriately (running to him and hugging his unclean body). He acted too generously, and killed the older son's calf. The tone in the son's voice seems clear in Luke's writing, "All these years I have been slaving for you . . ." In addition to this he refused to participate in the welcome home party.

I remember when I was a youth minister. The tradition of the church was to honor the high school graduates. We had four but one of the kids did not come to church or youth group. His grandparents were active but I made it known that we shouldn't invite him. I was convinced it was not a good example for the other seniors who had come regularly (two without their parents) and who were active in our youth group. I also felt it was a bad example for the other youth. The elders really encouraged me to reconsider and I relented, but I let them know it was because I respected them. The dinner went well, the church showered the seniors with love, and I gave them all cards. The young man hugged me afterward and thanked me. He had a good evening.

I was helping one of the elders carry the decorations out to his car and said, "Well, I guess you guys were right, but I still think it is a bad example for our kids." He stopped, put his arm around me, and said, "Ron, one thing you need to understand—this church has a lot of love for people. That's what we believe God has called us to do." It broke me.

The father met with the older brother and talked with him. The tension in the son's voice was strong and he seemed to have a valid point. He was faithful and loyal to his father, yet never received a celebration of that loyalty. However, the father reminded the son that he owned everything. He could have had a celebration any time, but he chose to consider his work slavery. He ran the farm and would one day replace the father when he died (the younger brother had nothing and would be at the mercy of his brother). There must be celebration at the repentance of sinners because they cannot experience life unless someone gives it to them. In addition to this, there must be a sense of joy in the older brothers/sisters who stay on the farm and work for the master. If we see it as slavery, we will not be able to offer mercy, forgiveness, and grace.

The older son was not only a challenge to the Pharisees but the disciples as well. The call to follow Jesus was a call to forgive, show mercy, and love whether people deserved it or not. In a world that valued intimidation, power, oppression, greed, and violence the role of the father, as shown in Jesus, was one that requires courage, sacrifice, and devotion. Not all can fulfill this call, but Luke reminded the disciples and the early readers that going to the margins of society provides hope and love for those struggling to find their way home.

Reversing the Stories

After reversing the stories of forgiveness and love Jesus told a parable concerning a dishonest slave manager. As mentioned earlier (Luke 12:47–49) business owners many times hired slaves as stewards/managers to manage their accounts. In this story a slave was dishonest with his master's money and was called to be audited by his master. Realizing he was caught, the slave adjusted the accounts of his boss's clients and gave them favorable discounts. By doing this the clients would feel indebted to the owner as well as the slave. The slave knew that he could not work on the streets (much less receive the physical beating he would be given if he was caught), so he adjusted the bill. He was dishonest. He cheated his master. However, his boss believed that he acted "shrewdly" or was "sneaky." The master would be praised by the clients for being generous and the slave would be welcome in homes as the man who orchestrated the generous blessing for the clients. The master was blessed and the slave accepted. The master couldn't punish the slave since he would be dishonored by the clients. In a sneaky way the slave brought honor to his master (from the clients) and honored the clients.[4]

It seems odd that Jesus would offer dishonesty as a condition of discipleship, but the issue was not honesty or financial integrity. The issue was that the slave knew that it was better to be generous (like the father in the

4. Landry and May, "Honor Restored," 302–3, 308.

previous parable) toward people than follow a law that punished relationships with others. In addition to this, he used material wealth to maintain/restore relationships.

> The master praised the unrighteous steward that he had done wisely because the children of this age are wiser than the children of light in this generation. I tell you, make your friends with unrighteous materials so that when it is gone they may receive you into eternal places to live (or be eternally grateful). Those who are faithful with small things will be faithful with many things. Those who are unfaithful with small things will be with many things. If you are not faithful with unrighteous materials then who will trust you with the truth? If you are not faithful with little things who will trust you with their own possessions? No one is able to serve two masters because they will hate the one and love the other. He will be devoted to the one and despise the other. You are not able to serve God and materialism," Jesus said. All the Pharisees heard this; they loved money and ridiculed him. (Luke 16:8–14)

While some might decide to make a case that suggests it is acceptable to be dishonest if you don't hurt anyone (much like the bumper sticker claiming "No One Died When Clinton Lied") the point of the parable concerns the religious leaders. The slave was dishonest but in the end he realized that people and relationships were more important than money. When his back was against the wall he knew that it was important to use his wealth to gain friends and support. Unfortunately, Jesus indicated, the Pharisees didn't understand this. They had become greedy and focused on money, status, power, and honor. The group of men who were to teach the concepts of the Torah in love, mercy, and faithfulness had become part of the upward mobility of society. They had sold themselves to the struggle of society to climb the economic ladder and maintain a level of status. Unfortunately, in doing this they had driven people to the margins. Unlike the dishonest slave, they had few friends who would take them because they provided grace, forgiveness, and a discount.

Reversing Behavior

After Jesus criticized the leaders for their greed Luke arranged a parable concerning riches and salvation. The parable of the "Rich Man and Lazarus" is a story that is unique to Luke. In the ancient world the poor were not confined to certain locations of the city, as they are in many urban contexts in U.S. cities. The poor were scattered through town, typically located at the gates of those with money. The rich would have to walk by the poor any time they left their homes and either give alms or ignore them.

> There was a certain rich man who was clothed in purple and linen and who feasted every day. At his gate was thrown a certain poor man named Lazarus, covered with sores, who desired to be fed with what fell from the rich man's table, even the dogs came and licked his sores. The poor man died and was carried by the angels to Abraham's chest. The rich man died and was buried. In Hades, while being tortured, he looked up and saw Abraham in the distance with Lazarus in his chest. He cried out, "Father Abraham, have mercy on me, and send Lazarus to dip the end of his finger in water to cool my tongue, for these flames are killing me!" But Abraham said, "Child, remember that you received your good things while living, and Lazarus received bad things. Besides all this, between us is a great chasm so that those who wanted to cross from here to you may not be able and none may cross from there to us." He said, "Then I beg you, father, to send him to my father's house—for I have five brothers—so that he may warn them, so that they don't come to this tortured place." But Abraham said, "They have Moses and the prophets; let them hear them." He said, "No, father Abraham, but if someone goes to them from the dead, they will repent." He said to him, "If they do not hear Moses and the prophets, one who rose from the dead will not persuade them." (Luke 16:19–31)

This story has been used to discuss levels or locations of hell, the judgment, or the identity of "Abraham." However the story involves more than that. First, *the story discusses boundaries*. As mentioned above the rich man would have had to step around or over Lazarus any time he left his house. The rich man refused to cross boundaries to help the poor man. In addition to this Lazarus was not able to cross the boundaries to enter the man's home; he was left at the gate. In ancient homes the front door was many times open and one could see through the front door into the dining room. In this story Lazarus longs to eat crumbs from the table, indicating that he could see the table and dinner from where he lay. Yet he was not welcomed into the man's home. In the afterlife the rich man could not cross boundaries to Lazarus nor could Lazarus cross them to help the suffering man. Because the rich man refused to cross boundaries through mercy, in the end those with compassion and mercy cannot either.

Second, *the story involves mercy*. The rich man refused to show mercy. The only merciful ones in the story were the dogs. In the end Lazarus was not allowed to show mercy on the rich man in torment. Mercy would not even be shown the family of the suffering man, because it was not shown to Lazarus.

Third, *the story involves comfort*. One man received comfort, praise, and honor while on earth. In the end things reversed and the one suffering received comfort.

Fourth, *the story provided divine reversal*. As Jesus mentioned in the Sermon on the Plain (Luke 6), those who were currently fed had already received their comfort while those who hungered would one day be fed. This "divine reversal" was the work of God. Those who received joy in this life, to the neglect of others, would be neglected in the end. It is odd that the man with a name and identity was the poor man. The rich man remains nameless, without status, and without honor. However, in the end Lazarus was in the arms of Abraham and received comfort.

Finally, *the story involves God's word*. Abraham clearly indicated that Moses and the prophets were enough to teach people to care for the poor. The rich man wanted to warn his brothers but in the story Jesus claimed that Moses and the prophets (something read weekly in the assembly) had ample information concerning treatment of the poor.

Luke's audience was again being challenged to care for those on the margins of society. This story was a clear condemnation to those who attended worship, listened to God's word, and ignored those suffering in society. The challenge for Luke's readers was that discipleship involved crossing boundaries and helping those in need.

When I was in Albania teaching Luke at one of the churches, I began the week by asking how many beggars my listeners had passed on the way to class. I had counted five in just my short walk as well as another dozen while on an early morning run. My students responded that they had not seen any beggars. As the week progressed and we read through Luke I would begin each morning with the same questions. They noticed more each day. By the end of the first week we had a discussion about these beggars. There were many myths concerning them, "They really weren't poor," or "They gouged out their children's eyeballs to get more money from sympathetic people," or "They deserved to be poor because they drank their money away," and even, "They are lazy and won't work." I shared with the group that these were the same comments people made in America about the poor. I then suggested that they stop and talk to these beggars and if God led them, maybe offer them something.

When our class discussed the Rich Man and Lazarus, I found it interesting that the students were noticing the people on the side of the road, some had talked to them and prayed with them, and others had offered them food. We also discussed how prevalent begging was on their trip to class since we were now opening our eyes to what was happening around us. Incorrect myths, false judgments, apathy, and business had kept us not only from seeing them as people, it kept us from understanding the mission and ministry of Jesus and the church. I was proud of the students as they identified these issues and found ways to treat the beggars as humans who needed compassion, love, and mercy. In addition to this we also discussed how the Hebrew Bible became more alive to them as it also gave messages of hope and mercy to the poor and those in need of love and compassion.

REVERSING RELATIONSHIPS

Luke continued to challenge the reader through divine reversal as this section drew to a close. Those who live on the margins have a way of living that seemed contrary to those living for status and honor in society. However those on the margins know that people and relationships are key to survival. The disciple must seek and embrace relationships, even when it means crossing boundaries and walls that separate us from others. This will be important when we enter Acts and discuss the division between Jew and Gentile.

> He spoke to his disciples, "It is not possible to live without offensiveness—but woe to those who face it. It is better if one has a boulder around their neck and is thrown into a lake than to offend one of these little ones. Be careful. If your brother/sister sins against you rebuke/confront them and if they repent, forgive them. If they sin against you seven times a day and turn to you seven times and say I repent, forgive them." The Apostles said to the Lord, "Increase our faith." The Lord said, "If you have faith the size of a mustard seed you could say to this tree, 'Pull yourself up by the roots and plant yourself in the lake,' and it would listen to you." (Luke 17:1–6)

For Jesus, relationships involved mercy, compassion, grace, and repentance. Christians have many times focused more on forgiveness than in healing and repenting in relationships. It is easy to tell someone to forgive; at least it is easy for me. However, to call someone to repentance is a different thing, as it requires that I invest in others and walk with them in the journey. In repentance we not only see one person heal, we experience all their victims' healing as well. In this text Luke called the early reader to help people repent and call them to a life of healing. As Jesus suggested, marginalized people many times understand better how to cultivate relationships, support others, and develop a network of friends.

My brother and sister-in-law live on a farm in Missouri. We love going back to visit and meet many of the people we knew in the small town and surrounding farms. One day he took me to visit a Mennonite family. This area of Missouri is settled by many Amish and Mennonite groups, which work together with their community and towns to help people and grow as groups. We were having a good visit when the Mennonite man asked me about living in Portland, our boy's school system, and some of the technologies we had as opposed to that in rural areas of Missouri. We were having a good visit when he said, "You know, times have changed so much. You have to be careful with technology as change demands sacrifice. Sometimes we have to sacrifice a lot of good things to accommodate change." I shook my head as I remembered having many of these conversations in the church where we worked in Missouri. Change is difficult for some people, especially those who are traditional, older, or tend to have bad experiences with living in urban areas. "Change happens," I said, "but fortunately much of what has changed has made us stronger as a people and nation." He nodded his head yes as I spoke, then said, "Well, I see your point, but change for change's sake is not always the best. Take this for instance, it used to be that you could say 'nigger' in this country and it was okay. Things have changed so that you can't say that and have to find some other words so you don't offend everybody." I laughed (not the ha ha laugh but the "I can't believe you just said that" laugh) and responded, "It's never been okay to say that word. I think as a country we have had to learn to respect people's feelings. Immigrant and ethnically diverse communities have changed our language not because someone told us to, but because we realized that words can hurt people and we need to be sensitive to the feelings of others." I don't think that he agreed with me and I don't want to call him a racist. I know many people from those communities who would never use negative language towards people of color, and this man may have been an isolated instance. However, it is interesting that those of us who are in a position of privilege (white males) can feel threatened when others confront us on our language and what we say about others. It is not about our intentions, what we really meant, or that others are "too sensitive." It is about how *we* make others feel in what we say and do. It is not really about change—because I thank God for change. It involves our willingness to allow change to make us better and more caring people. I find, however, that some people view change as bad rather than something healthy that takes work, sacrifice, and patience as a community strives to work together and values each member. Living in community requires this type of respect. Being a citizen of this country demands that we respect others and develop relationships with people, so that the empire of Jesus can grow.

10

Taking Risks on the Margins
Luke 17:11—19:27

THIS FINAL SECTION PREPARES the reader to begin the journey to Jerusalem and the crucifixion of Jesus.

HEALING OF THE SAMARITANS

As Jesus and the disciples were traveling to Jerusalem, they walked along the border of Samaria. Earlier the Samaritans would not accept Jesus (9:51–56), and this time Jesus and his band avoided the country. They were met by ten men with the dreaded skin disease called leprosy. These men were unclean and stood at a distance seeking mercy. While earlier the Samaritans refused to send a welcome party, in this text Jesus was greeted by those on the margins of their community. Again, Jesus was rejected by the "normal" but welcomed/accepted by outcasts. In response, Jesus healed them. They were cleansed as they went their way, yet one, a Samaritan, returned to give thanks to Jesus. The interesting theme of this story is that again a Samaritan, as well as other lepers, His emphasis on the poor.

LIFE IN THE EMPIRE

As the group traveled further a Pharisee inquired of Jesus when the empire of God would come. This would have been a loaded question as Galilee was full of revolutionaries and zealots who sought to overthrow both the Roman and the corrupt Jewish rulerships that existed.

> Being asked by the Pharisees when the empire of God would come, he answered, "The entrance of God's empire is not something one can observe, nor will they say, 'Hey, it's here or there.' The empire of God is in your midst." (Luke 17:20–21)

While many at this time were looking for a grand entrance of this empire, Jesus claimed that it already existed. In the days of the Maccabees, 160 BCE, the Jewish nation experienced wars, revolts, and heroic tales that ended in the expulsion of the Greek ruler, Antiochus Epiphanes, and his army. Simon Maccabaeus entered Jerusalem riding on a donkey, signaling the return God's empire/kingdom and restored worship at the temple. Rembering these events, the Judean people longed for the days when the kingdom would return, Jerusalem would become its own city, the temple would be holy, and oppressive government would depart (or be defeated). The Pharisee who asked this question must have been testing Jesus by suggesting that he would try to overthrow the current government. It would also have been odd for someone who worked among the marginalized and performed miracles for the sick to claim to lead a revolt against as powerful war machine as Rome. At least the Maccabee boys were fighters and proved their worth in combat. Jesus, however, had not fought a battle. He offered peace, forgiveness, and hope, rather than violence, power, or a victory over the Roman colonizers.

Jesus's response to the Pharisee was that the empire was here, among them. The empire/kingdom of Jesus was not something waiting to be established, it already existed. Even though they were under the "thumb" of the Romans, Yahweh was still king. Earlier Luke indicated that the empire came as Jesus cast out demons (11:20). While this would have made sense to the Pharisee it would not have been a reality he wanted to accept. To *acknowledge* that the empire is or may be present is one thing; to *accept* that the empire is present is a completely different response.

First, if we accept that God's empire is already here then we must look to Jesus's ministry to see evidence of his reign. Kingdom and empire are the same Greek words. I chose empire because it contrasts the Roman Empire. In addition to this, empire and reign/rule are also the same Greek words. The empire of God is the reign of God. Jesus and the early writers were not referring to buildings, castles, and land; they were referring to power, authority, and submission by subjects. When Jesus indicated that God's reign (Jesus's reign) was present then his ministry became a reflection of God's rule. Healing the sick, doing ministry to those on the margins, and offering love, forgiveness, and mercy become empire values that must be practiced if the reign of God is to continue to exist.

Second, if we accept that God's empire/reign is present then there is no need to wait for another kingdom or mission. If the empire of Jesus existed by the finger of God when he healed and fought evil, then the mission becomes clear. We are called to that mission, rule, and empire. There is no need to wait for anything else to be revealed because the kingdom has come and we must seek to do God's will. The church is called to go, witness, and spread the message of Jesus.

Finally, if we accept that God's empire/reign is already here then the ministry and empire values that Jesus was involved in should be our mission and values. The critique of Jesus by the religious leaders was very similar to the question that the disciples of John asked Jesus (7:18–21). However, the negative attitude involved Jesus's healing those who were demon possessed. This should have been a moment of rejoicing for the leaders of Jesus's day— as it was for the people who were enslaved by evil. Jesus claimed that his suffering and rejection were part of the entrance of his empire. These kingdom values included persistence, humility/humiliation, mercy, compassion, forgiveness, and risk.

Empire Values

Persistence

> He spoke this parable to them to show them that they should not get tired of praying often. "A certain judge in a certain city did not respect God or people. A certain widow in the city came to him saying, 'Give me justice against my opponent.' It happened after this that the judge said to himself, 'Since I don't respect God or humans, but this widow keeps harassing me, I will give her justice so that she doesn't dishonor/shame me by coming again.' Hear the unrighteous judge; won't God give justice to the chosen ones who cry out day and night even with patience? I tell you that justice will come soon. Will the Son of Man find faith on earth when he comes?" Jesus said. (Luke 18:1–8)

This parable did not suggest that "God had to be harassed" through prayer in order to act. As discussed earlier, Yahweh was unlike the gods of the pagan world. However, this parable was a story that honored the Father, unlike the unjust judge (who spoke to himself). The judge did require harassment and acted out of a sense of his own honor, protecting his reputation. He was concerned for himself, not the widow. He represented the colonizers who ruled the land for their own benefit and honor. Jesus taught that God cared for the victims.

God will bring justice because the victims need it. Disciples do not pray with persistence to motivate God to act, disciples pray persistently believing that God hears the cries of victims.

Years ago I was approached by two churches dealing with a case of child abuse. Both groups had leaders who were unaware of the abuse. It had happened a decade previously and came to light to the leaders recently. One group of leaders heard the accusation from the victims and their family directly. We met and talked about a proper course of action. I suggested that the leaders surround the victims and their families, hear their pain, acknowledge the sin of the offender, and offer healing, peace, prayer, and anything else they could do to help the victims and their families heal. I also suggested that they confront the oppressor and offer to walk with the victims in their counseling, healing, and any legal action they might take.

The second group of leaders had heard the allegations through a lawsuit presented by some of the victims. We also met to talk about a course of action. The offender was continuing to be present at the church and even lead prayer in the worship. I offered the same suggestion that I had offered the previous leaders. This group of leaders counseled with their lawyer and their insurance company, who suggested that they keep a distance from the victims and allow the courts to process the conviction.

This is a story about justice. This is also a story about support. This is a story about hearing the cries of the oppressed and holding oppressors accountable. One group acted out of a desire for justice and another group listened to counsel in order to save face. Disciples who pray persistently for justice know when God has called them to walk with victims and join the journey for justice.

Mercy

Luke wrote that one day a wealthy ruler (suggesting a Pharisee) came to ask Jesus the way to salvation. This story is common in Matthew and Mark (Matt 19:16–30; Mark 10:17–31), as well as Luke. In all three accounts the man was called to sell his possessions and give to the poor.

> A ruler asked him, "Good Teacher, what do I need to do to inherit life in the next age?" Jesus said, "Why do you call me good; only God is good. You know the commandments—do not commit adultery, murder, steal, lie about people, and honor your mother and father." He said, "I have kept these since I was a young man." Jesus said, "One thing you have left out: sell all you have and give it to the poor and you will have treasure in

the next age. Then come and follow me." When he heard this he became grieved because he had a lot of money. (Luke 18:18–30)

Matthew wrote that this was what the man must do to be mature (19:21). Maturity was represented by God's Agape love (Matt 5:43–48). In Mark's account the man was incomplete by not giving to the poor (10:21). Luke, however, indicated that the man had left out (*leipo*) something important in his relationship with God. He had left out giving to the poor (Luke 18:21). He had also left out the importance of this for salvation. His relationship with God was incomplete without caring for the vulnerable (in all three accounts) but Luke suggested to the early reader that they also may have left something out in their practice of their faith. Luke's emphasis on the poor and marginalized seems obvious in this text and his challenge to his audience to heed Jesus's passion for the vulnerable in society. For the rich ruler obeying Torah for one's own life/family was what God required. For Jesus, Torah (as with the rich man and Lazarus) required and included caring for the poor.

Discipleship involved the empire value of mercy. This was illustrated by three comments which Luke made. First, the ruler had followed the Torah since childhood, but had not been motivated to give to the poor. Second, when challenged by Jesus the man went away upset, because he was very rich. Instead of believing that God would provide for his doing the right thing, he believed he must depend on his own resources and material possessions. He was unable to renounce his "things" and unwilling to care for the marginalized (Luke 14:34–35). Finally, Jesus told Peter and the disciples that those in the empire of Jesus would be rewarded for their sacrifices. Practicing mercy and compassion involve risk, but God promised to provide and protect those who were willing to care for others.

Humility/Humiliation

In the ancient world *humility* was not a psychological term. The Hebrew and Greek words represent a class of people (poor, oppressed, vulnerable) as compared to those who were "honorable." The Latin term, *humiliors*, was reserved for this "lower class" of people. To be humble/humiliated did not mean that one spoke negatively of oneself. It did not represent an attitude or public presence. To be humble meant: 1) a person who lived and existed in the vulnerable class in society, and/or 2) one who associated with the humiliated. When the Apostle Paul wrote that Jesus was humble/humiliated, it referred to the company that he kept as well as the class of society where he lived (Phil 2:8). Paul's encouragement for the early Christians to "associate with the humiliated" meant that the wealthy should care for and embrace those in the church who represented the vulnerable/lower classes of society, or as the Romans called them the *humiliors* (Rom 12:16).[1]

As with the story of the lost son and elder brother, Jesus made a direct comparison to the religious leaders of his day.

> He spoke this parable to certain people who were confident in their own righteousness and looked down upon/despised others. "Two men went to the temple to pray. A Pharisee, and the other, a tax collector. The Pharisee stood by himself and prayed, 'God I am thankful I am not like the rest of people; thieves, unrighteous, adulterers, and this tax collector. I fast two times per week and I give a tithe of everything I possess.' But the tax collector stood at a distance and did not want to look to heaven, but hit/beat his chest and said, 'God have mercy on me, a sinner!' Which one descended to their home justified? All of those who lift themselves up will be humiliated and the humiliated will be lifted up/honored." (Luke 18:9–17)

The Pharisee in the story went to the temple (public religious space) to pray and affirm his faith toward God. While his prayer may seem arrogant or proud to the modern reader, ancient readers would have expected the Pharisee to perform this action. He, as a leader, was affirming his faith and commitment to God.

The tax collector, however, affirmed his faithlessness by standing at a distance, lowering his eyes, beating his breast, and pleading for mercy. The Pharisee made two mistakes in the story, according to the way of Jesus. First, *he marginalized the tax collector* (his fellow Israelite). "I am not like this man," was not just a true statement, it was said in the hearing of the tax collector, who responded with humiliation. Second, *as the tax collector cried out for mercy, the Pharisee did not offer him any*. This summarized much of what Luke wrote about the Pharisees, their attitudes toward others, and their neglect of those seeking mercy. The story ended with the question by Jesus, "who went to his home justified?" or "who received mercy?" The parable was similar to one Jesus told Simon the Pharisee (Luke 7:44–47). Which one showed mercy?

Barbara Ehrenreich holds a doctorate degree in science and left a lucrative research position to become an award-winning author. For her book *Nickel and Dimed* she went undercover and worked various minimum wage jobs and, as a reporter, explained how difficult it is to survive in America while working lower wage occupations. In one account she describes her

---

1. Clark, "Associating with the Humiliated," 68–72.

encounter with a homeowner, while working for a maid service, who heard Ehrenreich give a speech at a university.

> When I can find no more surfaces to wipe and have finally exhausted the supply of rooms, Maddy assigns me to do the kitchen floor. OK, except that Mrs. W. is *in* the kitchen, so I have to go down on my hands and knees practically at her feet. No, we don't have sponge mops like the one I use in my own house; the hands-and-knees approach is a definite selling point for corporate cleaning services like The Maids. "We clean floors the old-fashioned way—*on our hands and knees*" (emphasis added), the brochure for a competing firm boasts. In fact, whatever advantages there may be to the hands-and-knees approach—you're closer to your work, of course, and less likely to miss a grimy patch—are undermined by the artificial drought imposed by The Maids' cleaning system . . . A mop and a full bucket of hot soapy water would not only get a floor cleaner but would be a lot more dignified for the person who does the cleaning. But it is this primal posture of submission . . . that seems to gratify the consumers of maid services.
>
> I don't know, but Mrs. W.'s floor is hard—stone, I think, or at least a stone-like substance—and we have no knee pads with us today. I had thought in my middle-class innocence that knee pads were one of Monica Lewinsky's prurient fantasies, but no, they actually exist, and they're usually a standard part of our equipment. So here I am on my knees, working my way around the room like some fanatical penitent crawling through the stations of the cross, when I realize that Mrs. W. is staring at me fixedly—so fixedly that I am gripped for a moment by the wild possibility that I may have once given a lecture at her alma mater and she's trying to figure out where she's seen me before. If I were recognized, would I be fired? Would she at least be inspired to offer me a drink of water? Because I have decided that if water is actually offered, I'm taking it, rules or no rules, and if word of this infraction gets back to Ted, I'll just say I thought it would be rude to refuse. Not to worry, though. She's just watching that I don't leave out some stray square inch, and when I rise painfully to my feet again, blinking through the sweat, she says, "Could you just scrub the floor in the entryway while you're at it?"[2]

Ehrenreich's description of humiliation in this story suggests that we struggle as a nation to offer mercy, respect, and value to our own people who serve or work for us.

2. Ehrenreich, *Nickel and Dimed*, 83.

Not only did Jesus call his disciples to persistence as a value in his empire, but in this text he called them to offer mercy to others. In addition, disciples of Jesus do not humiliate others. Those who are vulnerable in society represent empire values. Humiliation is a key characteristic among those in the empire of Jesus. This was also represented in the story immediately following the tax collector and Pharisee. While most commentaries suggest that Jesus and the children indicate that disciples should view the empire of God through the eyes of innocent children, the story also addressed humiliation (18:15–17).[3]

In the ancient world children represented marginalized populations. Adult males, especially rabbis, did not spend time with or even touch/hold children. The disciples assumed that those bringing children were dishonoring Jesus. However, Jesus suggested that how disciples treated children (the humiliated/vulnerable) reflected their place in the empire of God. Instead of suggesting that disciples act like children he called them to act on behalf of them.

Humiliation is a value in the empire of Jesus, suggesting that those who are victims and vulnerable in society represent the heart of Jesus and are a group from whom God protects. The God of the exiles who protected and embraced the humiliated people of Judea continued in the way of Jesus, who called disciples to protect and embrace the marginalized of society.

Compassion

Jesus moved closer to Jerusalem in this next story. I find it interesting that in this text Jesus was not leading the group of followers/disciples. Luke 18:39 suggested that the group was leading the journey and had no time to stop to help this blind man (remember, he was part of the group whom Jesus came to set free—Luke 4:18–19). How easy it must have been to rush Jesus through this town in order to get him to the cross. How easy it must be for the church today to ignore the true mission because we assume his purpose was only to die on the cross for *our* sins.

> As he was nearing Jericho, a certain blind man sat beside the road spanging. Hearing the crowd walk through he asked who it was. They said that Jesus of Nazareth was passing by. He cried out, "Jesus Son of David, have mercy on me." Those leading the way rebuked him to be silent but even more he cried out, "Son of David, have mercy on me." Jesus stood there and called for him to be brought. Getting closer, he asked him, "What do you want

---

3. Clark, "Kingdoms, Kids, and Kindness," 235–48.

> me to do for you?" The man said, "Lord, I want to see." Jesus said to him, "Get up, your faith has saved you." Immediately he could see and followed him giving glory to God. All the people who saw this also gave glory to God. (Luke 18:35-43)

Jesus halted the fast moving mob and asked them to "lead him to me." Disciples were not called to neglect the mission of Jesus or become confused concerning their purpose. However, in this story it seemed that his disciples were rushing him through Jericho. Is it possible that they were rushing him to his death in Jerusalem? Much of Christianity has been focused on the death of Jesus (our symbol has been a cross for centuries). Sometimes we have done this to the neglect of the resurrection. However, as we will read in Acts, Luke heavily emphasized the resurrection over the death and crucifixion of Jesus.

> As the lightning flashes and lights up the sky from one side to the other, so will the Son of Man be in his day. But first he must suffer many things and be rejected by this generation. (Luke 17:24-25)

> He told the twelve this parable, "I am going up to Jerusalem and all that has been written by the prophets about the Son of Man will be completed. He will be handed over to the Gentiles, humiliated, mistreated, spit upon, flogged, killed, and on the third day raised to life." They did not understand this because it was hidden from them and they did not know what to say. (Luke 18:31-34)

As Jesus fulfilled his mission by giving sight to the blind man, the man followed him and gave glory to God, as well as the observant crowd. The church has been called to bring glory and praise to God, not just in words but by our actions—fulfilling the mission of Jesus. In the story of the blind man the disciples almost missed an opportunity to offer compassion to a man seeking Jesus.

> By making Christ seem otherworldly, even ethereal, the church has inadvertently put him out of reach to us as an example or a guide. Even though Jesus routinely called people to follow him, the church has often represented this following in purely metaphysical or mystical terms. We can follow Jesus "in our heart" but not necessarily with our actions. Even after the phenomenally successful What Would Jesus Do campaign, in which Christians were encouraged to ask themselves this question before every action, it seemed that Christians were more interested in

asking the question than in doing what Jesus would do. We have sanitized and tamed Jesus by encasing him in abstract theology, and in doing so we have removed our motivation for discipleship. When Jesus is just true light of true light, and not flesh and blood, we are only ever called to adore him, not follow him.[4]

To follow Jesus suggests that we be led by him rather than leading him past those who need his attention and compassion.

Forgiveness

He entered Jericho and was passing through. A man named Zaccheus, who was a rich chief tax collector, sought to see Jesus but was not able, because of the crowd and because he was short. He ran in front of the group and climbed a fig tree in order to see him, since he was about to pass by. When he came to that place Jesus looked up and said, "Zaccheus, hurry down, it is necessary that I stay at your home today." He quickly came down and eagerly welcomed him. People grumbled seeing this saying that this man goes into the home of a sinner, who is lost. But Zacchaeus stood and said to the Lord, "Hey, I give one-half of my possessions to the poor. If I have harassed/defrauded anyone I give back four times the amount." Jesus said to him, "Today salvation is in this house, since he is a son of Abraham. The Son of Man came to seek and to save the lost." (Luke 19:1–10)

Physiognomy was an ancient practice of judging one's spirituality or relationship to the gods based on a person's physical appearance.[5] The ancient world viewed the sick, malformed, and crippled as either punished by the divine ones or as being evil. Stature was also a characteristic of one's morality. "Throughout history it has been commonplace to associate outer physical characteristics with inner qualities; it was assumed that you can, as it were, judge a book by its cover.[6] Zaccheus was short and a chief tax collector. If tax collectors were separate from sinners, then this man, as their boss, would have been viewed as especially corrupt.

However the story, as has been common to Luke, took a twist. In contrast to the cautious stinginess of the Torah-following rich ruler (18:16), the unrighteous tax collector supervisor willingly offered to pay back twice the required amount to those he may have wronged as well as half of his goods

---

4. Frost and Hirsch, *ReJesus*, 19.
5. Parsons, *Body and Character in Luke and Acts*, 17.
6. Ibid., 12.

to the poor. We don't know if Zaccheus suggested that "if I have wronged people I would pay . . ." meaning that he claimed to be innocent, or that he was volunteering restitution. The point Luke seems to make was that this man understood repentance and social justice more than the rich young ruler. In addition to this, Jesus willingly invited himself to Zaccheus's home, as opposed to the disciples rushing him past the blind man. This text challenged the disciples to both embrace sinners—"he has gone to be a guest of a sinner . . ."—and demonstrated that the empire of Jesus had valued compassion and repentance. Those who repented received grace, mercy, and salvation.

Risk

> Then he added this parable as he was near Jerusalem, because some thought that the empire of God was going to appear. He said, "A certain noble man went to a country far away to receive his authority to rule then return home. He called his twelve slaves and gave them ten coins and said to them, 'Do business with this until I come.' But the citizens hated him and sent an embassy saying, 'We don't want him to rule us.' In time he returned having received the authority to rule and said, 'Call out the servants, whom I gave the money so I might find out how they did with the money. The first [servant] appeared saying, 'Master your one coin has grown to ten coins.' He said, 'Great job, you are a good servant and have been faithful in a little. I will give you authority over ten cities.' The second one came and said, 'Master, your coin has made five coins.' He said, 'You will be over five cities.' The other said, 'Master, your coin was put in a cloth and buried. I was afraid since you are a strict person, taking what you did not put down and reaping what you did not plant.' He said, 'Your own mouth has condemned you, evil servant. You knew I was a severe man, taking what I did not place down and reaping what I did not plant. You should have given my money to the tables to grow when I returned.' He said to those standing by, 'Take the one coin and give it to the one with ten.' Someone said, 'Lord, he already has ten!' I tell you, everyone who has will be taken away and those who do not have will be taken away. But those enemies, who did not want me to rule, go and slaughter them before me." (Luke 19:11–27)

The final empire value for Luke's call to discipleship involved risk. This parable of the coins also occurred in Matthew's Gospel (Matt 25:14–30). In

Matthew's account the servants were given various amounts of his property and entrusted with them. The servants were told to take care of his property. The story also occurred after Jesus spoke against the temple, while he was in Jerusalem, and along with two other parables discussing faithfulness before the crucifixion. In Matthew this parable called the disciples to faithfulness.

In Luke's account, Jesus told this parable on his way to Jerusalem while people thought the empire would appear quickly. This story also involved a man in a royal family (an heir to become ruler) who traveled to receive his right to rule the city. Luke's account would have been very familiar to the ancient reader. First, *the story seemed to reflect the Jewish story concerning Herod Antipater and his journey to Rome to be appointed king over Jerusalem, by Augustus.* As he returned those living in Jerusalem rebelled against his authority. Herod had the people destroyed and took control of the kingdom. While the master in the parable became ruthless the issue was not whether or not God was cruel, but the emphasis suggested that God required loyalty from disciples and followers.

Second, *the three servants were each given a coin and told to "do business with it."* They were also expected to put the money to work among the people of the city who were against the noble man. Unlike Matthew's account, these men were told to put the money to work in a hostile environment. The servants were expected to be faithful with what their master gave them, regardless of their location and environment.

Finally, *two of the servants invested their coins at tremendous risk.* To grow from one to ten, or one to five, in such a short time required a high interest investment. While we don't know if they were gambling it is clear that the growth of this money took risk, faith, and courage. They were rewarded for taking this risk with the man's money. However, the servant who hid his coin was playing it safe. He did not take a risk, did not display faith, and did not manifest courage. He was judged not because he only had one coin, but because he admitted (with his own lips) that his master expected a return on the investment. While the punishment of the servant seems contrary to God's grace, the point of the parable was that disciples were called to risk through faith, rather than play it safe.

This is such an important value in the empire of Jesus. Persistence/faith, humiliation, mercy, compassion, repentance, and risk are qualities of discipleship. Jesus risked everything to journey to Jerusalem. Jesus called disciples to likewise risk their lives to follow him. However, today disciples struggle to embrace this risk for the kingdom.

One Sunday afternoon my middle son Hunter and I were lying out in the sun, in our yard. I asked him about the lesson he had in the kids Sunday worship class and he told me it was from Luke, about the guys given the coins. This ten-year-old boy enjoys Bible stories but had trouble understanding this one. I shared with him that the story involved taking risks for Jesus. I asked him if he remembered when Lori and I left the large congregation where I preached to start a new church. We talked about the nine months we spent building a team in our living room, the launch of the new church, the many baptisms we had seen, the new people who came to us from the streets, and young people ready to quit church altogether. We talked about the many people who had been in our home for small group, meals, or just to visit. We talked about the new churches, AS IS Church and the Agape Rockwood Campus, that were begun a few months before. I asked him about many of the ministries in which he and his brothers accompanied us as we reached out to people in town or from other countries. Risk requires faith, forgiveness, mercy, compassion, and courage.

After a few minutes I mentioned that it was a big risk for mom and I to leave a stable preaching job, with security and financial support, to start something new. He said that it was a big risk. Then I asked, "So if we would not have taken this risk who would we have never met?" Hunter began to name people who we loved and cared for at Agape, the other churches, and who we met on the streets. It became clear to not only Hunter, but me as well, that while taking risks for Jesus takes faith, it also brings tremendous rewards. "I understand the parable now," Hunter said.

The journey next focused on Jerusalem. In ancient literary journeys the heroes met monsters, gods, and evil beings. They conquered lands and battled their foes on the way home. When returning home they were celebrated as heroes, gods, and honorable men.

Luke described the journey of Jesus as one that encountered those on the margins of society. However, these people joined the movement and added to the growing band of brothers and sisters.

In addition to this, when Jesus returned home, he did not receive a hero's welcome.

SECTION 4
The Long Journey Home

11

Jesus Comes Home

Luke 19:28—21:38

> It is understandable, therefore, that after the theme of Jesus' journey to the city is reiterated in the central section . . . his coming to the city must be viewed as climactic.[1]

THIS FINAL SECTION OF Luke's Gospel describes the homecoming Jesus faced as he journeyed to Jerusalem. This city was considered the city of God, city of the Great King, Zion, and the place where Yahweh lived. From the day that King Solomon built a temple or house for God, it was believed that Yahweh lived in that city.

> When the priests came out of the Holy Place, a cloud filled the house of Yahweh. The priests could not stand to do ministry because of the cloud, for the glory/honor of Yahweh filled the house/temple. (1 Kgs 8:10–12)

Even though God was in the heavens and was not confined to a building, tent, or body, Jerusalem claimed to be Yahweh's city. Even more Yahweh claimed that Jerusalem was to be devoted to God. In the years when foreign nations, including the northern tribes of Israel, attacked Jerusalem, Yahweh promised to protect it—if it stayed loyal to it covenant relationship with God.

Through time God's people turned to other gods, oppressed the poor, and became guilty of injustice and immorality. Jerusalem became the seat of this controversy. Therefore, Yahweh allowed the Babylonian king

---

1. Kinmen, "Parousia, Jesus,'" 279.

Nebuchadnezzar to destroy the city, including Yahweh's house. However, throughout the exilic prophets Yahweh promised to return the people home so that they could rebuild their city and God's house. Over four hundred years God continually threatened to return to the city and confront people for their corruption, or promised to visit those who sought their Lord with their heart.

WELCOME HOME, JESUS

As Jesus prepared to enter his city he sent some of the disciples to obtain a young donkey. Riding into the city on a donkey rather than a horse was a sign that Jerusalem was to become free. As mentioned earlier, Simon Maccabaeus entered the city almost two hundred years previously to promise freedom to this enslaved community. The kings Soloman and Jehu also entered Jerusalem with a royal welcome (1 Kgs 1:33; 2 Kgs 9:13). This time, Jesus did not enter after a victorious battle overthrowing the powerful colonizer. Jesus entered having freed the marginalized masses of sickness, sin, and hopelessness. Luke 19:37–40 records Jesus crossing the Mount of Olives (where one can view the east gate of the temple) to fulfill the common belief that the Messiah would enter from the East.[2]

> As he was drawing near—already on the way down the Mount of Olives—the crowd of his disciples began to rejoice and praise God with a loud voice for all the mighty works that they had seen, saying "Blessed is the emperor who comes in the Lord's name. *Shalom* in heaven and glory in the highest." Some of the Pharisees in the crowd said to him, "Teacher, rebuke your disciples." He answered, "I tell you, if these were quiet, the stones would scream this as well." (Luke 19:37–40)

If one were present during this scene it would seem logical that the Pharisees were anxious. First, it was their responsibility to keep crowds under control. Second, if the crowd was proclaiming Jesus to be emperor/Caesar on the hill overlooking the temple, the Roman detachment near the temple would hear this and become involved. Finally, this would also be an act of blasphemy, since the Messiah was viewed to be God or divine. This eruption of praise, treason, and blasphemy from the crowd was too much for the Pharisees to handle.

However, Jesus accepted the welcoming committee and their offer of praise to him. They were welcoming him as any city should by sending

---

2. Malina and Pilch, *Social-Science Commentary*, 24.

people to praise and honor Jesus as king. However, ancient Near Eastern customs required the city leaders to welcome the king first, followed by the people. This scene not only violated ancient codes of conduct but again displayed a reversal—the marginalized welcomed Jesus more than the elite.[3] In addition to this Jesus made it clear that praise was natural. All creation praises the creator (notice that Jesus here accepts this role of creator) and naturally responds to God. People are no different, especially the marginalized masses in front of him.

Luke differs from the other Gospel writers (Matt 21:6–9; Mark 11:4–10) in that he focuses more on the road and the trip along the Mount of Olives. He also adds "Peace in heaven and glory . . ." to the praise of the people. This recalls the statement the angels made to the shepherds (Luke 2:8–9), as if Jesus were a Roman Emperor entering a city after a victorious battle.

Creating a Safe and Sacred Space

> When he drew near and saw the city, he cried, saying, "If you knew that on this day you had the things that made *shalom*. But now they are hidden from you. The days will come when your enemies will fence you in, surround you, set up a siege, hem you in on every side, and tear you and your children apart. They will not leave one stone standing, because you did not know the time you were visited [by me/God]." He then entered the temple and began to drive out the merchants, saying to them, "The scripture says, 'My house shall be a house of prayer,' but you have made it a robbers' den/hideout." (Luke 19:41–46)

While the crowd gave Jesus a glorious welcome, and the Pharisees resisted praising their emperor, Jesus showed that he had not come to make a friendly visit. While in the prophets and Hebrew Bible the term for "visit," "discipline," and "look after" were similar to each other (*pqd*—notice that the Greek term of this is a term we translate *bishop* or *overseer*) the thought of Yahweh visiting the people had a sense of urgency and judgment. Yahweh claimed to visit the nation of Israel in judgment through terms very common in apocalyptic literature. Apocalyptic literature is a genre of writing that possibly developed in the schools where prophets and wisdom scholars wrote and produced their teachings for other scholars. Apocalyptic literature used symbols, pictures, and wild images to impress upon the reader that evil was active but would be confronted by the gods and their angels/messengers.

---

3. Kinmen, "Parousia, Jesus," 281–84.

The stories were not meant to be literal (no more than many of our songs, poetry, or figures of speech are meant to be taken literally) but were powerful forms of communication for an oral audience envisioning the story and application of the message. Typically, in apocalyptic literature when a god visited people, the god usually did so by riding a cloud/chariot and coming with anger and violence. Those who were privy to evil would face the wrath of the god or divine messenger. Those who were victims would see this "coming" or visitation as a time of redemption. In the Hebrew Bible these are referred to as the *Day of Yahweh, Great and Terrible Day, Coming of Yahweh*, or *God's Divine Visitation*.[4] In many cases this divine visitation was heightened by describing cataclysmic events such as stars falling, skies changing color, the sun and moon becoming dark, and earthquakes and storms occurring. These were terms meant to describe a terrible visit from a god. It would almost be similar to when our parents claimed, "When I come up there I am going to be fuming . . ." We all knew it wasn't literal but it did communicate that mom or dad was mad, so we better behave.

For Luke the scene is much different. The divine visitation of God/Jesus was a time of celebration for those marginalized in their communities. However, for those who were guilty, it was a time of violence and anger. This became clear as Jesus entered the temple. Instead of worshiping and enjoying praise with his disciples, he cleaned out those defiling God's house (or his house). He also quoted Jeremiah (a text used when Jeremiah confronted the leaders at the temple before the exile) and suggested that the temple was to be a place of prayer. Why was Jesus angry? The temple or house of God was to be a place of prayer, teaching, worship, and safety. Unfortunately it had become a place where merchants charged money so that others could purchase items to sacrifice for worship. It is also possible that those from the marketplace had spilled over into the portico of the Gentiles (since Gentiles weren't really welcome into the Jewish faith at that time) during this crowded Passover time of year. This would have prevented the Gentiles from seeking Yahweh or having space to worship. Jesus felt that God's house was once again corrupted and that those who needed to worship were hindered. Even more, the story was a challenge to the religious leaders who should have made certain that the temple was a safe place for people.

The final two verses of this section remind the reader of Jesus's presence in the temple when he was twelve. Once again God was in the holy place teaching people. Luke suggested that the people "hung on Jesus's words." However the chief priests, teachers, and leaders were convicted,

---

4. Clark, *The God of Second Chances*, 90–92.

and they did what they had always done to God's messengers. They tried to silence them by murdering them.

Jesus had come home, but unfortunately his home was not safe, neither was it sacred. People could not offer praise and worship to God because of the corruption and injustice not at the hands of the Romans, but the hands of God's own leaders. While the religious leaders, zealots, and other leaders may have blamed the Roman presence for their problems, the Romans did not prevent people from serving God. The leaders had. Once again Jerusalem had become a blemish on the pure canvas of God's creation. Once again the city of the great king had become the emperor's toilet.

Home Is Where the Heart Is/Was

Jesus then began to "clean house." If the city was corrupt, it would be time for God to take out the trash, sweep the floors, and remodel what the termites had eaten. However, it would take more than sweeping and remodeling. To create a safe and sacred space would require a major overhaul and demand that some people be evicted. Imagine the disciples' reactions during these days. These would have been long days filled with teaching, conflict, and arguments. Tensions would have been high. Crowds cheered, hissed, and some would have been silent as if to say, "I can't believe he said that and got away with it."

One can almost feel the tension as the religious leaders tested Jesus, questioned his authority, and asked him question followed by question. Jesus was disrupting the perceived *shalom* and safety of the city. No one else had a problem with life the way it was. Rome was happy, Pilate was happy, Herod was happy, so why wouldn't God be happy? Yet every time Jesus taught, spoke, or acted, a crowd would have erupted with joy and loud noises. It was one thing to do this in small Galilean towns; it was another thing to come to the big city and start changing the way things have always been done.

> A man planted a vineyard, hired farmers, and went away for a while. At the time of harvest he sent his slaves to the farmers to receive fruit from the vineyard, but the farmers beat him, and sent him away empty. Again he sent another slave, but they badly beat him, dishonored him, and sent him away empty-handed. He sent a third one and they abused him and cast him out. The master said, "What will I do? I will send my loved son because they will respect him." But when the farmers saw him they discussed among themselves, saying, "This is the heir, let's

> kill him so we can get the vineyard." They threw him out of the vineyard and killed him. What will the master of the vineyard do? He will take it from the farmers and give it to others to farm. When they heard this they said, "No way!" He looked at them and said, "It is written, the stone rejected by the construction workers became the main corner stone, and everything falling on it is smashed as it smashes what it falls upon." (Luke 20:9-18)

In this story Jesus didn't speak in apocalyptic language, nor did he mince words. He was plain and to the point. Luke wrote the story very similar to Matthew and Mark and emphasized the sending of many other prophets and messengers. However, Luke had the owner of the vineyard talk to himself (he is the only good guy in Luke to talk to himself) and convinced himself to send his son. Luke also had Jesus speak directly to the Pharisees and apply to parable to them. There was no mistaking the message of this story. The leaders of Jerusalem were opposed to God, God's love, and Jesus, just as they had been for years. The Incarnation is not a story of God becoming more loving by sending the son. The Incarnation was what it always has been: God reaching out to people—only in Jesus, God personally showed up. Jerusalem would fall and while it brought sadness to God, it would have to be done.

Sometimes in order to create safe and sacred spaces, one has to clean out the evil. I can think over the years at Agape we have had to ask a few people to leave our church. In the past when I worked at traditional churches we seemed to work hard to keep people (which ended up being a time to keep them happy) in our church and put up with a lot of negativity. While it was a struggle we felt that it was supposed to be done, or at least we called it "God's way." We also called it "shutting the back door." We were convinced that people would easily leave and it was our job to keep them in our church.

After planting Agape I became exposed to the view that we needed to keep the back door open. One church planter said that every body has to get rid of waste, otherwise the body becomes toxic. I have begun to realize that these illustrations are true. There have been abusive and controlling males who have not respected our desire to create a safe and sacred community at Agape. We have had to not only confront them but ask them to leave. There have been some males and females who in themselves were quite toxic and felt compelled to infect others, especially those trying to become healthy. There have also been people in prostitution who have thought our gathering was a place to connect sexually. Some have come to our worship intoxicated and carrying a bad attitude. In all of these cases we have had to state that

Agape is a safe place for people, including them. We have had to also state that before a place can become sacred it must be safe.

Some have left and chosen not to come back. Others have fought us but eventually left. Most have agreed and stayed to work things out. Even more, many who were vulnerable and stayed have told us that they feel safe at Agape. However, as leaders we know that creating a safe and sacred space as a church means that sometimes we have to clean the temple, meet with the vineyard owners to require fruit, or offer safety for those on the margins of society. Leaders who become self-centered and self-focused have a difficult time providing a sacred place, because they are not willing to do the hard work of opening the door and letting the toxicities escape.

CONTROL

God did not cause the vineyard to become unfruitful. As mentioned in Luke 13 with the unfruitful tree, Jesus's desire has always been for the children to show the world, through obedience and imitation of their father, that God is good. Jesus proved to be a faithful son by his obedience and love. Jesus offered us an example of what it means to be the child of a loving and compassionate God. However, those who rented the vineyard from their master did not display this obedience.

We live in a high crime area of Portland. Our area is full of apartment complexes and has high rates of transitory occupants. We many times watch families occupy rental homes in our neighborhood. Those who care for the house, property, and neighborhood are a blessing to us as well as the owner. However, those who do not become a problem to the neighbors. Then the house becomes dirty, the grass grows tall, the lawn becomes cluttered with trash, and the occupants violate noise ordinances. Everyone is affected. The owner receives complaints from neighbors, the police, and other businesses. Property values decrease. Sometimes neighbors are threatened or retaliated against by the renters. It becomes a miserable situation, but one that happens often. However, when the occupants are evicted the neighborhood becomes peaceful, the landlords gains control of their property, and the process of rebuilding relationships continues. Fear and anxiety abates and peace/*shalom* is restored.

I find it interesting that in my many years of observing this situation I have not met a neighbor who feels sad for the evicted family. This may seem cruel to some but those affected by destructive behavior feel that the owners are well within their rights to expect their property to be treated well. I have heard the tenants, upon their departure, express their dissatisfaction with their treatment and the fact that they were never given a fair chance. They call us all "judgmental" and "nosy neighbors." Their flagrant disrespect for all involved, including their landlord, who had to spend six months battling to get them to pay their rent (which they typically stop sending) and finally evicted, is surprising. It is as if they have no responsibility to be honorable in their behavior. However, the point still remains—one should always treat another person's property with respect and value.

The same was true with the owner of the vineyard. He deserved to have his offer of good will treated better than it was. The tenants not only affected the owner's vineyard, they injured the servants and son of the owner. God was not glorified through their actions and behavior.

First, the tenants misused the owner's gesture of good will through control. They were unwilling to share the fruit, as would have been expected. Like the leaders of Judah in the prophets, these corrupt leaders decided to control the fruit and other people.

Second, the tenants displayed a resistance to God. The owner represented God and the tenants the leaders of Judea. The Jews were the children of God. The leaders were God's servants who were entrusted with the nation to help it grow and bring glory to God. However, these leaders refused to empower people. As in the past, the leaders had become controlling and fear-based in that they refused to honor God by practicing honesty and integrity, thereby producing *shalom*.

Finally, these tenants/leaders destroyed the sacred space that needed to be shared with God's people. Even worse, they decided to kill the son of the owner. While this seems extreme, Luke suggests that this was the typical behavior of corrupt people in the empire of Jesus. Due to their controlling behavior and greed, they destroyed a place that was to provide safety and peace for God's people. These religious leaders had developed an illusion of power, control, and fear.

> In the hearing of all the people he said to his disciples, "Beware the scribes, who like to walk around in long robes, love greetings in the marketplaces, the best seats in the synagogues, places of honor at feasts, who devour widows' houses, and enjoy making long prayers. They will receive the greater condemnation." (Luke 20:45–47)

For Luke, it was important to flush out the hidden behaviors of the religious leaders of Jesus's day. It might have been convenient for Luke's audience to empathize with the religious leaders as they were in a position of authority, privilege, and power. However, Luke needed the privileged readers to know that with responsibility came the power and expectation to help people.

Often, if we are in the same social class as other leaders we might feel that they are misrepresented and misunderstood. We call this collusion.

When people in power abuse their authority those who are victims, and those who have been victims, feel a sense of anger and injustice, and are many times retraumatized. There is a sense of healing and peace when justice is enacted, even if it seems violent or hyper-violent. While this is a dangerous place to be it is understandable why so many times victims cheer when a bully, corrupt politician, or abusive parent is convicted. Unfortunately, it is also common that those who are in power feel that a mob mentality, cruel and unusual forms of punishment, or hasty response may be unjust. Too often when I present research on men's violence against women, clergy abuse, or child abuse I am reminded (almost always by males) that there also exist false allegations by victims. In addition I am reminded that the Gospel requires grace and we should not rejoice in the punishment of perpetrators. While I understand that vengeance, vigilantism, and revenge can create their own forms of injustice, the Gospels clearly suggest that the religious leaders were receiving what they deserved and that God had been victimized.

Luke was clear in these stories. Corrupt leadership not only angers God, it is not a behavior that is to be accepted among the disciples. In addition to this Jesus's message was that corruption in leadership happens because people seek their own needs rather than God's and the needs of others. Just as the tenants in our neighborhood affect the owner's home and those homes around them, so corrupt leadership affects a community.

THERE GOES THE NEIGHBORHOOD

Stone Walls Do Not Make a Home

Jesus, as did the prophets of old, stood at the temple and presented a negative sermon that suggested God would judge the holy place. The Jerusalem temple was a magnificent structure that was built with extremely large stones, all tightly packed together. While Solomon's temple was originally glorious, the rebuilt temple (after the Jews returned from Babylon) would not have been as wondrous. Because of this Herod Antipater, who was well known for building Jewish structures in the Roman style of large buildings that presented an image of power, reconstructed the temple to make it more beautiful.[5] Standing at the temple and looking up, would have brought a powerful sense of awe in the structure and the presence of God and holiness.

5. Netzer, *The Architecture of Herod the Great Builder*, 304.

> Certain people commented that the temple was adorned with beautiful stones and offerings, but he said, "Concerning these things, the days will come when they will be thrown down and not stand." They asked him, "Teacher, when will these things happen and what will be the sign when they are about to take place?" (Luke 21:5–7)

Imagine standing next to the Twin Towers in New York City, September 10, 2001. It would have been an amazing sight. To gaze at the marble, stone, metal, and glass would have created a sense of awe. Now imagine someone saying, "Do you see all of this? Tomorrow it will be a large pile of rubble." What would be your response? If you were someone from the first century you would not be familiar with explosions, bombs, or even airplanes. Your only thought would be that something divine or catastrophic would have to happen for these buildings to come crashing to the earth.

The disciples would have had the same reaction that we would. Matthew had the disciples suggest that this implied that the end of the world (Matt 24:3) or the coming (judgment) of Jesus/God. Mark, as with Luke, had the disciples ask Jesus in private when this would happen (Mark 13:3–4). The response of the disciples would be similar to any one of us standing in New York City, "When will this horrible event happen?" Notice that in Luke, the disciples' question did not involve the end of time, the final days, or the rapture to heaven. The question simply was in reference to Jesus's claiming that the temple would be destroyed. It had happened once by the Babylonians and it would happen again through the Romans.

Suffering Inside and Out

Why would the temple be destroyed? This question had been in the back of the mind of Luke's original reader. Scholars suggest that Luke's Gospel was written after the destruction of the Jerusalem temple (70 CE), indicating that the reader was already aware of this fact. Questions would arise in the reader's mind since Luke held a high regard for Jesus and the Torah. Yet his journey to Jerusalem began to flush out the true corruption and dishonesty that existed among God's leaders. Luke shared with the reader that the Pharisees were corrupt, dishonest, greedy, oppressive, driven by fear/anxiety, and losing honor in their communities. The people, who obviously knew their leaders were corrupt, were finally glorifying God because Jesus brought to light what the people already knew.

Even more, the leaders' corruption not only ruined their relationship with their God (the landlord), it destroyed their neighborhood, community, and relationship with people. Spiritually, the temple became an eyesore. While the stones were beautiful they could not hide the spiritual graffiti, yard damage, and structural corruption that ate away at the condition of God's house. Property values were decreasing in the city of Jerusalem and Roman gangs were moving into the neighborhood harassing and oppressing whoever they wanted. Those who spoke out, those who called the police, and those who reported the leaders to the neighborhood association would pay the price.

> But before all this they will put their hands on you and persecute you, delivering you up to the synagogues and prisons. You will be brought before emperors/rulers and governors for my name's sake. This will be your opportunity to witness to me. Don't meditate beforehand how to answer; I will give you a mouth/words and wisdom, which none of your adversaries will be able to withstand or contradict. You will be delivered up by parents, brother [and sisters], relatives, and friends, and they will kill some of you. You will be hated by all because of me. But not a hair of your head will be destroyed. By endurance you will gain your lives. (Luke 21:12-19)

The only way that the neighborhood would experience *shalom* would be if neighbors spoke up. Their houses would be tagged, their car tires slashed, and their kids harassed—but Jesus called them to clean up their spiritual neighborhoods. For Luke's audience a level of comfort was being challenged. Instead of seeking to move up the social scale the call of Jesus was to do the right thing. It may take a village to raise a child but it takes villagers to clean up the block and reclaim a neighborhood. Jesus promised that if they stood together and stayed in the neighborhood, property values would again thrive.

Divine Punishment/Jesus is Yahweh

> But when you see Jerusalem surrounded by armies, know that its desolation is near. Then let those who are in Judea flee to the mountains, and let those who are inside the city leave, and let those in the country not come back, because these are days of vengeance, to fulfill all that is written. (21:20-22)

Often this text and those in the other Gospels (Luke 21:5-38, Matt 24; Mark 13) are used to discuss the end of the world, the rapture, or the last days. While I do not have time to explain these views more fully, it is important to remember that the text is in response to the disciples' questions concerning the destruction of the Jewish temple (which occurred within a generation of their questions). In Matthew's and Mark's accounts the sign of the destruction was described as "the abomination of desolation," referring to Daniel's account (Matt 24:15; Mark 13:14; Dan 9:27) of the desecration of the temple by the Greek king Antiochus Epiphanus IV about 150 years before Jesus. However, Luke was clearer in that he used a term that would be understood by Gentiles, especially after the destruction had already happened. Luke wrote that Jerusalem would be surrounded by armies (70 C. E.) and the temple destroyed, and this was a sign that Jesus, who was Yahweh God, had judged Jerusalem. As the owner of the vineyard came to wipe out the corrupt tenants, so Jesus would come again to his home, this time in vengeance.

For Jesus the destruction of Jerusalem was not simply an act of the Roman Empire, it was ordained and supported by God/Jesus. As in the Hebrew Bible, God sent faithful leaders to Jerusalem and claimed to ordain and be present in their judgment on the city. The corrupt tenants in Jerusalem were being punished and expelled from the premises. Luke reminded the reader that God's new empire was transitioning from Jerusalem to the followers of Jesus. "When you see these things taking place, you know that the empire of God is near. Truly, I say to you, this generation will not pass away until all has taken place" (21:31–32). This transition would create a sense of hopelessness. With the destruction of the temple and the city of Jerusalem the neighborhood would spiritually have *shalom*, but there would be a sense of homelessness for residents. This would happen within one generation (forty years) from when Jesus spoke (33 C.E.). It happened by 70 C.E..

WHERE IS OUR HOME? JESUS AMONG THE HOMELESS

With the destruction of Jerusalem and the temple, a new neighborhood was formed. This neighborhood was not covered in precious stones, jewels, finished wood, or fancy linens. This neighborhood was a community of people who followed Jesus/God as refugees, exiles, and nomads. As Jesus redefined family in Luke 8:19–21 as those who heard and did God's word, so he redefined God's city, neighborhood, and community as those who embraced his teachings.

> The teachers of the law and the chief priests looked for a way to arrest him immediately, because they knew that he had spoken this parable against them, but they were afraid of the people. (Luke 20:19)

> Some of the teachers of the law responded, "Well said teacher!" No one dared to ask him any more questions. (Luke 20:39–40)
>
> Every day he was teaching in the temple, but at night he went out and lodged on the mount called Olivet. The people came early in the morning to the temple to listen to him. (Luke 21:37–38)
>
> He was teaching daily in the temple. The chief priests and the scribes and the prominent men of the people were seeking to destroy him, but they did not find anything they could do, for the people hung on his words. (Luke 19:47–48)

The neighborhood was changing because it had a new resident/leader. While God had always been present, Jesus came home and sought fruit from his vineyard, his house, and his community. Those who had rented his property decided to abuse their neighbors, not pay their rent, destroy the house, neglect their yards, and dishonor the owner. Through many citations, letters, and visits they were warned and threatened with expulsion. Unfortunately they did not believe that they were guilty of anything. Even as the Roman police entered their home with battering rams, tear gas, tazers, and a team of commandos, the house could not be salvaged. The neighborhood witnessed a massive bonfire and wondered—what now? Where will we live? Will our community ever be the same?

However, Luke shared that Jesus had come home. He also came to offer a vision for a new community, neighborhood, and home. This new home was not a house, condo, or apartment. Home and neighborhood were a community, a group of people who listened to Jesus, obeyed God, and treated neighbors with respect. This new neighborhood would become alive once the Spirit came upon the community and offered hope, courage, and peace. It would be a neighborhood with people who not only respected each other, but exposed those in darkness for who they were and created a community that was safe, supportive, and fruitful.

12

Jesus Is Evicted
Luke 22:1—23:56

A FINAL MEAL

Before Jesus faced the suffering and torture of the cross, as well as the stress of the final confrontation with the religious leaders, he decided to have a last meal with his followers. Luke often uses meals as a way to communicate key values in the empire of Jesus. He may have done this for various reasons. First, *in the ancient world writers often used the meal (or Symposium) as a backdrop for stories concerning the teachings of great philosophers.* Plato's *Symposium* is one example of a classical story involving Socrates and his friends who gathered at a meal and chose to abstain from drinking excessively (since they had done this at the meal before) so that they could engage in rational dialogue.[1] Typically *Symposia* were Greek and/or Roman meals, usually among the rich, where males gathered together and ate, discussed ideas, and enjoyed excesses both with food and sexual favors provided by male and female slaves. Prostitutes were a common presence at most Symposia, suggesting that "modest" females in the ancient world avoided eating in the presence of males. For Luke, meals were an opportunity to teach something profound concerning Jesus's teachings.

Second, *the meal was a very traditional event and involved strict etiquette concerning invitations, time of day, seating arrangements, order of food consumption, and those guests who were invited.* When we think of ancient

---

1. Plato, *Symposium*, 39.

meals it might be convenient to compare them to our traditional American Thanksgiving practices. In many cases each action involves a family or cultural tradition that is explained and passed down to each generation. For Luke, Jesus altered the important traditions of the ancient meal concerning guests, seating arrangements, who serves, and sexual purity. Luke used the meal scene as a non-traditional story concerning Jesus.

Third, *the meal scene in Luke 22:14–30 occurred during the Jewish Passover feast.* Typically this has become the model for communion, the last supper, or our Eucharist during worship services. We gather together, share a scripture and song, and either read this occurrence in the Synoptic Gospels or another verse discussing Jesus's death. Comparisons are made concerning the Passover lamb, sacrifice, and death of the Messiah. In my experiences I have found that the mood or moment is to be considered a somber or sad time. Sometimes it seems we are discouraged from entering the moment with joy, excitement, or celebration. We are being reminded of Jesus's suffering and are expected to reflect that to those around us.

I remember hearing many stories graphically displaying the suffering and pain of Jesus, as a reminder that the symbols (bread/cracker and juice/wine) were symbols of his death for us. We were able to go from a celebration worship song to a moment of guilt and sadness, all over juice and crackers. The tone was always that this was a Passover meal not a celebration.

However, it always amazed me that the early Church for centuries considered this communion meal the Eucharist (which is from the Greek word "Thanks"). Somehow this was not to be a moment of shame, or somberness, but joy.

> When the hour came, he reclined at table, and the apostles with him. He said to them, "I really want to eat this Passover with you before I suffer. I tell you I will not eat it until it is fulfilled in the kingdom of God." He took a cup, and when he had given thanks he said, "Take this, and divide it among you. I tell you that from now on I will not drink of the fruit of the vine until the empire of God comes." He took bread, and when he had given thanks, he broke it and gave it to them, saying, "This is my body, given for you. Do this in remembrance of me." Again he took the cup, after they had eaten, and said, "This cup is poured out for you. It is the new/renewed covenant in my blood. The hand of the one who betrays me/delivers me over is with me on this table. The Son of Man goes where it has been determined, but woe to that man who betrayed him." They began to question one another, which of them it could be who was going to do this. An argument also arose among them, as to which of them

was to be regarded as the greatest/best. He said to them, "The Gentile rulers exercise lordship/power over others, and those in authority are called benefactors. You don't do this. Instead, let the greatest/best among you become as the youngest, and the leader as one who ministers/attends. For who is greater, the one who reclines at table or the one who serves them? Is it not the one who reclines at table? But I am among you as the one who serves/ministers. You are those who have stayed with me in my trials, and I assign to you, as my Father assigned to me, an empire, that you may eat and drink at my table in my empire and sit on thrones judging the twelve tribes of Israel. (Luke 22:14–30)

Luke mentioned "two cups" during this meal. While this occurred during the Passover and it seemed likely that this took the form of a common *Symposium*, which would have involved dancing, music, and celebration. Except that this meal was Jesus style. In the *Symposium* the first cup signaled the main meal, while the second cup signaled the next stage of the meal. Sometimes this stage included excessive and violent behavior. At other times it was the stage of discussion, sharing, and prayers.

Stage One

In the first stage of this meal Luke seemed to summarize the key teachings of Jesus's ministry. First, *Jesus eagerly desired to share a meal with the disciples*, which is a comment unique to Luke. One might be reminded of Moses, Aaron, Nadab, Abihu, and the seventy elders eating in the presence of God after the commandment was ratified with the nation of Israel (Exod 24:8–11). God consistently throughout the Bible desired to connect with people and form an intimate relationship.

Second, *Jesus promised to eat with them again*. This would not be their last meal together and their journey would continue past Jerusalem. Jesus promised that they would again eat together in his empire.

Finally, *he gave them common elements, bread and wine, as reminders/symbols of his sacrifice*. Communion/breaking bread together was a common event in the early church, one that was practiced at least every Sunday. These common elements expressed the relationship God had with people, not in costly jewels or rich excessive meals, but in common food and drink. This first stage of the meal offered the disciples the reality that discipleship involved relationship, community, and symbols of forgiveness and grace.

Stage Two

The second cup introduced the *Symposium*, or the next stage of the meal. However, this stage would not involve drunkenness, sex, violence, and shameful behavior. This stage involved discussion, sharing, and conversation. These were also important concepts of discipleship. First, *Luke alone called the covenant "new covenant" and used the possessive "my blood."* While Matthew and Mark indicate that the blood of the covenant was symbolized by the cup of wine, Luke more directly associated this with the "new covenant" referred to by the prophets (Jer 31:31). When the temple of Jerusalem had been destroyed and the Jews were scattered throughout the land, the prophets promised a day when all people would return to Jerusalem and receive a new/renewed covenant. The first covenant had been violated by this nation. However, God offered a second chance. Jesus was again suggesting that the people who were once again spiritually scattered and marginalized would have a renewed/new covenant. Jesus was God's offer for a second chance, renewed covenant, and sacrifice. This would happen by his blood and sacrifice. Communion was not a symbol of forgiveness but a second chance and new relationship with God through Jesus. Discipleship involved embracing God's forgiveness and second chance at life. This was a costly relationship in that it came at the expense of Jesus's blood or life.

Second, *Jesus reminded them that the covenant could again be violated.* Someone was present who would betray God by turning against Jesus and the group. Luke's audience would remember that Judas was the one to betray Jesus. The problem was not only that he would betray him, but that he was eating with Jesus as well. The disciples were not aware of this individual (that's how sneaky Judas must have been) and thought they might be part of the plot. However, he was guilty and there would be no mercy for him. Discipleship involved choosing to do the right thing as a person who embraced the covenant of Jesus.

Finally, *Jesus warned the disciples concerning controlling behavior.* They had journeyed with Jesus and witnessed his confrontation of the leaders, their corruption, and their oppression of others. Jesus had challenged the disciples to be compassionate to those who were on the margins of society. During this discussion, Jesus reminded them that being a servant and caring for people would provide the manifestation of discipleship and ministry in the mission of Christ. Their Roman Caesars built the foundations of Rome and *Pax Romana* through patron/client relationships and offered good will at a price. However, the empire of Jesus was not to do this. Leaders were to be servants, and offer good will without conditions.

Stage Three

Communion today should be no different than Jesus's "Last Supper." Instead of focusing on the sacrifice, guilt, shame, and somberness of the moment, our churches have an opportunity to provide a *Symposium* atmosphere of Jesus's meal with the disciples. First, there should be celebration, joy, and a festive atmosphere—in the ancient world meals were like that. Second, the emphasis should be less on the emblems/symbols and more on the discussion. Communion opens opportunities to share ideas, confess struggles, and offer hope to those who come seeking a stronger relationship with God. At Agape I find that when we, as well as our church plants, offer smaller multiple communion stations/groups with leaders who start a discussion with a question, more people share, engage, and ask for prayer. Our homeless guests will have had something to eat from our breakfast team before entering worship, and they feel free to share in a smaller group.[2] Communion involves the invitation to join a community, share thoughts, and realize that covenant is not something I receive, it is something I embrace and support.

A FINAL PRAYER

After the meal Jesus and the disciples not only discussed discipleship, but Jesus was honest with them. Judas would not be the only one to turn on the group. Peter was singled out by Jesus, as well as Satan. Jesus told Peter, and the group, that Satan wanted to attack him, but he was praying for him, Notice that Jesus believed that Peter could succeed, however he, like all humans, was weak and struggled to know his purpose.

> He came out and went, as was his custom, to the Mount of Olives, and the disciples followed him. When he came to a place, he said to them, "Pray that you may not enter into temptation." He withdrew from them about as far as one can throw a rock, and fell down and prayed, saying, "Father, if you want, remove this cup from me. However, it is not to be what I want but you." There appeared to him an angel from heaven, strengthening him. Being in an agony he prayed more earnestly; and his sweat became like great drops of blood falling down to the ground. When he rose from prayer, he came to the disciples and found them sleeping because of their sorrow, and he said to them,

---

2. For more concerning communion, early Christian meals, and those attending church hungry, see Clark, *The Better Way*, 108–11.

"Why are you sleeping? Rise and pray that you may not enter into temptation." (Luke 22:39–46)

The disciples had joined Jesus on his final journey to prayer. They would not be able to accompany him any further, but they were with him in his final hours. It is interesting that Luke alone suggested that the disciples all followed Jesus. Three times Jesus asked them to pray to avoid the temptation to flee (Luke 22:32, 40, 46). While he was praying and agonizing with the prayer but they had fallen asleep. Luke indicated that they were tired due to grief/sorrow (22:45). They were not sleepy from the meal, the wine, or the late night, they were overwhelmed with sadness. All that Jesus had told them concerning his suffering, death, and crucifixion had become clearer to them. Judas had left them while their best friend was a few yards away (Luke alone wrote it was a stone's throw) in pain. Jesus's stress was so great that his sweat became drops of blood. The capillaries close to the skin around his skull had burst due to the stress and found an opening in his sweat glands.

Jesus, the friend of sinners, tax collectors, and common people was alone. He was truly by himself. He was not in peaceful bliss, solitude, or reflecting prayer. One can imagine the apostles sitting together hearing their best friend scream out in agony. Luke also wrote than an angel accompanied him to strengthen him. The angel did not rescue him, nor did it transport him to heaven. The angel wrestled with him in prayer and stood with him. One can almost imagine a similar scene in Daniel 9 where Michael the archangel wrestled with evil angels/demons, taking a stand with Yahweh in the battle with monsters from the deep. God and Satan have been fighting since Genesis 3, and angels have joined in that battle. In the Garden of Gethsemane the angel stood beside Jesus, fully awake, and fully aware of what would happen next.

For Luke's readers this would have been an odd scene. Angels typically came to the rescue in ancient literature. Gods and heroes who cried out were given answers, aid, special armor, or victory. Again, Luke has changed the story. The journey was not complete until the hero died, and this hero would die. The divine plan was not to escape but to face the end. If Jesus's friends were not fully present, the divine messengers would be.

Can We Blame Peter?

After Jesus was arrested the disciples fled. Luke's readers would not have been hard on the disciples—history has shown us all that good people falter at times. Even Jesus knew that this would happen. One of the most familiar stories of abandonment is that of the Apostle Peter.

When I was four or five years old I went to visit my grandparents in Lubbock, Texas. They lived in a normal neighborhood and when I would visit I would play with the kids along the block. In those days (1966) most of us could run the length of a block and feel safe. I spent a lot of time at Ramone's house. He was two years older than me and had many brothers and sisters. Because I had blond hair and blue eyes I stood out quite a bit in my grandparent's neighborhood.

One day Ramone and I were playing in his driveway. His parents left in their station wagon with a few of his brothers and sisters. We were playing in the yard when some boys from another block came and started calling him names that I had never heard before. I told them to shut up and they started throwing dirt clods (hard clumps of dirt/clay) at us.

The dirt clods stained the driveway and the boys eventually left. Ramone and I were sweeping the driveway when his parents came home in the station wagon. Ramone grabbed my broom and said, "Go home now." I said, "I want to help clean it up." He said, "No, you better go home now." I ran home to my grandmother's house. She gave me a Popsicle and I decided to go back to Ramone's house.

I was on the other side of the street walking toward his home. As I approached his house I heard a lot of yelling and screaming. The garage door was opened and I saw Ramone's dad standing there with a whip and yelling. Ramone was yelling back but he was afraid. The rest of the family was sitting quietly. The look of terror on all of their faces was clear to my four-year-old mind. I heard the whip crack and the screaming. It was unclear why Ramone was being punished, but the sounds were terrible. I ran back to my grandmother's house, my heart pounding, and my breathing heavy. My grandmother saw me coming and opened the door. "Get in here and don't go back out," she said. She grabbed me and hugged me. I never saw Ramone again.

I think of this story when I read the text involving Peter in the courtyard. Luke wrote that Jesus looked at Peter (Luke 22:61), indicating that the distance between the courtyard and the upper room of the high priest's house was not very far. Imagine Peter in the courtyard following Jesus. He would have heard screaming, yelling, slapping, punching, thuds, moans, cries, and other horrible sounds. Only a few hours earlier he heard his friend screaming in the garden, then while in the courtyard he would have heard his friend being abused at the hands of others. Just as my heart was racing at the screams and crack of the whip, so Peter's heart must have been racing at the suffering of his friend. We should not be too hard on Peter, at least he was in the midst of the battle.

While all the Gospel writers wrote that Peter followed at a distance, they also suggested that he was in the courtyard—close enough to see and hear what was happening (ancient homes didn't have glass windows). Luke indicated that he sat near a fire, stayed in the courtyard when questioned, and was able to see Jesus. Of course he denied Jesus three times. He was traumatized. He was confused. He was tested more than any of the other disciples. True, he failed. But while the other disciples were hiding and Judas was swinging from a tree, Peter was by the fire near his friend.

> Then they seized him and led him away, bringing him into the high priest's home. Peter followed at a distance. When they had kindled a fire in the middle of the courtyard and sat down together, Peter sat down among them. A servant girl saw him as he sat in the light and looked at him, and said, "This man also was with him." But he denied it, saying, "Woman, I do not know him." A little later someone else saw him and said, "You also are one of them." But Peter said, "Man, I am not." After about an hour another person said, "Certainly this man also was with him, for he s a Galilean." Peter said, "Man, I do not know what you are talking about." Immediately, while he was still speaking, the rooster crowed. The Lord turned and looked at Peter, and he remembered that the Lord had said, "Before the rooster crows today, you will deny me three times." He went out and wept. (Luke 23:54–62)

Luke reminded us that Peter wept after his last denial. Not only would they have been tears of regret, they would have been tears of trauma, confusion, and fear. I don't know that the early reader would have viewed Peter as a failure, but they would have understood his situation. Peter, like so many disciples, came face to face with the truth concerning following Jesus. Sometimes doing the right thing means suffering even if it calls us to stand in the fire.

Peter had the last word. When we read Acts he preached the first Christian sermon. He was a reminder that Jesus offers grace, second chances, and a renewed covenant.

Justice for Jesus?

Luke's description of the trial of Jesus clearly displayed injustices. For Luke the point was obvious to any reader; the religious leaders wanted to kill him and they did whatever it took to get the job done. They met in the night, they made decisions without the full council present, they offered false witnesses to trap Jesus, they accused him of crimes that were much more extreme than his actions, and they did not take into account the good work he had done for God. Luke indicated later in the Gospel that a Joseph of Arimethea (Luke 23:50–51) was a member of the council and did not consent to the judgment of the council. The council may have met without his knowledge and support. In all events, the evidence was clear: there was no justice for Jesus. As with the response to Yahweh in the Hebrew Bible, the people of God not only committed injustice, they approved of it.

> They began to accuse him, saying, "We found this man misleading our nation and forbidding us to give tribute to Caesar, and saying that he himself is Christ, an emperor." Pilate asked him, "Are you the King of the Jews?" He said, "You are saying this." Then Pilate said to the chief priests and the crowds, "I don't find any accusation against this man." But they were urgent, saying, "He stirs up the people, teaching throughout all Judea, from Galilee even to this place." . . . Pilate then called together the chief priests and the rulers and the people, and said to them, "You brought me this man as one who was misleading the people. After examining him I did not find this man guilty of any of your charges, neither did Herod, for he sent him back to us. He has done nothing deserving death. I will punish him and let him go." . . . Pilate addressed them once more, desiring to release Jesus, but they kept shouting, "Crucify, crucify him!" A third time he said to them, "Why, what evil has he done? I have found no reason to have him executed. I will therefore punish him and let him go." . . . So Pilate decided that their demand should be granted. He released the man who had been thrown into prison for terrorism and murder, for whom they asked, but he delivered Jesus over to their will. (Luke 23:1–25)

Pilate, the Roman governor, of Judea was no better.

While some scholars have questioned whether Luke was pro-Roman Empire or against the establishment, this text suggested it was neither. It becomes clear, in Acts, that the Roman Empire became a convenient vehicle for Paul and the mission team to spread the gospel throughout the Roman world. Luke was also fond of Roman centurions (he mentioned four in Luke/Acts) and resists judging their presence in Judea. However, in this text Luke also sent a clear message to the original audience—the government that claimed to provide justice throughout the known world, was powerless to acquit Jesus.[3]

First, while some might suggest that Pilate made an honest attempt to free Jesus, the reality was that he could do what he wanted. Pilate was ruthless and acted without reason concerning some of his actions in Palestine. He did not have a fondness for the Jewish leaders and did little to appease them. In addition to these characteristics, as a Roman Pilate could have done whatever he wanted to maintain peace. Jesus, according to Pilates's responsibility, presented no threat to the Roman Empire's presence in Jerusalem. Even though he claimed to be king/Caesar, this was a common claim of many rebels, bandits, and terrorists. Upon questioning Jesus he found nothing critical or offensive in his response. Pilate could have freed Jesus without any reservation.

Second, his delegating the task to Herod (only Luke wrote about this) was a ploy to avoid dealing with this "small matter." Herod likewise found nothing offensive in Jesus's defense. Herod had been seeking to meet with Jesus since Luke 9:9. Unfortunately when he met Jesus he must not have been impressed. But he also found no reason to execute Jesus, nor did he listen to the charges of the religious leaders.

Luke indicated that Pilate and Herod formed a friendship over the trial of Jesus. In one way, Jesus brought enemies together (Eph 2:12–16). In another way, injustice colluded with injustice. Neither leader brought justice to their communities, only political bargaining. Luke suggested in this text that those who could provide justice did not. Jesus was handed over to the mob for crucifixion not because Pilate tried to free him, but because the colonizer did not want to provide true justice. The crucifixion of Jesus was, as was always true with the suffering of God, due to leadership's unwillingness to provide justice to the community.

Luke's readers would have been confronted with a powerful message. The empire that promised justice and peace/*shalom* failed to provide justice when needed. As we see in Acts, Roman leaders were as corrupt as the religious leaders in Judea.

FACES AT THE CROSS

Jesus was sentenced by the Jews and allowed to be tortured and killed by the Romans. The government that was to provide justice had become privy and supportive to those driven by fear, anxiety, anger, and jealousy. However,

---

3. Pickett, "Luke and Empire," 7.

the journey continued and Jesus, once again, encountered others along the road to his glory.

> As they led him away, they seized Simon of Cyrene, who was coming in from the country, and made him carry the cross behind Jesus. A crowd of people and women followed him. Some women who were mourning and lamenting for him also followed. Jesus turned to them and said, "Daughters of Jerusalem, do not weep for me, weep for yourselves and for your children. The days are coming when they will say, 'Blessed are the barren and the wombs that never bore and the breasts that never nursed!' Then they will begin to say to the mountains, 'Fall on us,' and to the hills, 'Cover us.' For if they do these things when the wood is green, what will happen when it is dry?" Two others, who were criminals, were led away to be put to death with him. When they came to the place that is called the Skull, there they crucified him, and the criminals, one on his right and one on his left. Jesus said, "Father, forgive them, for they know not what they do." They cast lots to divide his garments. The people stood by, watching, but the rulers scoffed at him, saying, "He saved others; let him save himself, if he is the Christ of God, his Chosen One!" The soldiers also mocked him, coming up and offering him sour wine and saying, "If you are the King of the Jews, save yourself!" There was also an inscription over him, "This is the King of the Jews." One of the criminals who were hanged railed at him, saying, "Are you not the Christ? Save yourself and us!" But the other rebuked him, saying, "Do you not fear God, since you are under the same sentence of condemnation? We indeed suffer justly, for we are receiving the due reward of our deeds; but this man has done nothing wrong." He said, "Jesus, remember me when you come into your kingdom." He said to him, "I tell you the truth, today you will be with me in Paradise." ... Then Jesus, calling out with a loud voice, said, "Father, into your hands I commit my spirit." Having said this he took his last breath. When when the centurion saw what had taken place, he praised God, saying, "Certainly this man was innocent!" All the crowds that had assembled for this spectacle, when they saw what had taken place, returned home beating their chests. All his acquaintances and the women who had followed him from Galilee stood at a distance watching these things. (Luke 23:26–45)

Jesus's final journey to the hill of Golgotha was again a journey where people met him along the way. First, Simon was a man from Northern Africa/Egypt.

Mark's Gospel listed his sons as Rufus and Alexander, who may have been leaders in the Roman church (Mark 15:21; Rom 16:13). Luke mentioned that Simon came from the country (margins) and was expected to carry Jesus's cross for him. Simon was forced to join the journey but in some way he was influenced enough by his encounter with Jesus that his sons became Christians.

Second, a group of women mourners were following Jesus to his death. In the ancient world there were women who made sure that everyone had someone to mourn for them in death. The thought of leaving this earth without sorrow would have been culturally dishonorable. These women, professional mourners, were accompanying Jesus to his death. However, Jesus reminded them that this was not a time to mourn his death but the destruction of Jerusalem. Jesus had been teaching that the temple would once again fall by the hands of the enemy, Rome, and would be the judgment of God. He quoted Hosea 10:8, which referenced the destruction of Jerusalem by Babylon.

Third, Jesus encountered two robbers/bandits on his journey to death. Roman protocol during a triumphant parade of a general and king required the hero to be flanked by two high ranking officers (one on right and other on left). This is a practice continued when the United States President speaks in Congress and is flanked by the Vice President and Speaker of the House. In the Roman triumph the king paraded through the streets with joy and cheers as he arrived at the capitol (head) of the city. For Jesus, his triumph went through the streets of Jerusalem with mourning, abuse, and pain. He arrived at the head (skull) outside the city and was flanked by two criminals. One criminal criticized Jesus, while the other expressed faith. Jesus again encountered people on the margins while on his way to heaven. He also offered salvation to the second criminal simply because of his confession of faith.

Finally, the crowd witnessing the death of Jesus encountered this hero on his way to death. Some responded in a display of repentance/remorse. The Roman centurion responded by claiming his innocence. Those who were close to Jesus, even in crucifixion, were impacted by his life and death.

Stay Close

Jesus's followers were standing in the distance. Luke seemed to suggest that salvation and the experiences of discipleship were best experienced in the midst of tension, battle, and the fire. Those who drew close to Jesus would see the glory of God. For Luke, it did not matter what a person believed, only that they stayed close. Those who struggled suffered because they chose to stand back. Discipleship involved courage, faith, trust, and love. While Jesus had returned home to see his neighborhood, his people had lost their way. Those who were leaders had become corrupt, comfortable, and afraid. Therefore they had affected their community. Fear, injustice, and corruption permeated the neighborhood and Jesus paid the price for speaking out. However, his witness would not be the end of the story. Someone else would have to carry the banner, proclaim the message, and share the news.

It would need to come from someone who was close, who stood in the fire, and who embraced courage and hope.

13

Jesus Returns

Luke 24

THE DEATH OF JESUS would have been a very traumatic event for the disciples. I remember watching *The Passion of the Christ* many years ago. The movie must have traumatized many audiences. The media seems bent on sharing the gory details of the torture and crucifixion of Jesus, almost as an attempt to motivate us to deeper appreciation and sympathy for the death of Jesus. However, the Gospel writers give few details concerning the final hours of Jesus. They focused more on what Jesus said and did rather than what was done to him. Motivating disciples of Jesus to deeper appreciation does not involve traumatizing them, but reminding them of the mission of Jesus.

Imagine living in a neighborhood with families, children, and elderly neighbors. Through time two of the homes become locations to manufacture methamphetamines, provide illegal automobile trades, and kidnap young boys and girls to use in prostitution. Unfortunately all of the neighbors know the business of these homes, yet because of fear and extortion they keep quiet. Often neighbors gather to discuss what to do or how to "clean up the neighborhood," yet the residents in the violent homes threaten those who gather for the meetings. Some neighbors move away. Others claim that they have lived there their whole life, and do not want to move.

One day a family moves into the neighborhood and begins to clean their lot, their house, and connect with the neighbors. They are a large family with a father who is very caring, compassionate, and open, with strong feelings of right and wrong. It is clear that this man is loved by his family and friends. He has a strong sense of justice and believes that being a community means helping each other and protecting those who are vulnerable in this community. Over the years you watch him talk to the occupants of the two homes that seem to be causing trouble on the blocks. It becomes clear to the neighbors that he has crossed the line, but he tells you he doesn't care. One night the neighborhood has a block party, hosted by the new neighbor. In the middle of the meal he states, "Tomorrow I am going to those two homes and asking their residents to leave. I'm telling them I have evidence that they have broken countless laws and that I'm going to get a lawyer and take them down." What would be the response of the people at the party?

Some would say, "It's about time."

Others might suggest he do nothing, as they have been doing for years.

Others might say, "Go ahead, but leave me out of it. I don't want trouble."

A few might say, "We are with you."

Then he says, "I know that one of you has told them I'm coming, but I don't care. It is time to do the right thing." You wonder which neighbor has been feeding information to the troublemakers down the street. Was this neighbor threatened, was he coerced, or was he a coward?

The next morning you wake up, look out your window, and there on your neighbor's lawn you see it. His body is hanging from the tree in the front yard, badly beaten, and dismembered. His children and wife are trying to get his body down from the tree. They are screaming, crying, and sobbing.

What do you do?

What do you say?

Where do you go now?

I find it interesting that many people would remember that last meal of the neighbor as the time when he provided a vision for the neighborhood. At the funeral the neighborhood would not discuss the bloody carcass, the rope in the tree, or what might have happened when he confronted the corrupt neighbors. You would focus less on his death and more on the fact that he had a vision. "We should all be a neighbor like him," or "He believed in a safe neighborhood," or even, "He showed us that in order to have peace we would have to stand up to evil."

What would happen in the neighborhood?

Would everyone stay in their homes or would they go out on the street to speak out?

Even more, would the focus of those in the neighborhood be the death of their courageous neighbor or the vision he had for peace?

SEEING JESUS THROUGH FAITH AND OBEDIENCE

> Early in the morning, on the first day of the week, they went to the tomb, taking the spices they had prepared. They found the stone rolled away from the tomb, but when they went in they did not find the body of the Lord Jesus. While they were confused about this, two men in bright clothes stood by them. They were frightened and bowed their faces to the ground, but the men said to them, "Why do you seek the living among the dead? He is not here, but has risen. Remember how he told you, while he was still in Galilee, that the Son of Man must be delivered into the hands of sinful men, crucified, and on the third day rise." They remembered his words, and returning from the tomb they told all these things to the eleven and to all the rest. Now it was Mary Magdalene and Joanna and Mary the mother of James and the other women with them who told these things to the apostles, but these words seemed to them an idle tale, and they did not believe them. Peter rose and ran to the tomb; stooping and looking in, he saw the linen cloths by themselves; and he went home marveling at what had happened. (Luke 24:1–12)

The empty tomb did present a problem for the early Christians. First, in the ancient world, resurrection was not a well-taught theme. For the Jewish community the Messiah was to come and lead the nation to freedom and victory. The concept of death, burial, and resurrection was not present in the teachings of the Jews. While Daniel 12 offered a belief that the just would be resurrected to a glorious life (Dan 12:1–4) this did not refer to returning to earth and walking among the people. The empty tomb was a curiosity for the women and apostles as they visited it. Even though Jesus had taught that he would suffer and raise throughout the journey, the disciples would have struggled with this concept.

It is no surprise that the first ones to minister to Jesus at the tomb were females. The mission of Jesus was to those on the margins and Luke is full of stories discussing the faithfulness of the marginalized. These women were part of that neglected community and, in this story, proved their faithfulness. It didn't matter why they were at the tomb nor did it matter that they did not believe when they went to attend to what they thought would be the dead body. Luke's point was that they were there, they were obedient, and they displayed respect and honor for their rabbi. Because of this faithfulness, they were the first witnesses to the resurrection and took the prestigious place in Christian history of being the first to proclaim the resurrection of Jesus.

One of my doctoral students shared with me during one of our advisor/dissertation meetings that she was frustrated. "I have always believed that my denomination has empowered women and feel passionate about serving in ministry," she said. I agreed and had always believed that they had. "Unfortunately," she expressed, "the understanding is that when a woman becomes a pastor she is supposed to cut her hair short, wear longer dresses, and gain at least ten pounds." I could see tears well up in her eyes. "It's sad because I was raised in this group, yet now that I am ordained and finishing my doctorate, I see a side I don't know that I like. It forces me to either stay and accept it or leave and go where God calls me." I understood what she was saying. I also could see that this was a very painful issue and decision for her to address. Even more, it challenged me as a minister in a church that typically doesn't empower women in ministry to realize how many women suffer in a faith that Jesus brought to free captives, including them. Even more I realize that empowering women, and others, involves more than giving them titles. Earlier research was cited suggesting that while females have been able to enter ministry they continue to experience higher rates of harassment, sexual abuse, and oppression—even by male colleagues.[1]

The apostles, all male, not only abandoned Jesus in his death, but also lacked the faith to accept the resurrection. While they not only chose not to believe the women, they chose to continue life as if Jesus was permanently gone. For Luke's readers belief and understanding of the resurrection was not the driving force in the church. While the apostles claim to proclaim a risen Jesus based on firsthand knowledge, the church continued to grow by those who had not witnessed Jesus returning alive. Luke's emphasis in this text suggested that faith and obedience, in spite of what we know to be true, was a driving force in the growth of the church. For the early reader of Luke's Gospel the empty tomb meant that the mission and journey of Jesus must continue.

It was also a time to celebrate the hope of his resurrection. While the disciples may have been overcome with grief, they were learning that joy exists in the midst of sorrow, death, and loss. When our oldest son was five years old I was preaching at a small church in south Missouri. One of our members, who we were very close to, was dying of cancer. We had been with her through the long journey of diagnosis, treatment, remission, reoccurrence, and hospice. Now she was in the final stages. She had been moved to

---

1. Fortune and Poling, *Sexual Abuse by Clergy*, 5.

a care facility where one of our church members worked. She was especially fond of our son and we were all grieving as a church and family.

At midnight we received the call from the care facility and decided to take our son with us to say goodbye. Lora Vureen was in her last hours, was struggling to breath, and fighting to hold on. As we walked in the door we were met by the night staff, including the member from our church. They offered to take Nathan while we were inside praying and holding Lora's hand. Since Lora's family lived out of town we knew that they would not arrive until the next day. A hospice nurse was present holding her hand and singing to her. We prayed, talked to her, and encouraged her to continue to fight (it is the natural reflex of the body) as long as she wished. She was not aware of anyone's presence but we believed that she heard our prayers and felt our touches.

Suddenly we heard a loud "Wheeee." It was one o'clock in the morning and no one was awake, except the staff. Then we heard it again, "Wheeee." It was our son's voice. Lori stood up to go ask him to be quiet. "What is he doing yelling 'wheee' while everyone's asleep and our friend is dying?" As Lori stepped to the door our son sped by on a wheelchair. Both Lori and I thought the same thing, "He's is so in trouble." Then we saw the night nurses chasing him and yelling "Wheee, I'm gonna get you . . ." As we stepped into the hall the nurses station had bowls of chocolate ice cream and we saw three night staff pushing our son around in the rolling chair. Our friend from church stopped, smiled, and said, "Hey mom and dad—we thought we would get him sugared up for you. It gets kind of dismal here at night. We don't get to play with too many kids around here." Our son was smiling and having the time of his life.

A part of me felt that we should have been somber, respectful, and in mourning. But the staff felt that it was a time to enjoy life, since it was passing away from us as we spoke. Lori and I just looked at each other, laughed, said, "Have fun," and went back to our friend. Some might have called it disrespectful. Others might say that it was a reminder that life continues on. The staff and our son would just call it enjoying life while it is here. Sometimes we can become so preoccupied with grief that we miss the present hope in front of our eyes.

SEEING JESUS BY WELCOMING THE STRANGER

Luke's narrative continued with the story of another journey. Two of the early followers of Jesus were traveling away from Jerusalem. In Acts when the followers left Jerusalem they proclaimed the resurrected Jesus. In this story the followers left Jerusalem with intent to return home, back to their normal lives. Along the way they met a stranger.

> He said to them, "What is this conversation that you are having with each other as you walk?" They stood still, looking sad. Then one of them, named Cleopas, answered, "Are you the only visitor to Jerusalem who does not know the things that have happened there recently?" He [Jesus] said, "What things?" They said to him, "Concerning Jesus of Nazareth, a man who was a prophet powerful in works and word before God and all the people, and how our chief priests and rulers delivered him up to be condemned to death, and crucified him. But we had hoped that he was the one to redeem Israel. Yes, and besides all this, it is now the third day since these things happened. Some women of our company amazed us. They were at the tomb early in the morning, and when they did not find his body. They came back saying that they had even seen a vision of angels, who said that he was alive. Some of those who were with us went to the tomb and found it just as the women had said, but him they did not see." He said to them, "O foolish ones, and slow of heart to believe all that the prophets have spoken! Was it not necessary that the Christ should suffer these things and enter into his glory?" Beginning with Moses and all the prophets, he interpreted to them all the scriptures the things concerning him. (Luke 24:13–36)

One might wonder how these men missed the fact that Jesus was the individual speaking to them. If they had spent time with Jesus they would have recognized his voice, mannerisms, and appearance. Luke only wrote that they were prevented from recognizing Jesus. Whether this was a divine act, Jesus was wearing a hood, or they were overcome with grief and sorry that they didn't pay attention, the point Luke made was clear; the person speaking to them was not worth noticing. Jesus, here, represented the stranger or the common person who is so often neglected by Christians as they go about their business serving, teaching, believing, and praising God. It is easy to neglect the Jesus in all of us because we, like Martha, become burdened with much ministry.

During this journey the disciples again mention the suffering, death, and resurrection of Jesus. They repeat almost word for word what Jesus had been telling the apostles for months, yet they end with, "We had hoped . . . " One can almost imagine Jesus listening thinking in his mind, "Yes, yes, yes, you got it. No, you blew it with that last sentence . . ." They were so close to understanding this truth, yet they did not recognize Jesus or could they understand the repeated phrase about the "third day" that was so characteristic of Luke's Gospel.

It was not until the two disciples compelled Jesus to join them for dinner that they recognized him and his teaching. When he broke the bread they understood. For Luke the message was that Jesus and his mission is revealed in the practice of hospitality toward strangers. Luke's readers would have understood this point very well. Jesus is seen when we accept the stranger, those who dwell on the margins, and those who need hospitality.

Luke's readers had heard the stories of Jesus. Yet they seemed to have missed some important points. One was prevalent in this story. Modern readers have also missed some important points in our spirituality. The church has failed to connect with those on the margins. Our elaborate, expensive, and beautiful buildings have been designed to attract people. Somehow we have believed that if we open the door to our cathedrals those on the margins will flock to our worship services. However, this has not happened and the reality of Luke's epic narrative reminds us that we cannot compel strangers to join us for a meal unless we leave the comforts of our homes and safe buildings to engage them on the street. Too often God's people miss Jesus and continue to eat our bread in sadness believing that "We had hoped he was . . ." We will not recognize our own Messiah unless we embrace his mission. The friend of sinners and tax collectors has called us to compel his community into our communities so that we can see/recognize Jesus.

REMEMBER THE MISSION

Jesus reappeared to the apostles and their group. He ate with them, taught them, and spent time enjoying their presence. It must have been a wonderful time. "I can't believe you are really here . . ." might have been said a few times. Yet Jesus took this opportunity to remind them of the mission. First, he fulfilled the mission by taking the journey to Jerusalem, suffering, and enjoying new life. It was clear to the disciples, you can't kill God. However it was also clear that he did not come to do this just for them. Too often the church has confined the incarnation, passion, crucifixion, and resurrection to something done for us. However, Luke's readers were realizing that these are done *with* us. We join Jesus in this mission. Not only do the Law, prophets, and Psalms teach us about Jesus—they teach us about us. This section, which was unique to Luke, reminded the reader that Jesus came for a mission and vision, and they too were being called to that same mission and vision.

Second, they were being commissioned to join and fulfill the mission. They were not to stay put in Jerusalem, the fatal end of Jesus's journey, but the Spirit would lead them to leave and spread throughout the world. The mission of the church was bigger than the mission of Jesus, for as Jesus went to one small city the church would go to the largest cities of the world. While Jesus came to his own, the disciples would go to those who were not like them, but were also Jesus's own. As Jesus came to his home and was rejected, so the disciples would become strangers in an alien world that would accept Jesus's message.

> "These are my words that I spoke to you while I was still with you, that everything written about me in the Law of Moses and the prophets and the Psalms must be fulfilled." He opened their minds to understand the scriptures, and said, "The scripture says, that the Christ should suffer and on the third day rise from the dead, and that repentance and forgiveness of sins should be preached in his name to all nations/Gentiles, beginning from Jerusalem. You are witnesses of these things. I am sending the promise of my Father upon you. But stay in the city until you are clothed with power from on high." Then he led them out as far as Bethany, and lifting up his hands he blessed them. While he blessed them, he left them and was carried up into heaven. They worshiped him and returned to Jerusalem with great joy, and were continually in the temple blessing God. (24:44–53)

What would it mean if Jesus died for a vision rather than that Jesus died for me? I have heard many ministers suggest that the incarnation was Jesus moving into our neighborhoods. They share that Jesus was the neighbor who would have us in his home, have a beer with us, and/or be a light in the community. This is true.

However, if he were in the neighborhood he would also be vocal concerning evil, oppression, and the marginalizing of people. He would not just invite us to dinner, he would ask us to host the next meal. He would ask us why we allow the religious leaders to corrupt the way of God. If we saw him hanging from the tree he would have also told us that we must be willing to hang on our trees as well. Imagine getting up each morning, looking out the window at the tree in your front yard, and wondering if this was the day you would hang from it?

I could only ask that question if I were busy with the vision and mission he left in my neighborhood. My tree would not be a symbol of what "I might be willing to do" but a real place for my corrupt neighbors to hang me. If they came to my yard and said, "See that tree? You're next . . ." the tree would be more than a symbol. The tree would strike fear in me. It would ruin my appetite for breakfast. It might be something I would want to chop down. Yet it would stand as a reminder that vision, mission, and outreach came with a cost.

The tree would not be something I would boast about, it would be something that reminded me why I lived where I did. It would also be a reminder that our friend died, not just for us, but for a belief that truth and justice were worth laying one's life down.

And it be a reminder that as long as people stand for truth and justice, they will suffer at the hands of those who reject them.

All of this is true. Yet Jesus speaks beyond the tree. Jesus also showed us that the empty tomb speaks louder than any enemy because it suggested that there is victory in the truth, justice, and the mission of God's mercy.

14

The Church Continues Onward

ONE OF OUR AGAPE members encouraged our church to donate plasma at the center where he worked. He presented this to the church one Sunday and gave compelling reasons for us to become involved. First, we could make money and give it to the church. Second, we could help people. Third, there were people there whose lives had been wrecked by addictions and bad choices and we could share our faith with them while we donated. It all seemed good. We joked about "power in the plasma" and the "plasma of Christ." Eventually some of us started donating plasma. Since then we have had a baptism from the center, many visitors at both Agape campuses, and all of our male ministers and interns donate. It has been a hard ministry, but one that offers opportunity to talk, listen, and share people's lives, visions, and hopes. Even more, the plasma center staff work hard and receive little income—it is a great opportunity to hear people's frustrations.

I don't broadcast I am a minister, except when one of our people yells out, "Hey pastor, great sermon yesterday." Then my cover is blown. I don't try to hide anything but just want to visit with people and have them feel that I am a guy willing to listen. However, I have noticed an older man who comes to the plasma center with a big Bible and reads it, but rarely says a word to people. The technicians talk to us, those in the beds next to us talk, and those taking our vital signs talk to us. You cannot avoid a conversation, unless you choose to. Yet this guy says nothing. He reads his big Bible and doesn't speak.

I know he can speak because I have visited with him in the past. He doesn't say a lot, just smiles, and turns away. I posted in our class about him one day with my seminary students. George Fox Evangelical Seminary both Quaker and evangelical. Many of the students felt I was being harsh.

Maybe the guy was self-reflecting, focusing on spiritual development, or an introvert. Their point was well taken. Maybe they were right.

But here is my point. What message is communicated to people when we read our big Bibles and don't acknowledge humans or thank them for their service? Would Jesus not speak to his creation? Would Jesus be nice, or at least acknowledge appreciation? While I have heard people talk about introverts, being quiet, or struggling to talk to people, doesn't the incarnation suggest that our presence should be appreciated, seen, and valuable? Or, is it enough to just read our big Bibles and go about our business while others struggle, suffer, experience joy, work hard, and/or serve us? I am wondering if this is why many view Christians as arrogant, judgmental, or rude.

Luke wrote an epic narrative of the founding of the Jesus movement, the Christian church, or the empire of Jesus. Luke wrote this against the backdrop of the return from exile. As the Judean people returned from Persia and the surrounding areas to rebuild their home, Jerusalem, God called prophets to inspire them, offer them hope, and remind them that they were forgiven. Through years of struggle, repentance, sin, and wars the nation again found itself in captivity. Only this time it was social captivity. The Roman government controlled the Jewish nation as local elites became power brokers tried to placate their captors. Through corruption, anxiety, power, and social oppression they created a new form of captivity. Those who were vulnerable and resisted Roman rule were forced to the margins of their society. Those who were marginalized longed for relationship, connection, and the voice of God. Because they were on the margins of life, they somehow felt that they were outside of salvation.

Jesus was God in the flesh, who came to lead the captives home. This home was also not geographical but social. This home was not a building, house, or city. This home was *shalom*. This home was a new family—one that obeyed God's word. This home was a community living and practicing God's justice and experiencing divine reversal. The poor were now blessed. Those who were currently hungry would be fed. The sick, the crippled, the blind, and those afflicted by evil and addictions would experience healing, relationship, and acceptance. No longer would they grasp the wind while outside the borders of holiness. No longer would they feel alone. No longer would they carry shame. Jesus, the epic hero who took the journey, would meet them on the margins and gather them to his army and his caravan. Instead of the hero meeting monsters and killing them, Jesus met people and saved them. Luke's narrative was one that not only proclaimed Jesus as hero, it proclaimed the birth of a new movement, community, and empire. This new movement would reflect the qualities of its founder and carry out the passion of his ministry.

Luke's Gospel was a narrative to Theophilus and his community. This church knew the stories of Jesus, but it had forgotten some important themes in the Christian epic. Luke shared unique stories, as compared to the other Gospels, in an attempt to complete and create a sense of safety for the early Christians. First, *Luke reminded them that Jesus expected the community to care for the poor, have a passion for those on the margins, and become personally involved in reaching sinners.* They were to follow Jesus, which meant that they were called to do what he did. If he was the friend of sinners, they were expected to be as well.

Second, *Luke reminded them that carrying the cross to Jerusalem meant fully embracing Jesus's ministry.* John's disciples may have been disappointed at what Jesus was doing (Luke 7), but Jesus indicated that this was his ministry, and those who were offended would not belong. Jesus's mission was to face Jerusalem and confront corruption. By setting his face to the city he proved to his disciples, as well as the readers, that discipleship calls for courage, vision, and conviction.

Finally, *Luke indicated that shalom happens when God's people call for justice.* It happens when God's people practice justice. It happens when God's people stand for justice. It happens when God's people venture out of their comfort zones and go to the margins, to the people who are outcasts and are in darkness. These captives are to be set free so that they can experience Jesus, God, the Holy Spirit, and freedom. The Jubilee of the Lord is for those on the margins.

The church today has a similar challenge. We too have heard the story. We too have practiced the sanitized religion of Christianity. We too have been brainwashed by the belief that money and things are more important than people. We too have become embarrassed by the Jesus who is the "friend of sinners and tax collectors." The Christian faith in some ways has become static, comfortable, or easy. As Brandon Hatmaker once wrote, "We as church leaders tell our people to go. We tell them to be good news. And we assume they do. We assume they know how. While we've been charged to 'equip the saints' for works of service, the brutal truth is that most of us have reduced our expectations of 'serving' to a once-a-month tour of duty as an usher or greeter. We've settled for serving ourselves and serving as an event rather than serving those in need and living a new way of life that Jesus has called us to. There's got to be more to church than this."[1]

We were created for more. Our story, our movement, our vision, our mission, and our purpose is not a story but an epic adventure. The Journey of Jesus is a journey for the church. Luke's Book of Acts, which could be

---

1. Hatmaker, *Barefoot Church*, 16.

called *The Spirit of Jesus Unleashed on the Church,* continues that epic story. The church follows Jesus. The church models Jesus. The church sets its face toward Jerusalem and stands toe to toe with Satan. The church is clothed with power from the Spirit and boldly shares the unbelievable story of Jesus to an unbelieving but seeking world. If Jesus is the friend of sinners then the only way that the church does the same is by choosing to follow and imitate Jesus. If Jesus practiced love, so must we. If Jesus offered acceptance, so must we.

I was riding mass transit from downtown and was fading in and out of sleep. Earlier that day I had met with a couple people to discuss baptism and God's love, had meetings with a leadership group, a police chaplain friend, the police commander of Central Precinct, and finally visited some of our homeless sites. I was pretty tired. A couple guys got on at a stop near a drug rehab clinic and began talking loudly. I had my eyes closed when I heard, "Go Ducks, hey?" I opened my eyes to see one of the guys smiling at me. He had an Oregon Ducks hat on. He was referring to my sweatshirt.

I smiled. "Yes, they are doing well." He said, "I'm a cougar. Cougars eat ducks and beavers."

I laughed and said, "You're right, they do. You must be a Washington State fan."

"Yep, born and raised in Washington. I just borrowed the Ducks hat."

"Well," I smiled, "we moved out from Missouri years ago but our son goes to U of O so in some way we are proud financial supporters of the Ducks," which brought some laughter to others sitting around me. "Did you like Washington State?" I asked. He said, "Yeah, good school. I studied Agriculture, but didn't finish." I said, "Great, I got a minor in Ag. That's a hard degree, takes a lot of work." He asked, "So you did Ag in Missouri?"

"Yes, but I'm sure you know more about agriculture here in the Northwest than I do," I said. The MAX came to my stop. "I gotta get off here," I said. "Nice to meet you." He said, "Sure."

The next statement stopped me in my tracks and made me tense up. No, it wasn't "I've got a gun," or "give me your money," or something life threatening. We assume that's all that happens on public transportation, and that's why many people avoid traveling this way. What he said was in a way sadder than that.

"Thanks for acknowledging me," he said.

That's what stopped me in my tracks. I turned around to say, "No problem," and he was headed off to the other end of the train. Everyone else was looking down at their smart phones.

In a crowded place with people elbow to elbow, someone can feel unacknowledged? Someone can feel lonely? Someone can feel unappreciated? Someone can be marginalized?

That's what stopped me in my tracks.

On the way to my car I had to ask myself if it is really that much work to talk to someone, acknowledge them, or even smile at them.

It shouldn't be. It wouldn't have been for Jesus.

If we want to see Jesus, we must accept and love the stranger.

Bibliography

Adams, Dwayne H. *The Sinner in Luke*. Eugene, OR: Pickwick, 2008.
Allison, Dale C., Jr. "Rejecting Violent Judgment: Luke 9:52–56 and Its Relatives." *Journal of Biblical Literature* 121:3 (Fall 2002) 459–78.
Anderson, Paul. *The Fourth Gospel and the Quest for Jesus*. Edinburgh: T and T Clark, 2008.
Anderson, Ray S. *The Shape of Practical Theology: Empowering Ministry with Theological Praxis*. Downers Grove, IL: InterVarsity, 2001.
Arlandson, Janet Malcolm. *Women, Class, and Society in Early Christianity*. Peabody, MA: Hendrickson, 1997.
Bachmann, Michael. "Jerusalem and Rome in Luke-Acts: Observations on the Structure and the Intended Message." In *Luke-Acts and Empire: Essays in Honor of Robert L. Brawley*, edited by David Rhoads, David Esterline, and Jae Won Lee, 60–83. Eugene, OR: Pickwick, 2011.
Bailey, Jon Nelson. "Looking for Luke's Fingerprints: Identifying Evidence of Redactional Activity in 'The Healing of the Paralytic' (Luke 5:17–26)." *Restoration Quarterly* 48:3 (2006) 143–56.
Bailey, Kenneth E. *Finding the Lost: Cultural Keys to Luke 15*. St. Louis: Concordia, 1992.
———. *Jesus Through Middle Eastern Eyes: Cultural Studies in the Gospels*. Downers Grove, IL: InterVarsity, 2008.
———. *Poet and Peasant and Through Peasant Eyes: A Literary-Cultural Approach to the Parables of Luke*. Grand Rapids: Eerdmans, 2005.
Bird, Phyllis A. "Prostitution in the Social World and Religious Rhetoric of Ancient Israel." In *Prostitutes and Courtesans in the Ancient World*, edited by Christopher A. Faraone and Laura K. McClure, 40–59. Madison: University of Wisconsin Press, 2006.
Bonz, Marianne Palmer. *The Past as Legacy: Luke-Acts and Ancient Epic*. Philadelphia: Fortress, 2000.
Borgman, Paul. *The Way According to Luke: Hearing the Whole Story of Luke-Acts*. Grand Rapids: Eerdmans, 2006.
Bouma-Prediger, Steven, and Brian J. Walsh. *Beyond Homelessness: Christian Faith in a Culture of Displacement*. Grand Rapids: Eerdmans, 2008.
Brawley, Robert L. *Luke-Acts and the Jews: Conflict, Apology, and Conciliation*. Atlanta: Scholars, 1987.

Bringle, Mary Louise. *The God of Thinness: Gluttony and Other Weighty Matters*. Nashville: Abingdon, 1992.

Brueggemann, Walter. *The Practice of Prophetic Imagination: Preaching an Emancipating Word*. Minneapolis: Fortress, 2012.

———. *The Prophetic Imagination*, 2nd edition. Philadelphia: Fortress, 2001.

Burke, John. *No Perfect People Allowed: Creating a Come As You Are Culture in the Church*. Grand Rapids: Zondervan, 2005.

Burridge, R. A. *What Are the Gospels? A Comparison with Graeco-Roman Biography*, 2nd ed. Grand Rapids: Eerdmans, 2004.

Cancik, Hubert. "The History of Culture, Religion, and Institutions in Ancient Historiography: Philological Considerations Concerning Luke's History." *Journal of Biblical Literature* 116:4 (1997) 673–95.

Carson, D. A., Douglas J. Moo, and Leon Morris. *An Introduction to the New Testament*. Grand Rapids: Zondervan, 1992.

Carter, Warren. "Getting Martha Out of the Kitchen: Luke 10:38–42 Again." *Catholic Biblical Quarterly* 58:2 (1996) 264–80.

———. "Singing in the Reign: Performing Luke's Songs and Negotiating the Roman Empire (Luke 1–2)." In *Luke-Acts and Empire: Essays in Honor of Robert L. Brawley*, edited by David Rhoads et al., 84–106. Eugene, OR: Pickwick, 2011.

Cartlidge, David R. and David L. Dungan, eds. *Documents for the Study of the Gospels*. Minneapolis: Fortress, 1994.

Cassidy, Richard J. "Paul's Proclamation of *Lord* Jesus as a Chained Prisoner in Rome: Luke's Ending Is in His Beginning." In *Luke-Acts and Empire: Essays in Honor of Robert L. Brawley*, edited by David Rhoads et al., 142–53. Eugene, OR: Pickwick, 2011.

Clark, Ron. *Am I Sleeping With the Enemy? Males and Females in the Image of God*. Eugene, OR: Cascade, 2010.

———. "Associating With the Humiliated: Using Victim's Testimonies in the College Classroom." *Journal of Religion and Abuse* 7:1 (2005) 61–79.

———. *The Better Way: The Church of Agape in Emerging Corinth*. Eugene, OR: Pickwick, 2010.

———. *Emerging Elders*. Abilene, TX: Abilene Christian University Press, 2005.

———. *The God of Second Chances: Finding Hope in the Prophets of Exile*. Eugene, OR: Cascade, 2012.

———. "Kingdoms, Kids, and Kindness: A New Context for Luke 18:15–17." *Stone Campbell Journal* 5:2 (2003) 235–48.

———. *Setting the Captives Free: A Christian Theology for Domestic Violence*. Eugene, OR: Cascade, 2005.

———. "Open Your Eyes." *Journal of Religion and Abuse* 4:1 (2002) 27–36.

Conn, Harvie M. and Manuel Ortiz. *Urban Ministry: The Kingdom, the City, and the People of God*. Downers Grove, IL: InterVarsity, 2001.

Conway, Colleen M. *Behold the Man: Jesus and Greco-Roman Masculinity*. New York: Oxford University Press, 2008.

Corley, Kathleen E. *Private Women, Public Meals: Social Conflict in the Synoptic Tradition*. Peabody, MA: Hendrickson, 1993.

Cosgrove, Charles H. "A Woman's Unbound Hair in the Greco-Roman World, with Special Reference to the Story of the 'Sinful Woman' in Luke 7:36–50." *Journal of Biblical Literature* 124/4 (2005) 675.

Croatto, J. Severino. "Jesus, Prophet Like Elijah, and Prophet-Teacher Like Moses in Luke-Acts." *Journal of Biblical Literature* 124:3 (Fall 2005) 451–65.

Crossan, John Dominic. *Cliffs of Fall*. New York: Seabury, 1980.

———. *The Cross that Spoke*. San Francisco: Harper and Row, 1988.

———. *The Historical Jesus: The Life of a Jewish Mediterranean Peasant*. San Francisco. HarperOne, 1991.

———. *In Parables*. San Francisco: Harper and Row, 1973.

———. *Who Killed Jesus? Exposing the Roots of Anti-Semitism in the Gospel Story of the Death of Jesus*. HarperOne, 1996

Danby, Herbert, ed. *The Mishnah: Translation from the Hebrew with Introduction and Brief Explantory Notes*. New York: Oxford University Press, 1987.

De Silva, David. *Honor, Patronage, Kinship, and Purity: Unlocking New Testament Culture*. Downers Grove, IL: InterVarsity, 2000.

De Vos, Craig Steven. *Church and Community Conflicts: The Relationships of the Thessalonian, Corinthian, and Philippian Churches with Their Wider Civic Communities*. Atlanta: Scholar's, 1999.

Dunn, Richard R. and Jana L. Sundene. *Shaping the Journey of Emerging Adults*. Downers Grove, IL: InterVarsity, 2012.

Ehrenreich, Barbara. *Nickle and Dimed: On (Not) Getting By in America*. New York: Holt, 2001.

Elliott, John H. "Temple Versus Household in Luke-Acts: A Contrast in Social Institutions." In *The Social World of Luke-Acts: Models for Interpretation*, edited by Jerome H. Neyrey, 211–40. Peabody, MA: Hendrickson, 1991.

Evans, Craig A. *Jesus and His Contemporaries*. New York: Brill, 1995.

———. "Jesus and the Continuing Exile of Israel." In *Jesus and the Restoration of Israel: A Critical Assessment of N. T. Wright's* Jesus and the Victory of God, edited by Carey C. Newman, 77–100. Downers Grove, IL: InterVarsity, 1999.

Evans, Craig A., and Peter W. Flint. *Eschatology, Messianism, and the Dead Sea Scrolls*. Grand Rapids: Eerdmans, 1997.

Evans, Craig A., and James A. Sanders. *Luke and Scriptures*. Minneapolis: Fortress, 1993.

Evans, Craig A., and Stanley E. Porter, eds. *The Historical Jesus*. Sheffield: Sheffield Academic, 1995.

Finley, M. I. *Ancient Slavery and Modern Ideology*. Harmondsworth: Penguin, 1980.

Fitzmeyer, Joseph A. *The Gospel According to Luke I–IX*. Garden City, NY: Doubleday, 1981.

Fortune, Marie M., and James N. Poling. *Sexual Abuse by Clergy: A Crisis for the Church*. Eugene, OR: Wipf and Stock, 2008.

Friedrichsen, Timothy A. "The Temple, a Pharisee, a Tax Collector, and the Kingdom of God: Rereading a Jesus Parable (Luke 18:10–14A)." *Journal of Biblical Literature* 124:1 (2005) 89–119.

Friesen, Steven J. "Prospects for a Demography of the Pauline Mission: Corinth Among the Churches." In *Urban Religion in Roman Corinth*, edited by Daniel N. Schowalter and Steven J. Friesen, 351–70. Cambridge: Harvard University Press, 2005.

Frost, Michael. *Exiles: Living Missionally in a Post-Christian Culture*. Peabody, MA: Hendrickson, 2006)

———. *The Road to Missional: Journey to the Center of the Church*. Grand Rapids: Baker, 2011.

Frost, Michael, and Alan Hirsch. *ReJesus: A Wild Messiah for a Missional Church.* Peabody, MA: Hendrickson, 2009.

Gehring, Roger W. *House Church and Mission: The Importance of Household Structures in Early Christianity.* Peabody, MA: Hendrickson, 2004.

Grassi, Joseph. *Peace on Earth: Roots and Practices from Luke's Gospel.* Collegeville, MN: Liturgical, 2004

Hall, Douglas John. *The Cross in Our Context: Jesus and the Suffering World.* Minneapolis: Fortress, 2003.

Hatmaker, Brandon. *Barefoot Church: Serving the Least in a Consumer Culture.* Grand Rapids: Zondervan, 2011.

Hauerwas, Stanley. *The Peaceable Kingdom.* Notre Dame: University of Notre Dame Press, 1986.

Hellerman, Joseph H. *The Ancient Church as Family.* Minneapolis: Fortress, 2001.

Hirsch, Alan. *The Forgotten Ways: Reactivating the Missional Church.* Grand Rapids: Brazos, 2006.

Ipsen, Avaren. *Sex Working and the Bible.* Oakville, CA: Equinox, 2009.

Johnson, Luke Timothy. *The Acts of the Apostles.* Collegeville, MN: Liturgical, 1992.

———. *Messianic Exegesis.* Fortress, 1988.

———. *Prophetic Jesus, Prophetic Church.* Grand Rapids: Eerdmans, 2011.

Juel, Donald. *Luke-Acts: The Promise of History.* Atlanta: John Knox, 1983.

Keener, Craig S. *A Commentary on the Gospel of Matthew.* Grand Rapids: Eerdmans, 1999.

Kimball, Dan. *They Like Jesus But Not the Church.* Grand Rapids: Zondervan, 2007.

King, Martin Luther, Jr. *Why We Can't Wait.* New York: Mentor, 1964.

Kinman, Brent. "Parousia, Jesus' 'A-Triumphal' Entry, and the Fate of Jerusalem (Luke 19:28–44)." *Journal of Biblical Literature* 118:2 (Summer 1999) 279–94.

Kinnaman, David. *You Lost Me: Why Young Christians Are Leaving the Church. . .and Rethinking Faith.* Grand Rapids: Baker, 2011.

Landry, David, and Ben May. "Honor Restored: New Light on the Parable of the Prudent Steward (Luke 16:1–8a). *Journal of Biblical Literature* 119:2 (Summer 2000) 287–309.

Lee, Jae Won. "Pilate and the Crucifixion of Jesus in Luke-Acts." In *Luke-Acts and Empire: Essays in Honor of Robert L. Brawley,* edited by David Rhoads et al., 84–106. Eugene, OR: Pickwick, 2011.

Lewis, Robert, and Rob Wilkins. *The Church of Irresistible Influence.* Grand Rapids: Zondervan, 2001.

Malina, Bruce J. *The New Testament World,* rev. ed. Louisville: Westminster John Knox, 1993.

———. *Windows on the World of Jesus.* Louisville: Westminster John Knox, 1993.

———. "Reading Theory Perspective: Reading Luke-Acts." In *The Social World of Luke-Acts: Models for Interpretation,* edited by Jerome H. Neyrey, 3–23. Peabody, MA: Hendrickson, 1991.

Malina, Bruce J., and Jerome H. Neyrey. "Honor and Shame in Luke-Acts: Pivotal Values of the Mediterranean World." In *The Social World of Luke-Acts: Models for Interpretation,* edited by Jerome H. Neyrey, 25–65. Peabody, MA: Hendrickson, 1991.

Malina, Bruce J., and John J. Pilch. *Social-Science Commentary on the Book of Acts.* Minneapolis: Fortress, 2008.

Marshall, I. Howard. *Luke: Historian and Theologian*. Grand Rapids: Zondervan, 1971.

Martínez, Roberto. *The Question of John the Baptist and Jesus' Indictment of the Religious Leaders: A Critical Analysis of Luke 7:18–35*. Eugene, OR: Pickwick, 2011.

Maxwell, Kathy R. "The Role of the Audience in Ancient Narrative: Acts as a Case Study." *Restoration Quarterly* 48:3 (2006) 171–80.

McIntosh, Gary L. *Biblical Church Growth: How You Can Work with God to Build a Faithful Church*. Grand Rapids: Baker, 2003.

———. *One Size Doesn't Fit All*. Grand Rapids: Baker, 1999.

Messner, Brian. "'In the Fifteenth Year' Reconsidered: A Study of Luke 3:1." *Stone-Campbell Journal* 1:2 (Fall 1998) 201–12.

Mitchell, Don. *The Right to the City: Social Justice and the Fight for Public Space*. New York: Guilford, 2003.

Moo, Douglas J. "'Gospel Origins': A Reply to J. W. Wenham." *Trinity Journal* 2 (1981) 24–36.

Moxnes, Halvor. *The Economy of the Kingdom*. Overtures to Biblical Theology. Philadelphia: Fortress, 1988.

———. "Patron-Client Relations and the New Community in Luke-Acts." In *The Social World of Luke-Acts: Models for Interpretation*, edited by Jerome H. Neyrey, 241–68. Peabody, MA: Hendrickson, 1991.

———. *Putting Jesus in His Place: A Radical Vision of Household and Kingdom*. Louisville: Westminster John/Knox, 2003.

Multnomah County. *2013 Point in Time*. Online: https://www.portlandoregon.gov/phb/article/451470.

Nelson, Peter K. *Leadership and Discipleship: Study of Luke 22:24–30*. Atlanta: Scholars, 1994.

Netzer, Ehud. *The Architecture of Herod the Great Builder*. Grand Rapids: Baker, 2006.

Neusner, Jacob, ed. *The Babylonian Talmud: A Translation and Commentary on CD ROM*. Peabody, MA: Hendrickson, 2005.

Neyrey, Jerome H., ed. *The Social World of Luke-Acts*. Peabody: Hendrickson, 1991.

———. *Prophecy in Its Ancient Near Eastern Context*. SBL Symposium Series 13. Atlanta: Scholars, 2000.

Nissinen, Martti. "The Exiled Gods of Babylon in Neo-Assyrian Prophecy." In *The Concept of Exile in Ancient Israel and Its Historical Contexts*, edited by Ehud Ben Zvi and Christoph Levinson, 189–206. Boston: de Gruyter, 2010.

Nolland, John. *Luke*, 3 vol. Word Biblical Commentary. Dallas: Word, 1989

Osiek, Carolyn. "Archaeological and Architectural Issues and the Question of Demographic and Urban Forms." In *Handbook of Early Christianity: Social Science Approaches*, edited by Anthony J. Blasi, Jean Duhaime, and Paul-Andre Turcotte, 83–104. New York: Alta Mira, 2002.

Palmer, Darryl W. "Acts and the Ancient Historical Monograph." In *The Book of Acts in Its First Century Setting: Volume 1 Ancient Literary Setting*, edited by Bruce W. Winter and Andrew D. Clarke, 1–30. Grand Rapids: Eerdmans, 1993.

Papias. "Fragments of Papias." In Eusebius, *Hist. Eccl.* 3:39. *The Apostolic Fathers*, edited by J. B. Lightfoot and J. R. Harmer. Grand Rapids: Baker, 1987.

Parsons, Mikeal C. *Body and Character in Luke and Acts: The Subversion of Physiognomy in Early Christianity*. Waco, TX: Baylor University Press, 2011.

Peabody, David B., et al. *One Gospel from Two: Mark's Use of Matthew and Luke: A Demonstration by the Research Team of the International Institute for Gospel Studies*. Harrisburg, PA: Trinity, 2002.

Penner, Todd. *In Praise of Christian Origins*. New York: T and T Clark, 2004.

Pickett, Raymond. "Luke and Empire: An Introduction." In *Luke-Acts and Empire: Essays in Honor of Robert L. Brawley*, edited by David Rhoads et al., 84–106. Eugene, OR: Pickwick, 2011.

Pilch, John J. *Visions and Healing in the Acts of the Apostles: How the Early Believers Experienced God*. Collegeville, MN: Liturgical, 2004.

Plato. *Plato: The Symposium*. Translated by Walter Hamilton. New York: Penguin, 1983.

Powell, Mark A. "The Religious Leaders in Luke: A Literary-critical Study." *Journal of Biblical Literature* 109:1 (1990) 93–110.

The Proto-Gospel of James. In *The Other Bible*, edited by Willis Barnstone, 385–92. New York: Harper and Row, 1984.

Rainer, Thom S. *The Book of Church Growth: History, Theology, and Principles*. Nashville: Broadman, 1993.

———. *Breakout Churches: Discover How to Make the Leap*. Grand Rapids: Zondervan, 2005.

———. *Effective Evangelistic Churches: Successful Churches Reveal What Works and What Doesn't*. Nashville: Broadman and Holman, 1996.

———. *The Unchurched Next Door*. Grand Rapids: Zondervan, 2003.

Rauschenbusch, Walter. *A Theology for the Social Gospel*. Nashville: Abingdon, 1917.

Reid, Barbara E. "Women Prophets of God's Alternative Reign." In *Luke-Acts and Empire: Essays in Honor of Robert L. Brawley*, edited by David Rhoads et al., 45–59. Eugene, OR: Pickwick, 2011.

Resseguie, James L. *Spiritual Landscape: Images of the Spiritual Life in the Gospel of Luke*. Peabody, MA: Hendrickson, 2004.

Roetzel, Calvin J. *The World that Shaped the New Testament*. Louisville: Westminster John Knox, 2002.

Robinson, Anthony B., and Robert W. Wall. *Called to Be Church: The Book of Acts for a New Day*. Grand Rapids: Eerdmans, 2006.

Roth, Martha T. "Marriage, Divorce, and the Prostitute in Ancient Mesopotamia." In *Prostitutes and Courtesans in the Ancient World*, edited by Christopher A. Faraone and Laura K. McClure, 21–39. Madison: University of Wisconsin Press, 2006.

Rousseau, John J., and Rami Arav. *Jesus and His World: An Archaeological and Cultural Dictionary*. Fortress, 1995.

Saldarini, Anthony J. *Pharisees, Scribes, and Sadducees in Palestinian Society: A Sociological Approach*. Grand Rapids: Eerdmans, 2001.

Schaberg, Jane. "How Mary Magdalene Became a Whore." *Bible Review* 8 (Oct 1992) 31–37, 51–52.

Schmidt, Thomas. *A Scandalous Beauty*. Grand Rapids: Brazos, 2002.

Seccombe, David Peter. *Possessions and the Poor in Luke-Acts*. Linz: Studien zum Neuen Testament und Seiner Umwelt, 1982.

Shepherd, William H.. Jr. *The Narrative Function of the Holy Spirit as a Character in Luke-Acts*. Atlanta: Scholars, 1994.

Skarsaune, Oskar. *In the Shadow of the Temple: Jewish Influences on Early Christianity*. Downers Grove, IL: InterVarsity, 2002.

Smith, D. Moody. "When Did the Gospels Become Scripture?" *Journal of Biblical Literature* 119:1 (2000) 3–20.
Snodgrass, Klyne. "*Anaideia* and the Friend at Midnight (Luke 11:8)." *Journal of Biblical Literature* 116: (Fall 1997) 505–13.
Spencer, F. Scott. *Journeying through Acts: A Literary-Cultural Reading*. Peabody, MA: Hendrickson, 2004.
Stein, Robert H. *Jesus the Messiah*. Downers Grove, IL: InterVarsity, 1996.
Stetzer, Ed. *Planting New Churches in a Postmodern Age*. Nashville: Broadman and Holman, 2003.
Stivers, Laura. *Disrupting Homelessness: Alternative Christian Approaches*. Philadelphia: Fortress, 2011.
Strauss, Mark L. *The Davidic Messiah in Luke-Acts*. Journal for the Study of the New Testament Supplement Series 110. Sheffield: Sheffield Academic, 1995.
Stronstad, Roger. *The Charismatic Theology of St. Luke*. Peabody, MA: Hendrickson, 1984.
Thompson, Alan J. *The Acts of the Risen Lord Jesus*. Downers Grove, IL: InterVarsity, 2011.
Tisdale, Leonora Tubbs. *Prophetic Preaching: A Pastoral Approach*. Louisville: Westminster John Knox, 2010.
Tripolitis, Antonia. *Religions of the Hellenistic-Roman Age*. Grand Rapids: Eerdmans, 2002.
Turan, Ainai (Tamas). "A Neglected Rabbinic Parallel to the Sermon on the Mount (Matthew 6:22–23; Luke 11:34–36)." *Journal of Biblical Literature* 127:1 (Spring 2008) 81–93.
Udoh, Fabian E. "The Tale of the Unrighteous Slave (Luke 16:1–8 [13])." *Journal of Biblical Literature* 128:2 (Summer 2009) 311–35.
Van Til, Ken A. "Three Anointings and One Offering: The Sinful Woman in Luke 7:36–50." *Journal of Pentecostal Theology* 15:1 (2006) 73–82.
Walton, Steve. "Trying Paul or Trying Rome? Judges and Accused in the Roman Trials of Paul in Acts." In *Luke-Acts and Empire: Essays in Honor of Robert L. Brawley*, edited by David Rhoads, David Esterline, and Jae Won Lee, 122-41. Eugene, OR: Pickwick, 2011.
Wilkins, Michael. *Discipleship in the Ancient World and Matthew's Gospel*. Grand Rapids: Baker, 1995.
Witherington, Ben III. *The Acts of the Apostles: A Socio-Rhetorical Commentary*. Grand Rapids: Eerdmans, 1998.
———. *The Jesus Quest: The Third Search for the Jew of Nazareth*. Downers Grove, IL: InterVarsity, 1995.
———. *New Testament History: A Narrative Account*. Grand Rapids: Baker, 2001.
Woodward, J. R. *Creating a Missional Culture: Equipping the Church for the Sake of the World*. Downers Grove, IL: InterVarsity, 2012.
Wright, N. T. *Jesus and the Victory of God*. Minneapolis: Fortress, 1996.
Zvi, Ehud Ben. "Introduction: Writings, Speeches, and the Prophetic Books—Setting an Agenda." In *Writings and Speech in Israelite and Ancient Near Eastern Prophecy*, edited by Ehud Ben Zvi and Michael H. Floyd, 1–29. Atlanta: Society of Biblical Literature, 2000.

www.ingramcontent.com/pod-product-compliance
Lightning Source LLC
Chambersburg PA
CBHW031356230426
43670CB00006B/558